VISUAL QUICKSTART GUIDE

PowerPoint 4
for Windows

Rebecca Bridges Altman

Peachpit Press

Visual QuickStart Guide
PowerPoint 4 for Windows
Rebecca Bridges Altman

Peachpit Press
2414 Sixth Street
Berkeley, CA 94710
510/548-4393
510/548-5991 (fax)

Peachpit Press is a division of Addison-Wesley Publishing Company.
Copyright © 1995 by Rebecca Bridges Altman

Cover design: The Visual Group

Notice of Rights
All rights reserved. No part of this book may be reproduced or transmitted in any form by any means, electronic, mechanical, photocopying, recording, or otherwise, without the prior written permission of the publisher. For information on getting permission for reprints and excerpts, contact Trish Booth at Peachpit Press.

Notice of Liability
The information in this book is distributed on an "As Is" basis, without warranty. While every precaution has been taken in the preparation of the book, neither the author nor Peachpit Press, shall have any liability to any person or entity with respect to any loss or damage caused or alleged to be caused directly or indirectly by the instructions contained in this book or by the computer software and hardware products described in it.

ISBN 1-56609-168-3

9 8 7 6 5 4 3 2 1

Printed and bound in the United States of America

Printed on recycled paper

Dedication

To my two-year old daughter, Erica, who thought this book was "cute."

Acknowledgments

I'd like to thank the following people for their help with this book:

Carol Henry at C² Editorial for copy editing

Jan Altman at Express Train for developmental and technical editing

Nolan Hester at Peachpit Press for proofreading

Roslyn Bullas for coordinating this project

And my husband, **Rick Altman**, for his font and layout expertise.

Table of Contents

Chapter 1   **INTRODUCING POWERPOINT**

Presentation Graphics 2
The PowerPoint Window 4
Key to the PowerPoint Window 5
Mousing Around 6
The Menu, Please 7
Using Shortcut Menus 7
Understanding Pull-Down Menus 8
The File Menu 9
The Edit Menu 9
The View Menu 10
The Insert Menu 10
The Format Menu 11
The Tools Menu 12
The Draw Menu 12
The Window Menu 13
The Help Menu 13
Conversing with Dialog Boxes 14
The Toolbars 15

Chapter 2   **A QUICK TOUR OF POWERPOINT**

About the Tour 17
Launching PowerPoint 17
Choosing a Template 18
Choosing a Layout 19
Creating a Bulleted List 20
Creating a Graph 21
Formatting a Graph 22
Navigating a Presentation 23
Saving, Opening, and Closing Presentations 24
Printing a Presentation 25
Outline View 26
Slide Sorter View 27
Viewing a Slide Show 28

Chapter 3   **CREATING TEXT SLIDES**

About Text Slides 29
Choosing a Text Layout 30

TABLE OF CONTENTS

Entering Text into a Placeholder 31
Creating a Text Placeholder 32
Manipulating Text Placeholders 33
Moving Text 34
Using the Spelling Checker 35
Changing Case 36
Adding Periods 36
Changing the Bullet Shape 37
Adjusting the Bullet Placement 38
Changing the Font 39
Adding Text Effects and Color 40
Aligning Paragraphs 41
Setting Anchor Points in a Text Placeholder 42
Controlling Line and Paragraph Spacing 43
Copying Formatting Attributes 44

Chapter 4 INSERTING GRAPHS

About Graphs 45
Graph Terminology 46
Inserting a Graph Slide 47
Entering Data 48
Importing Data 49
Linking Data 50
Choosing a Chart Type 51
Inserting Titles 52
Rotating an Axis Title 52
Inserting Data Labels 53
Repositioning Data Labels 53
Revising a Graph 54
Creating Two Graphs on a Slide 55

Chapter 5 FORMATTING GRAPHS

Ways to Format Graphs 57
Formatting the Legend 58
Repositioning the Legend 59
Changing the Color or Pattern of a Data Series 60
Formatting Data Markers 61
Inserting/Removing Gridlines 62
Formatting Gridlines 63
Formatting the Tick Marks 64
Scaling the Axis 65
Formatting the Axis Numbers 66

TABLE OF CONTENTS

Formatting Graph Text 67
Adjusting 3-D Effects 68
Formatting the Plot Area 69
Formatting a Graph Automatically 70
Defining a Custom AutoFormat 71
Applying a Custom AutoFormat 72

Chapter 6 **CREATING PIE CHARTS**

About Pie Charts 73
Inserting a Pie Slide 74
Entering Pie Data 75
Showing Labels, Values, and Percents 76
Formatting Slice Labels 77
Exploding a Slice 78
Coloring the Slices 79
Rotating a Pie 80
Formatting 3-D Effects 81
Resizing and Repositioning a Pie 82
Creating a Doughnut 83
Sizing the Doughnut Hole 83
Creating Two Pies on a Slide 84

Chapter 7 **BUILDING ORGANIZATION CHARTS**

About Organization Charts 85
Inserting an Org Chart Slide 86
Entering Text into Boxes 87
Inserting a Box 88
Rearranging Boxes 89
Selecting Boxes 90
Choosing a Style 91
Choosing a Style 92
Formatting Box Text 93
Formatting the Boxes 94
Formatting the Lines 95
Zooming In and Out 96
Revising an Organization Chart 97

Chapter 8 **CREATING TABLES**

About Tables 99
Inserting a Table Slide 100
Entering Text into a Table 101

vii

TABLE OF CONTENTS

Revising a Table 102
Selecting Cells 103
Adjusting Column Widths 104
Adjusting Row Heights 106
Inserting Rows and Columns 107
Deleting Rows and Columns 108
Formatting Text 109
Adding Borders and Shading 110
Aligning Text Within a Cell 112
AutoFormatting a Table 113
Summing Columns 114

Chapter 9 — ADDING GRAPHIC OBJECTS

Types of Graphic Objects 115
Drawing Lines 116
Formatting Lines 117
Drawing Rectangles 118
Drawing Ellipses 119
Filling an Object 120
Drawing an Arc 122
Creating Polygons and
Freehand Drawings 123
Creating Other Shapes 124
Inserting Clip Art 125
Searching for Clip Art 126
Inserting Graphic Files 127
Pasting Graphics 128

Chapter 10 — MANIPULATING GRAPHIC OBJECTS

About Graphic Manipulation 129
Using Rulers and Guides 130
Using Grid Snap 131
Zooming In and Out 132
Aligning Objects 133
Grouping Objects 134
Copying Graphic Attributes 135
Recoloring a Picture 136
Scaling an Object 137
Cropping a Picture 138
Changing the Stack Order 139
Rotating Objects 140
Flipping Objects 141

TABLE OF CONTENTS

Chapter 11 — MAKING GLOBAL CHANGES

Formatting a Presentation 143
Replacing a Font 144
Changing Default Colors in a Presentation 145
Creating a Gradient Background 146
Choosing Compatible Colors 147
Editing the Slide Master 148
Changing the Default Format for Text 149
Adding Background Items 150
Inserting Page Numbers 151
Applying a Template 152
Using the Pick a Look Wizard 154

Chapter 12 — WORKING IN OUTLINE VIEW

Introducing Outline View 155
Hiding Text Formatting 156
Displaying Slide Titles Only 157
Creating Bulleted Lists 158
Reordering the Slides 159
Outlining a Presentation 161
Importing an Outline 162
Editing an Outline in Word 6 163

Chapter 13 — WORKING IN SLIDE SORTER VIEW

Introducing Slide Sorter View 165
Zooming In and Out 166
Reordering the Slides 167
Copying Slides 168
Moving Slides Between Presentations 169
Copying Slides Between Presentations 170
Deleting Slides 172

Chapter 14 — PRODUCING A SLIDE SHOW

About Slide Shows 173
Organizing a Slide Show 174
Displaying a Slide Show 175
Annotating a Slide 176
Hiding a Slide 177
Adding a Transition Effect to a Slide 178
Creating a Self-Running Slide Show 180
Rehearsing the Slide Show 181

ix

INTRODUCING POWERPOINT

Introduction

Visual QuickStart Guides offer a unique way to learn a software package. Each page contains concise step-by-step instructions on how to perform a certain task and is accompanied by a number of illustrations, each with explanatory captions and callouts. For the most part, each page is self-contained with a single topic. This type of organization makes it less overwhelming to learn an extensive program such as PowerPoint, and allows you to master just the features you need to.

At the end of each topic, you'll find a list of helpful tips. These tips provide you with shortcuts, alternate techniques, additional information, and related topics. Some of these tips are undocumented or are buried so deep in the documentation or Help files that it's unlikely you would ever learn about them elsewhere.

Time permitting, you may want to read the book cover-to-cover, but in all likelihood, you will probably just turn to a specific chapter or topic you want to learn about. And the way this book is organized, you will be able to do so quickly and efficiently.

For those who are new to the Windows environment, it is especially important to go through Chapter 1 carefully. This chapter covers the basics of using a mouse, as well as working with menus, dialog boxes, and toolbars.

Chapter 2 is a great way to learn the main features of PowerPoint, especially if you have a presentation that needed to be out the door yesterday.

Chapters 3 through 11 explain how to create different types of slides (bulleted lists, graphs, tables, and organization charts) and format your presentations. Chapters 12 and 13 illustrate two additional ways to view and organize presentations: Outline and Slide Sorter views. Chapters 14 and 15 show you different ways to output your presentation: on screen in a slide show, in printed form, and in 35mm slides.

Happy learning!

CHAPTER 1

Presentation Graphics

What exactly can a presentation graphics software package do? This type of software provides you with tools for creating the components of your presentations. You can create bulleted lists, numerical tables, organization charts, and business graphs (pies, bars, lines, and more).

You also get tools for adding graphic elements to your slides. For example, you can create designs for the background of your slide using the Rectangle, Ellipse, Arc, and Line tools. But don't worry if you aren't artistically inclined—you can always insert a ready-made drawing from the clip art library or use a professionally designed template (Figure 1).

You might be thinking, "Hey, I can type bulleted lists and tables in my word processor, I can create business graphs in my spreadsheet program, and with my drawing package I can produce nice art. Why, then, would I need a presentation graphics package?"

Here are three good reasons. First, as its name implies, this type of software *presents graphics*. You can present the graphics in a variety of ways:

- In an onscreen slide show (complete with special transition effects)
- On paper (one per page, or several per page for audience handouts)
- On 35mm slides

Second, a presentation graphics package is an environment in which you can bring all the components of a presentation together, into a single file. You can use the package to create the slides, or, if you prefer, you can use your favorite programs to create the data or art and then import them into slides in the presentation graphics program.

The software offers convenient ways to organize the presentation—the third reason for using a presentation graphics program. Using the Outline (Figure 2) or Slide Sorter views (Figure 3), you can see the structure of the presentation as well as take steps to reorganize the slides, if necessary. Changing the order of the slides is a snap in these two special views.

As you can see, there are quite a few advantages to creating your presentations in a presentation graphics package, and PowerPoint for Windows is an excellent choice for these tasks.

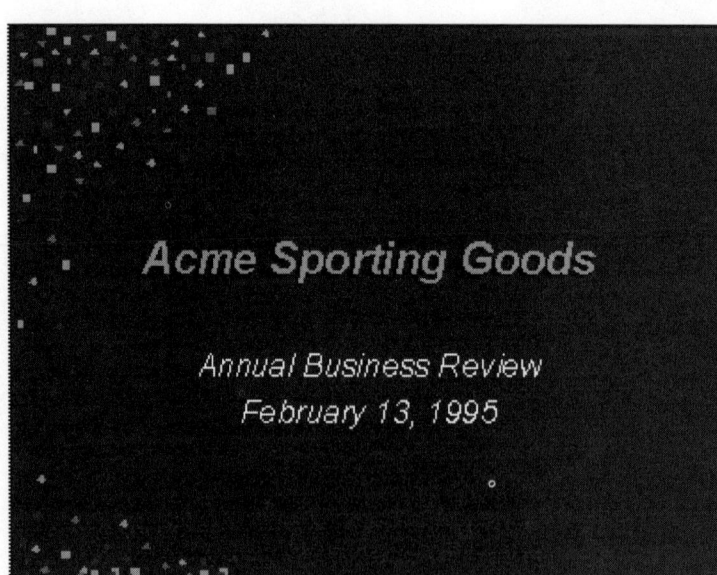

Figure 1. The confetti on this slide was produced by applying a professionally designed template.

INTRODUCING POWERPOINT

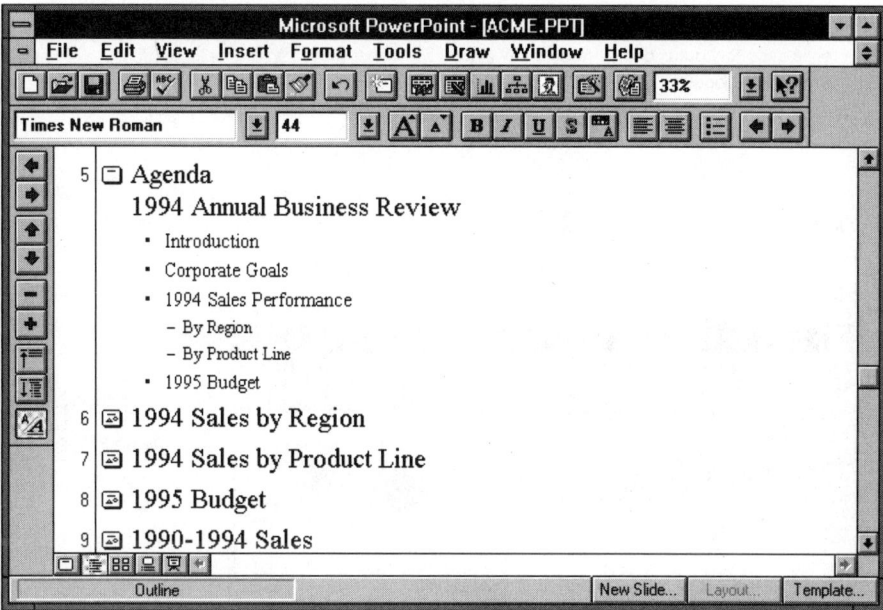

Figure 2. Outline view shows you the structure of your presentation, letting you reorganize the outline if necessary.

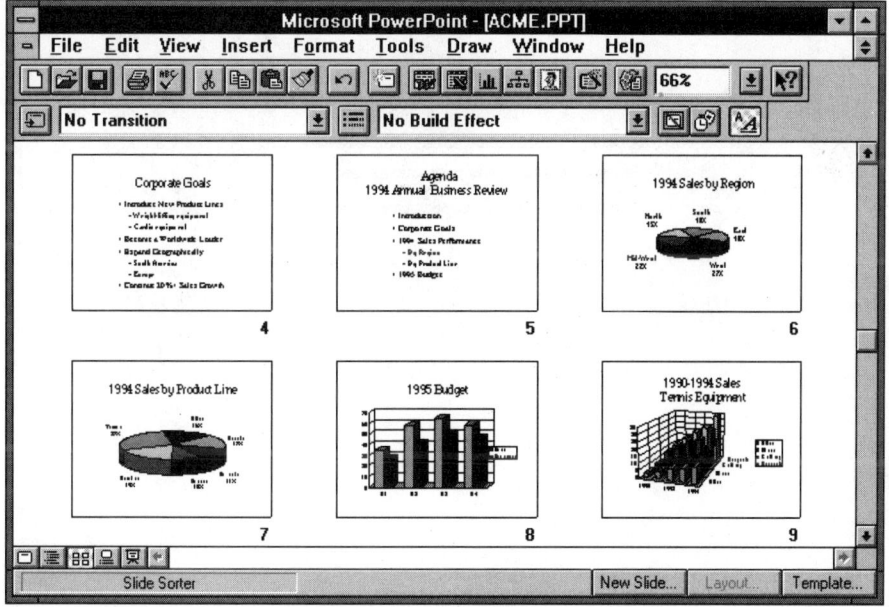

Figure 3. Slide Sorter view lets you see many slides at once.

3

CHAPTER 1

The PowerPoint Window

Figure 4. Here are the important areas of the PowerPoint window. For further details on any of these areas, refer to the numbered key on the opposite page.

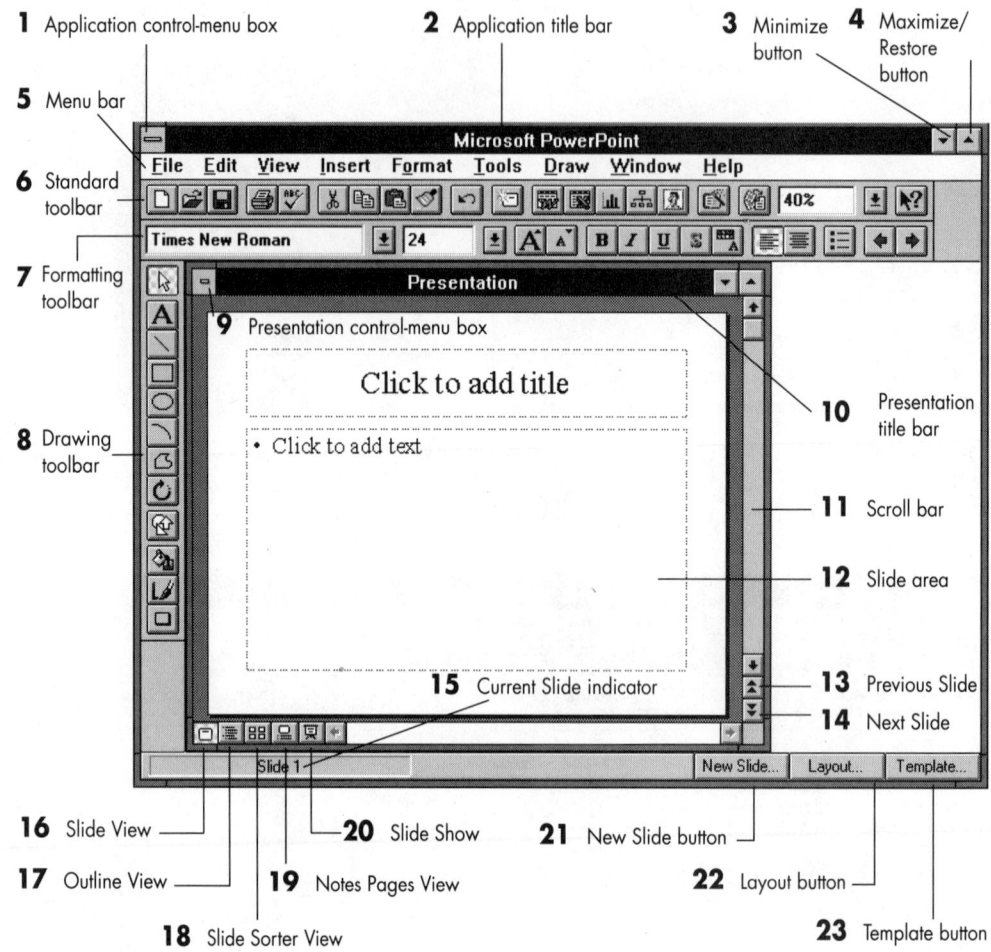

1 Application control-menu box
2 Application title bar
3 Minimize button
4 Maximize/Restore button
5 Menu bar
6 Standard toolbar
7 Formatting toolbar
8 Drawing toolbar
9 Presentation control-menu box
10 Presentation title bar
11 Scroll bar
12 Slide area
13 Previous Slide
14 Next Slide
15 Current Slide indicator
16 Slide View
17 Outline View
18 Slide Sorter View
19 Notes Pages View
20 Slide Show
21 New Slide button
22 Layout button
23 Template button

INTRODUCING POWERPOINT

Key to the PowerPoint Window

1   Application control-menu box
Displays the menu for controlling the PowerPoint window.

2   Application title bar
Displays the name of the current application (Microsoft PowerPoint).

3   Minimize button
Shrinks the application to an icon on the desktop.

4   Maximize/Restore button
Enlarges the window so that it fills the screen or restores the window to its previous size.

5   Menu bar
The main menu of choices. Clicking on a menu item displays a pull-down menu.

6   Standard toolbar
Contains buttons for frequently used tasks, such as saving and printing.

7   Formatting toolbar
Contains buttons for formatting text.

8   Drawing toolbar
Contains buttons for drawing and formatting objects.

9   Presentation control-menu box
Displays the menu for controlling the presentation window.

10   Presentation title bar
Shows the name of the current presentation.

11   Scroll bar
Displays other slides in the presentation.

12   Slide area
This is where you create, format, and modify the slide.

13   Previous Slide button
Displays the previous slide in the presentation.

14   Next Slide button
Displays the next slide in the presentation.

15   Current Slide indicator
Indicates the number of the slide currently shown.

16   Slide View button
Displays a single slide in the presentation window.

17   Outline View button
Displays an outline of the presentation (slide titles and main text).

18   Slide Sorter View button
Displays miniature versions of each slide, allowing you to see multiple slides at once.

19   Notes Pages View button
Displays speaker notes pages, allowing you to type notes about the slide. These notes can be printed and referred to during a slide show.

20   Slide Show button
Presents the slides one at a time in an onscreen slide show.

21   New Slide button
Inserts a new slide after the current slide.

22   Layout button
Allows you to change the layout of the current slide.

23   Template button
Applies a template (new design) to the current presentation.

CHAPTER 1

Mousing Around

Until you've used the mouse for a while, you are likely to feel awkward and uncoordinated; that clumsy feeling is perfectly normal. With practice, though, using the mouse will become as natural as using the keyboard. Here are a few techniques that every "mouser" needs to know.

Click

This technique is used to select menu items, to make selections in dialog boxes, and to choose toolbar buttons.

Move the mouse until the mouse pointer is on the object you want to click and tap the *left* mouse button. When you click the *right* mouse button, a shortcut menu displays.

See opposite page for more information on the shortcut menu.

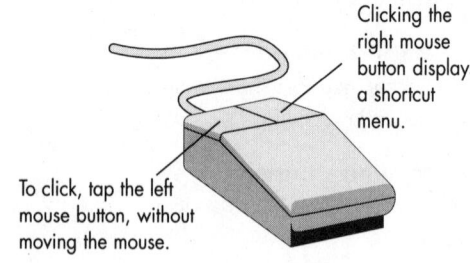

Clicking the right mouse button displays a shortcut menu.

To click, tap the left mouse button, without moving the mouse.

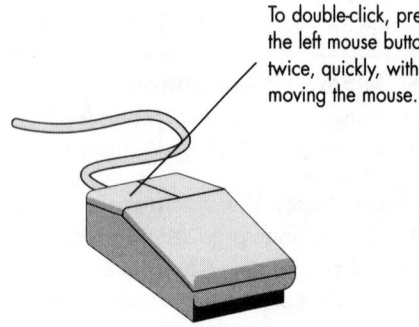

To double-click, press the left mouse button twice, quickly, without moving the mouse.

Double-Click

This technique is used to open a program group and to launch an application (such as PowerPoint for Windows). It's also used as a shortcut in dialog boxes: By double-clicking on an item (such as a file name), you select that item and close the dialog box.

Place the mouse pointer on the object and press the left mouse button twice, quickly. The proper speed at which you need to make the two clicks depends on your system; you may need to practice double-clicking several times until you get the feel for it.

Click and Drag

This technique is used to move an object from one place to another or to select a block of text.

Place the mouse pointer on the object you want to move or select. Press and *hold down* the left mouse button as you move the mouse in the direction you want to move the object, or across the passage of text you want to select. Release the mouse button when you are finished.

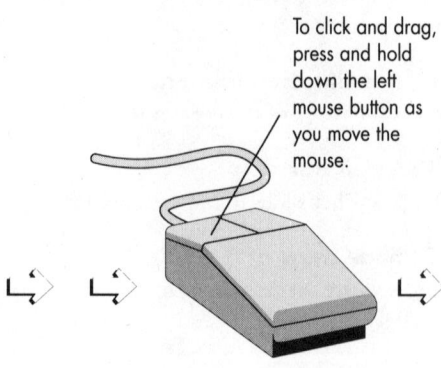

To click and drag, press and hold down the left mouse button as you move the mouse.

The Menu, Please

PowerPoint uses the standard Windows conventions for accessing menus. Figure 5 describes these conventions.

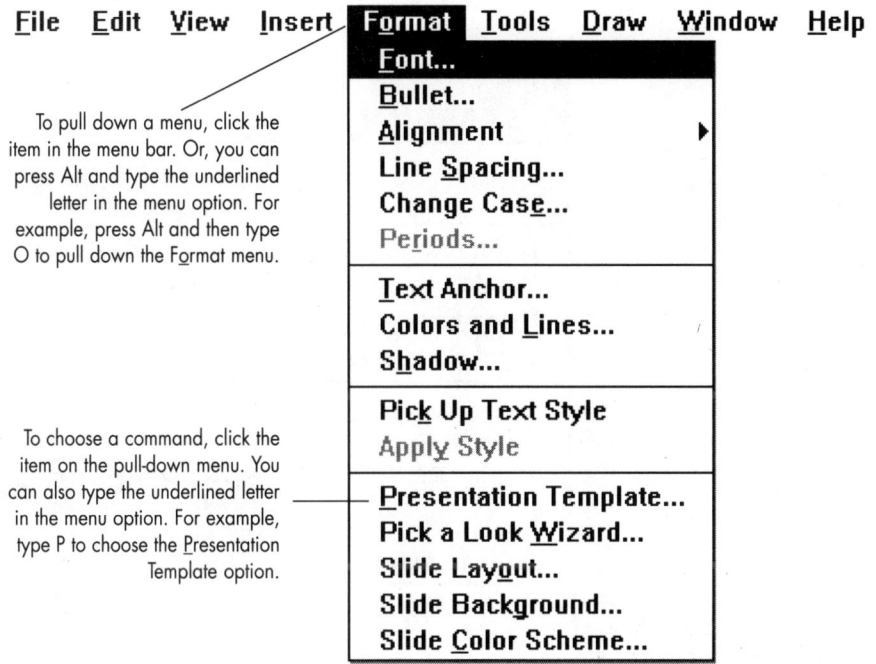

To pull down a menu, click the item in the menu bar. Or, you can press Alt and type the underlined letter in the menu option. For example, press Alt and then type O to pull down the Format menu.

To choose a command, click the item on the pull-down menu. You can also type the underlined letter in the menu option. For example, type P to choose the Presentation Template option.

Figure 5. Ways to access menu commands

Using Shortcut Menus

A shortcut menu displays the most common commands used with a particular object. The menu shows only commands and actions that are relevant to the selected object. If no object is selected, a menu with editing and view options will appear.

Figure 6 shows the shortcut menu that is displayed when a graphic object (the star) is selected.

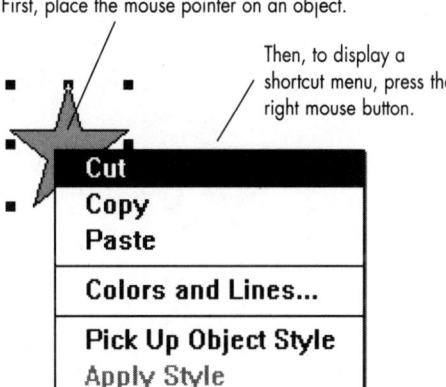

First, place the mouse pointer on an object.

Then, to display a shortcut menu, press the right mouse button.

Figure 6. Pressing the right mouse button displays a shortcut menu.

CHAPTER 1

Understanding Pull-Down Menus

Figure 7 below explains the different types of commands you'll find on a pull-down menu. In Figures 8 through 16 you'll find descriptions of the commands on all of PowerPoint's menus.

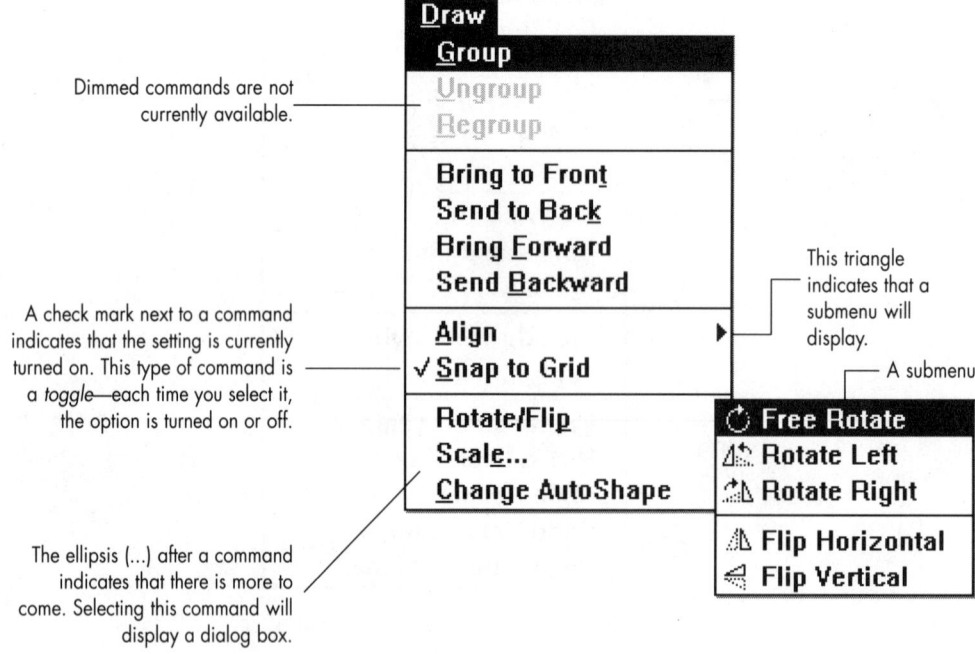

Figure 7. A pull-down menu

INTRODUCING POWERPOINT

The File Menu

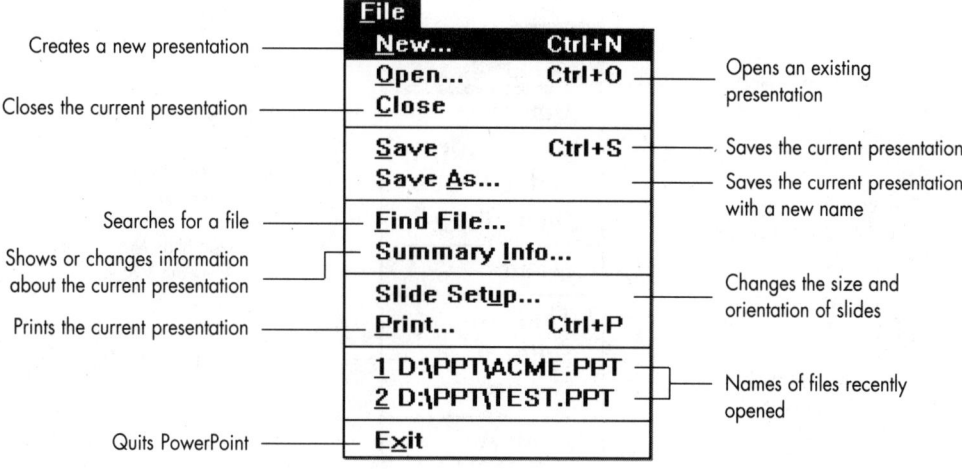

Figure 8. The File menu

The Edit Menu

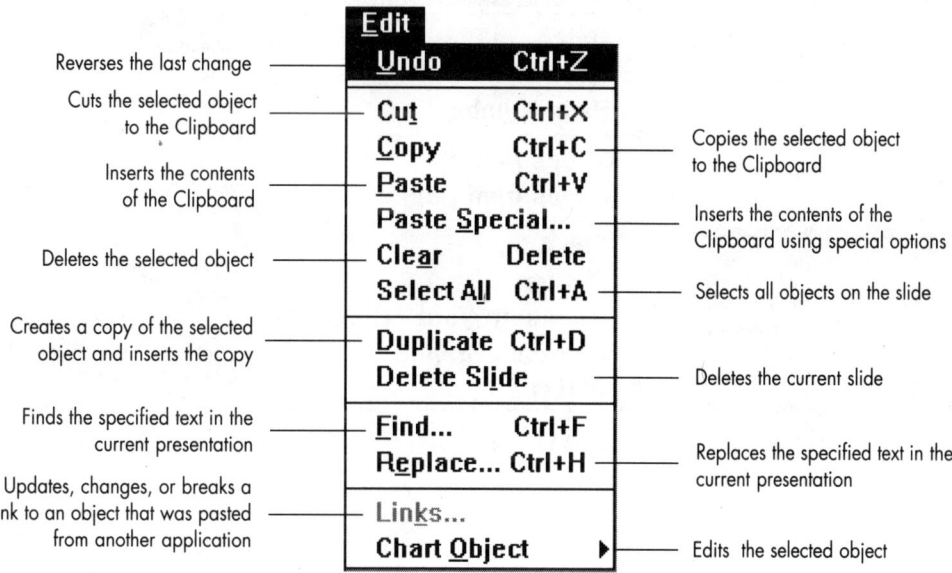

Figure 9. The Edit menu

9

CHAPTER 1

The View Menu

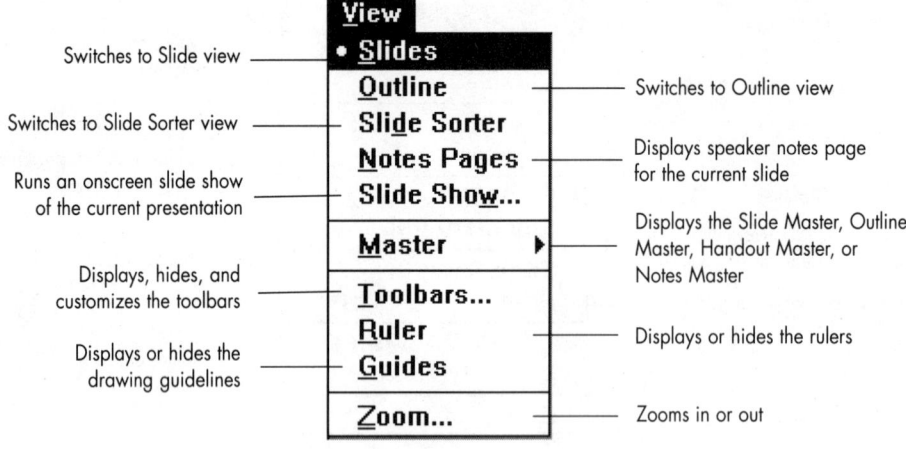

Figure 10. The View menu

The Insert Menu

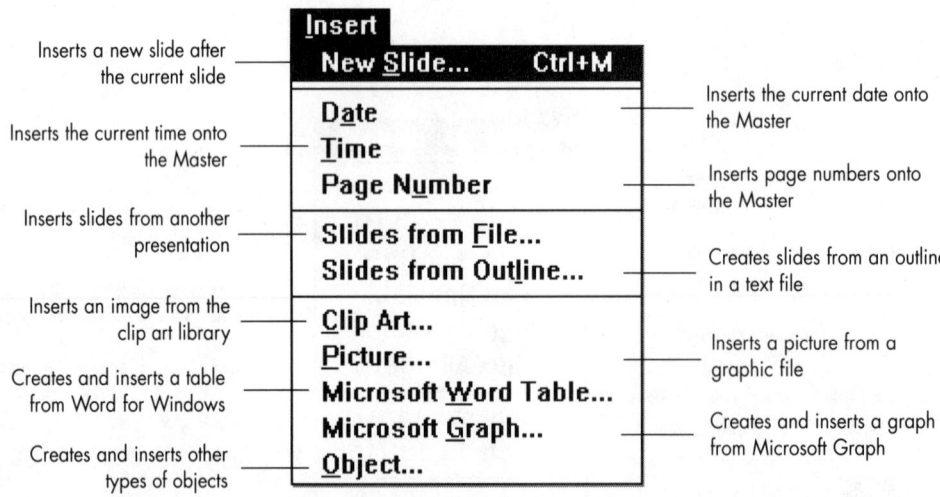

Figure 11. The Insert menu

INTRODUCING POWERPOINT

The Format Menu

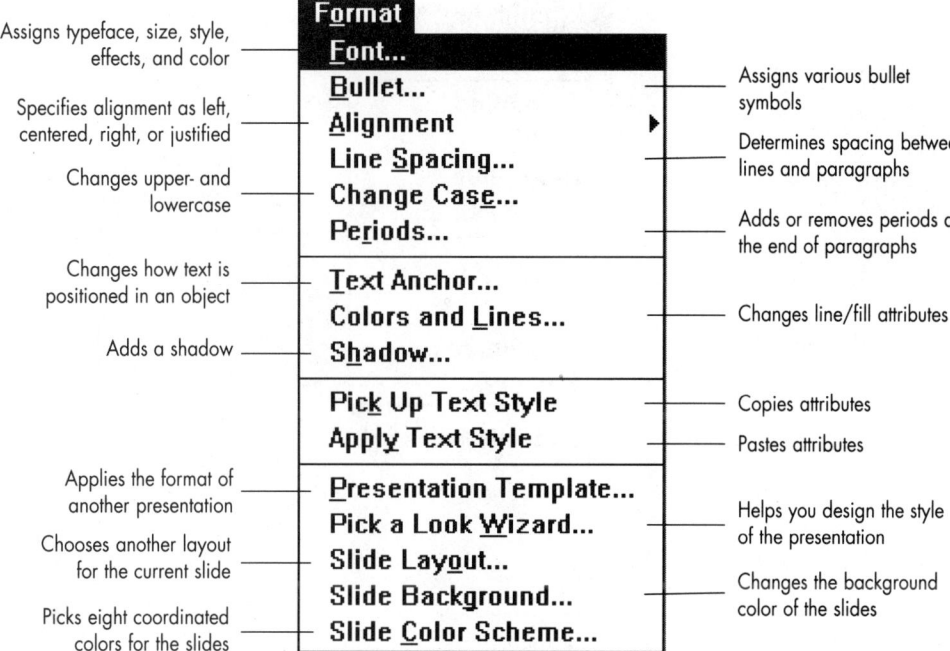

- Assigns typeface, size, style, effects, and color — Font...
- Specifies alignment as left, centered, right, or justified — Alignment
- Changes upper- and lowercase — Change Case...
- Changes how text is positioned in an object — Text Anchor...
- Adds a shadow — Shadow...
- Applies the format of another presentation — Presentation Template...
- Chooses another layout for the current slide — Slide Layout...
- Picks eight coordinated colors for the slides — Slide Color Scheme...

- Bullet... — Assigns various bullet symbols
- Line Spacing... — Determines spacing between lines and paragraphs
- Periods... — Adds or removes periods at the end of paragraphs
- Colors and Lines... — Changes line/fill attributes
- Pick Up Text Style — Copies attributes
- Apply Text Style — Pastes attributes
- Pick a Look Wizard... — Helps you design the style of the presentation
- Slide Background... — Changes the background color of the slides

Figure 12. The Format menu

11

CHAPTER 1

The Tools Menu

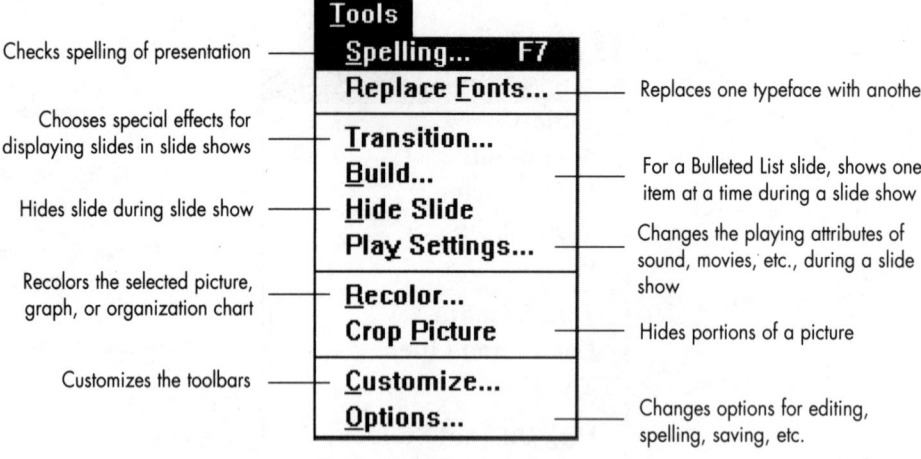

Figure 13. The Tools menu

The Draw Menu

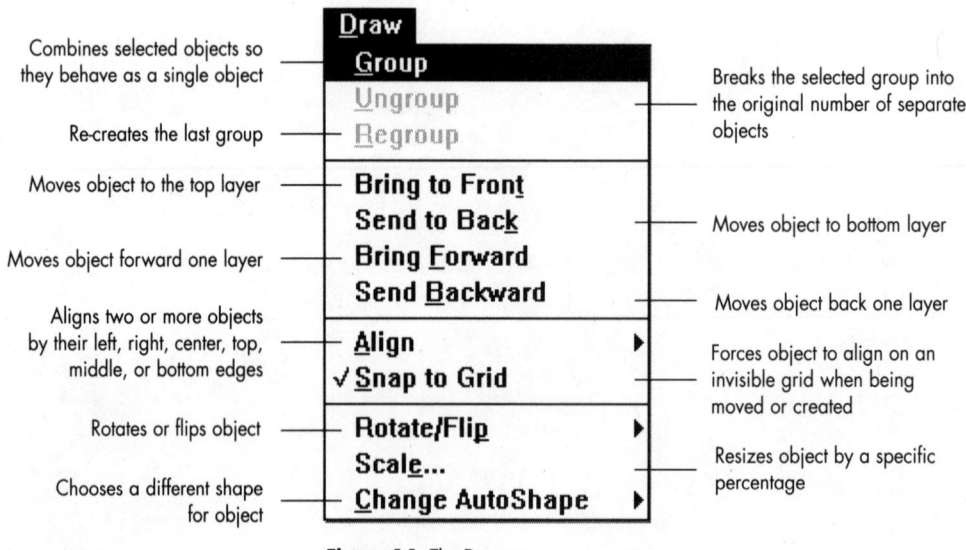

Figure 14. The Draw menu

INTRODUCING POWERPOINT

The Window Menu

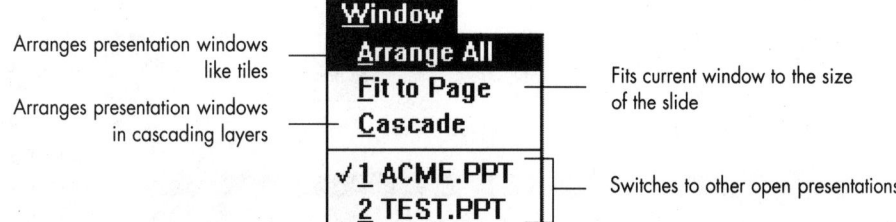

Figure 15. The Window menu

The Help Menu

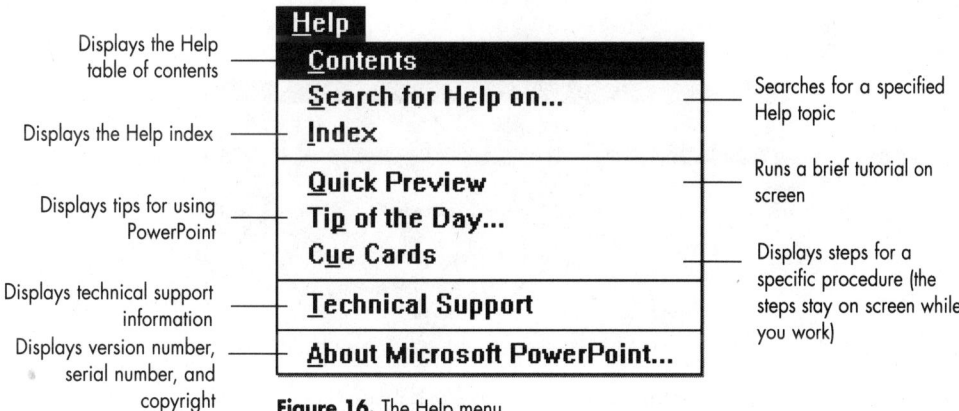

Figure 16. The Help menu

13

CHAPTER 1

Conversing with Dialog Boxes

Figures 17 and 18 point out the various types of options found in dialog boxes.

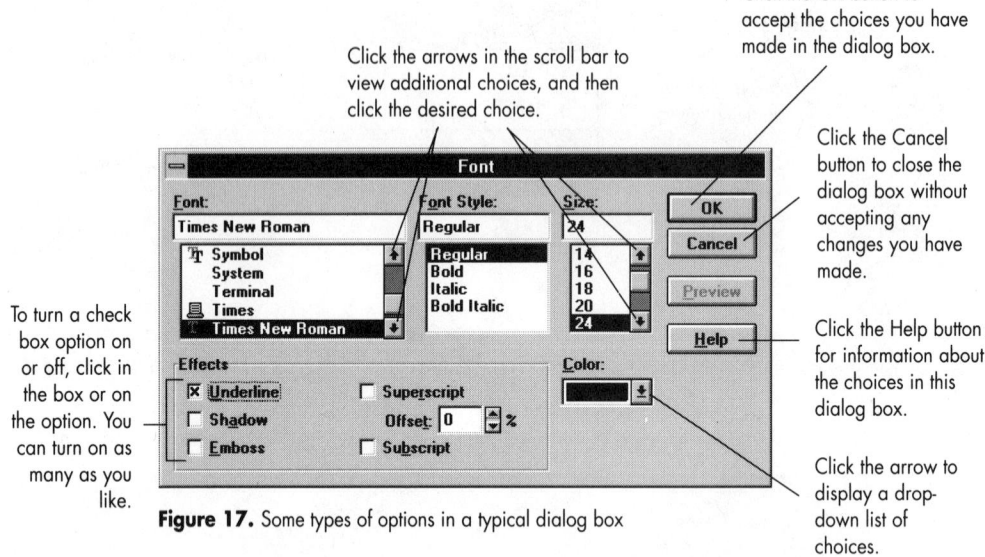

Figure 17. Some types of options in a typical dialog box

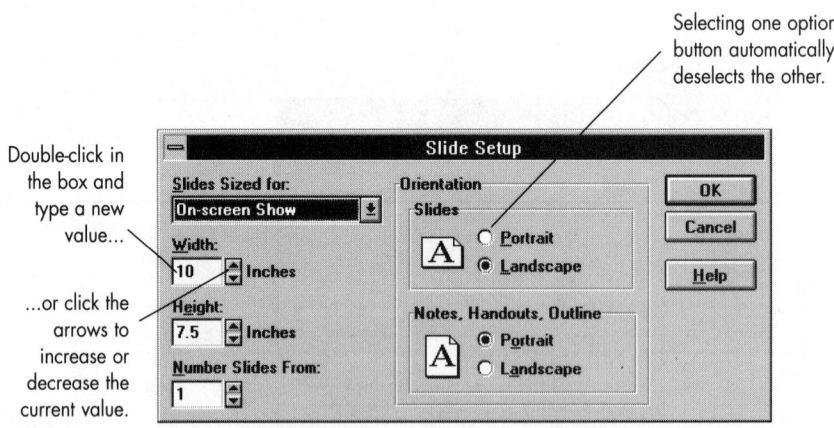

Figure 18. Other types of options found in a typical dialog box

INTRODUCING POWERPOINT

Figure 19. The Drawing toolbar offers buttons for creating, manipulating, and formatting objects (such as lines, boxes, and circles).

The Toolbars

The toolbars contain buttons that offer you a faster way to give commands to PowerPoint. Instead of choosing a command from a menu, you can simply click the appropriate button on the toolbar.

By default, three toolbars are displayed in Slide view: the Drawing toolbar (Figure 19), the Standard toolbar (Figure 20), and the Formatting toolbar (Figure 21).

To find out what a particular button does, place the mouse pointer on the button. (Do not actually click the button.) You will see a little yellow bubble (called a *ToolTip*) that gives a short description of the button; the status bar at the bottom of the window gives a lengthier description.

To hide one of the default toolbars or to display a different toolbar, use the View/Toolbars command. Use the Tools/Customize command to add and remove buttons from a toolbar.

Figure 20. The Standard toolbar offers buttons for everyday tasks such as saving files, opening files, printing, editing, and so forth.

Figure 21. The Formatting toolbar makes it easy to format text with a different typeface, size, or style.

15

A QUICK TOUR OF POWERPOINT

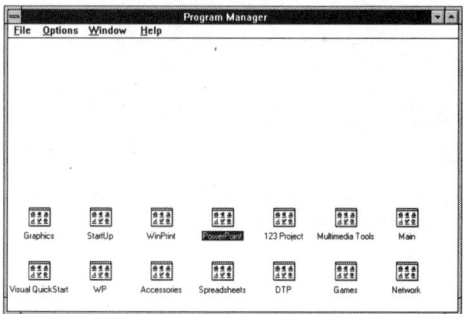

Figure 1. Windows Program Manager

Double-click here to launch PowerPoint

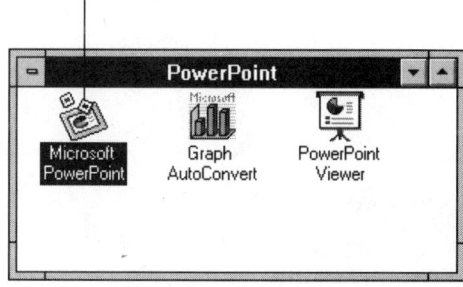

Figure 2. In this example, the Microsoft PowerPoint icon is located in the PowerPoint group. On your system, it may be located in a different group.

About the Tour

Suppose you need to create a set of charts by the end of the day, but you have never used PowerPoint. What will you do? Don't panic—just read this chapter. We understand that in today's busy world, people may not have time to read an entire book before they dive into a real-life project. So this chapter shows you the most important things you need to know about creating a presentation in PowerPoint for Windows.

After reading this chapter, you will be able to create bullet lists and graphs, format the slides, print the slides, view an onscreen slide show, and use Outline and Slide Sorter views to reorganize the presentation. This chapter gives you the bare bones information; for details, turn to the referenced chapters.

Launching PowerPoint

1. Load Windows and make sure you are in Program Manager (Figure 1).

2. If you don't see the PowerPoint icon in Program Manager, double-click the program group that contains your PowerPoint icon.

3. Double-click the PowerPoint icon (Figure 2).

■ Tip
✓ If you aren't sure which program group contains the PowerPoint icon, look for a group named Microsoft Office or PowerPoint. If you don't have these groups, open each program group until you find the icon.

17

CHAPTER 2

Choosing a Template

A *template* controls the overall look of your presentation—the colors, the format of the text, graphics placed on each slide, and so forth. PowerPoint comes with over 100 templates.

1. If the opening dialog box (Figure 3) is not displayed, choose File/New.
2. Choose Template and click OK.
3. In the Directories list, choose the appropriate template subdirectory (Figure 4).
4. In the File Name list, click a .PPT file (Figure 5). Look at the preview box to see what this template looks like.
5. When you find a template you like, click Apply.

To learn more about templates, see page 152.

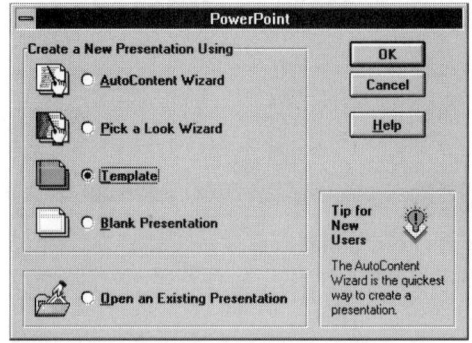

Figure 3. The opening dialog box that displays after you launch PowerPoint for Windows

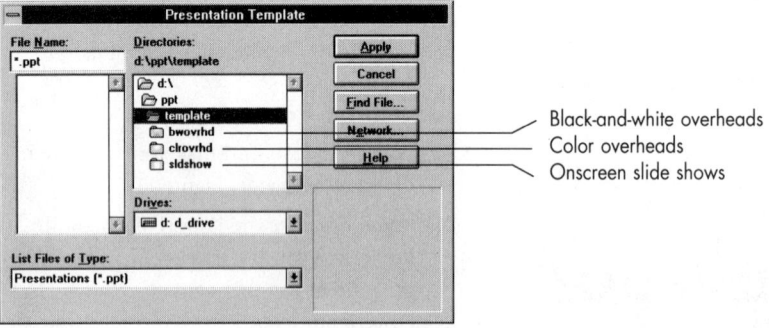

Figure 4. Choose the appropriate template subdirectory.

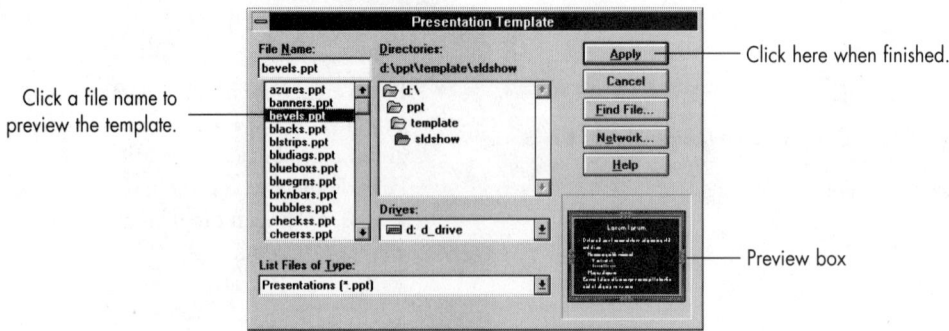

Figure 5. Choose a template in this dialog box.

A QUICK TOUR OF POWERPOINT

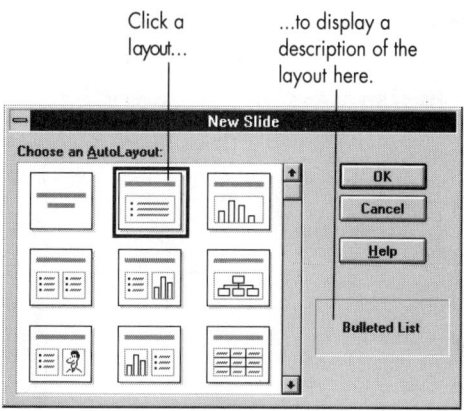

Figure 6. Choose an AutoLayout as you create a new slide.

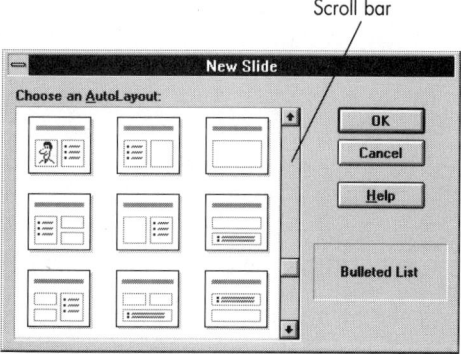

Figure 7. By using the scroll bar, you can see additional layouts.

Choosing a Layout

PowerPoint offers 21 different *AutoLayouts* to help you define what you want on a slide: a bulleted list, a graph, a table, an org chart, and so forth.

1. You choose a layout from the New Slide dialog box shown in Figure 6. This dialog box automatically displays when you create a new presentation or add a new slide.

2. Click the desired layout (scroll to see more layouts). Figure 6 shows the first set of layouts; Figure 7 shows the second set. Figure 8 describes the layouts you'll probably use most often (the first set).

3. Click OK.

On the following pages you will see examples of two types of layouts: Bulleted Lists and Graphs.

■ Tips

✓ When you click a layout in the New Slide dialog box, a description of the layout displays in the box (Figure 6).

✓ Instead of clicking on the layout and clicking OK, you can double-click the layout in the New Slide dialog box.

✓ To choose a different layout for an existing slide, click the Layout button at the bottom of the PowerPoint window or choose F_o_rmat/Slide Lay_o_ut.

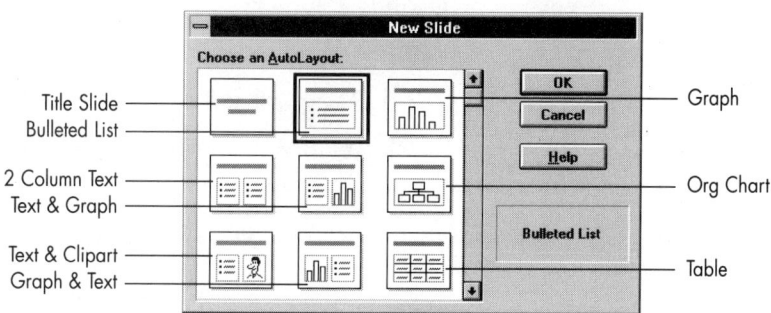

Figure 8. Descriptions of the first set of layouts

19

CHAPTER 2

Creating a Bulleted List

1. If the New Slide dialog box is not displayed, click the New Slide button at the bottom of the PowerPoint window.
2. In the New Slide dialog box, choose the Bulleted List layout.
3. Click the *title placeholder* (Figure 9), and type the title of your bulleted list.
4. Click the *text placeholder* (Figure 9), and type your bulleted text. Follow these simple rules:
   - Press Enter to type another bullet.
   - Press Tab to indent the current line (Figure 10).
   - Press Shift+Tab to unindent the current line.

■ Tip

✓ To change the bullet shape, use the Format/Bullet command.

See Chapter 3, starting on page 29, for additional information on creating and formatting text charts.

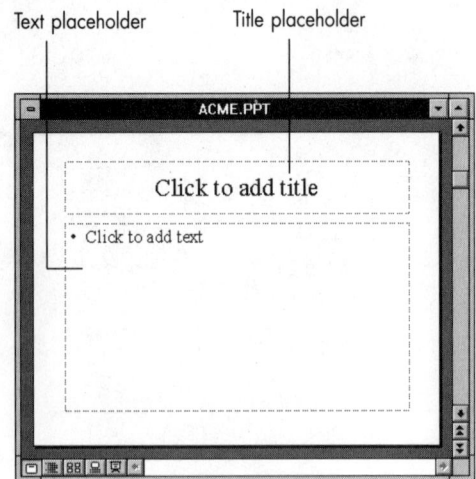

Figure 9. A new Bulleted List slide before any text has been added

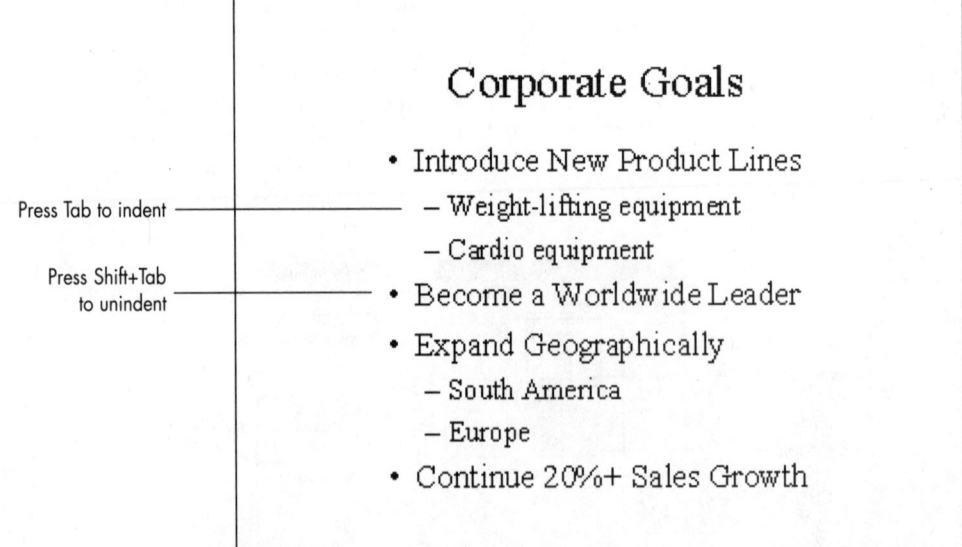

Figure 10. A slide with two levels of bullets

A QUICK TOUR OF POWERPOINT

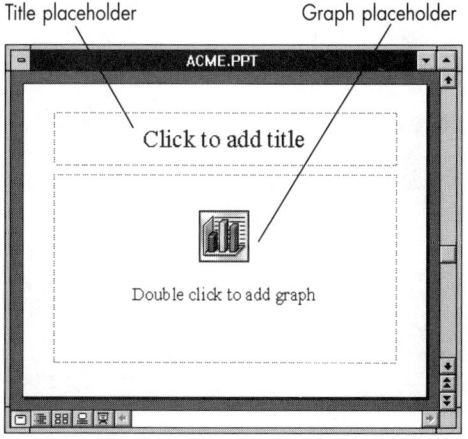

Figure 11. A slide with a graph placeholder

Creating a Graph

1. If the New Slide dialog box is not displayed, click the New Slide button.
2. In the New Slide dialog box, choose the Graph layout.
3. Click the title placeholder (Figure 11), and type the title of your graph.
4. Double-click the *graph placeholder* to load Microsoft Graph. A datasheet with sample data appears.
5. To erase the sample data, click the Select All button (Figure 12) and press Delete.
6. Enter the graph data (Figure 12).
7. To close the datasheet and view the graph, double-click the datasheet's control-menu box. Figure 13 shows a column chart of the data in Figure 12.

		A	B	C	D	E
		1990	1991	1992	1993	1994
1	Other	3	5	8	9	11
2	Shoes	4	6	9	10	15
3	Clothing	8	12	16	20	27
4	Racquets	9	15	21	25	35

Figure 12. Enter your chart data in the datasheet.

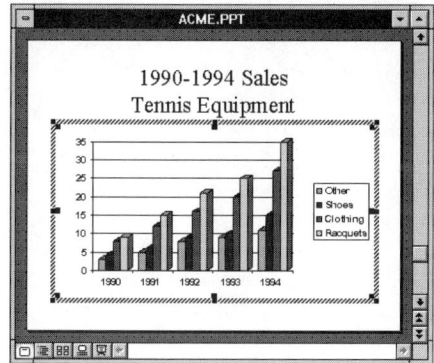

Figure 13. A column chart

■ Tips

✓ To redisplay the datasheet, click the View Datasheet button on the toolbar.

✓ To exit from Microsoft Graph, click the slide, outside of the graph placeholder.

✓ To reload Microsoft Graph, double-click the graph.

See Chapter 4, starting on page 45, for more information on inserting bar, line, and other graphs that have x- and y-axes.

See Chapter 6, starting on page 73, for information on creating pie charts.

CHAPTER 2

Formatting a Graph

To format a graph, you must still be in Microsoft Graph. If the graph has a border around it (like the one in Figure 16), you are still in Graph. If you don't see the border, double-click the graph placeholder to load Microsoft Graph.

1. To change the chart type (column is the default), choose F_ormat/_Chart Type (Figure 14).
2. Select _2-D or _3-D.
3. Click the desired chart type and click OK.
4. To format the graph quickly, choose F_ormat/_AutoFormat (Figure 15).
5. Select one of the sample graph formats, and click OK. Figure 16 shows a column chart formatted with the sixth AutoFormat option.

■ Tip

✓ The chart type can be selected before you fill in the datasheet.

See Chapter 5, starting on page 57, for additional information on formatting graphs, and Chapter 6, starting on page 76, for information on formatting pie charts.

Select a chart dimension...   ...then choose a chart type.

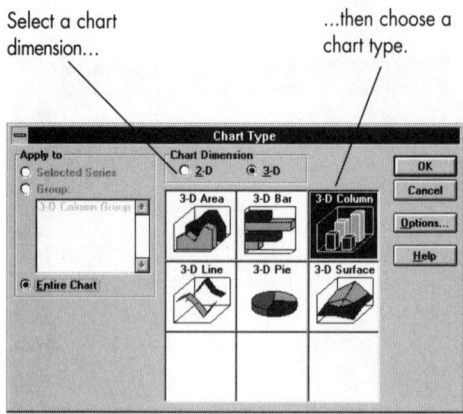

Figure 14. Selecting a chart type

You can choose a different chart type before choosing a format.

Each of the samples is formatted with different chart options.

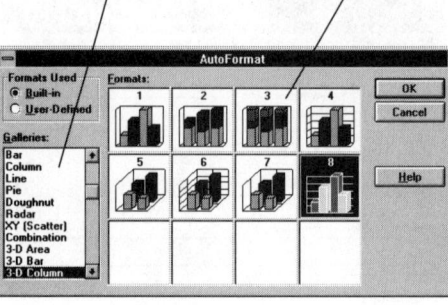

Figure 15. With the F_ormat/_AutoFormat command, you can click one of the sample charts to quickly format your chart.

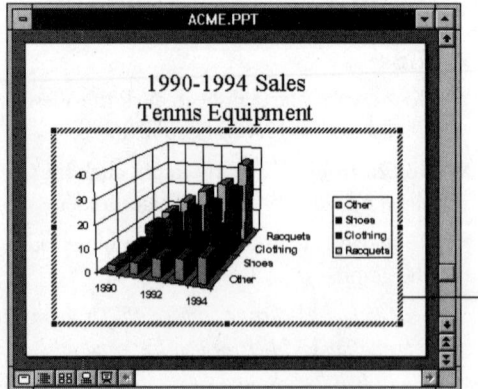

When a chart has a border around it, you are in Microsoft Graph.

Figure 16. This column chart was formatted using the sixth AutoFormat option.

A QUICK TOUR OF POWERPOINT

Navigating a Presentation

The status line at the bottom of the PowerPoint window indicates the current slide number (Figure 17). In Slide view, you can use the following keyboard commands to display other slides in the presentation:

Next Slide	Page Down
Previous Slide	Page Up
First Slide	Ctrl+Home
Last Slide	Ctrl+End

You can also use the Next Slide and Previous Slide buttons in the scroll bar. To navigate the presentation using the scroll box, do the following:

- Drag the scroll box to the top of the scroll bar to go to the first slide.
- Drag the scroll box to the bottom of the scroll bar to go to the last slide.
- Drag the scroll box up or down to go to a specific slide. (Slide numbers will display to the left of the scroll bar as you drag.)

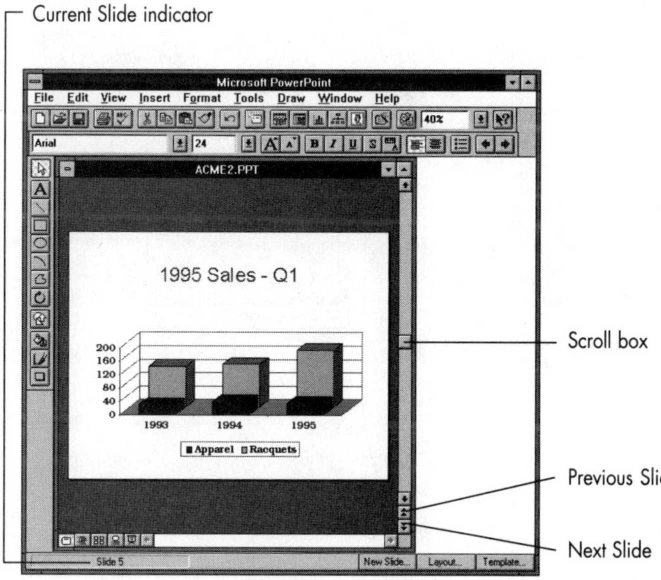

Figure 17. You can use the mouse in the scroll bar to display other slides in the presentation.

23

CHAPTER 2

Saving, Opening, and Closing Presentations

The commands for saving, opening, and closing presentations are available on the File menu (Figure 18).

Saving a New Presentation

1. Select File/Save As. This dialog box is shown in Figure 19.
2. In the File Name field, type a descriptive name (as descriptive as you can get in eight characters...).
3. To save to another drive, click in the Drives field and choose the desired drive letter.
4. To save to another directory, navigate the Directories list (Figure 19).
5. Click OK.
6. Fill in the Summary Info dialog box, if desired, and click OK.

The file is saved with a .PPT extension (for example, ACME.PPT).

Opening a Presentation

1. Select File/Open.
2. To open a file on another drive, click in the Drives field and choose the desired drive letter.
3. To open a file in another directory, navigate the Directories list.
4. Click the name in the File Name list and click OK.

Closing the Current Presentation

1. Select File/Close.

■ Tips

✓ The shortcuts for saving are Ctrl+S and the Save button (Figure 20). The shortcuts for opening are Ctrl+O and the Open button.

✓ Use the Tools/Options command to turn off the automatic display of the Summary Info dialog box.

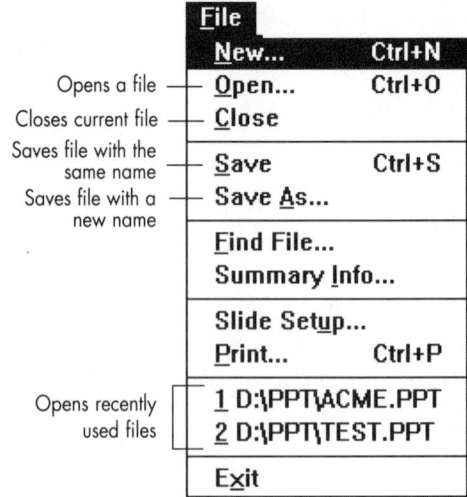

Figure 18. The File menu

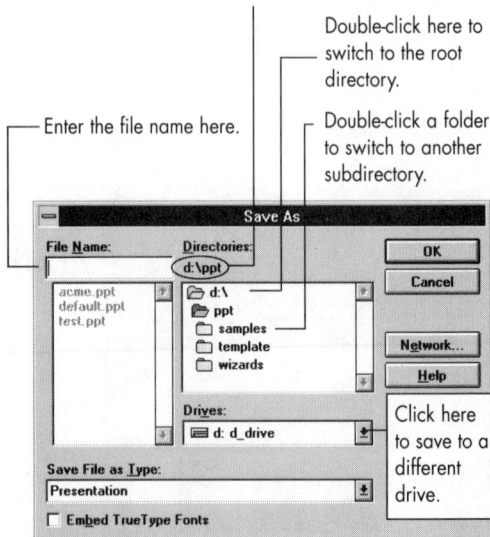

Figure 19. Issuing the File/Save As command displays this dialog box.

Figure 20. The Standard toolbar

A QUICK TOUR OF POWERPOINT

To print full-page slides, make sure the Print What option says Slides. (The other choices allow you to print an outline, speaker notes, and handouts.)

Be sure to select a slide range.

Current printer

Click the Printer button to select a different printer.

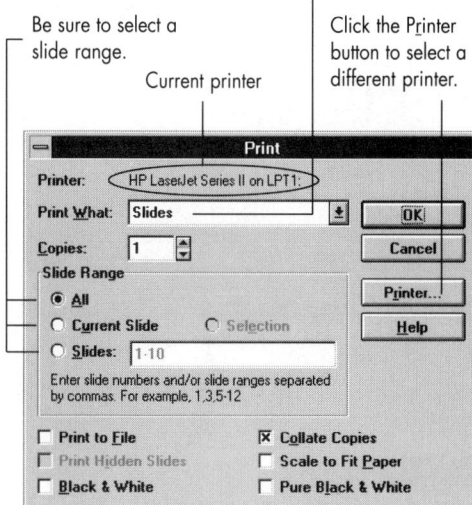

Figure 21. To display the Print dialog box, choose File/Print.

Print

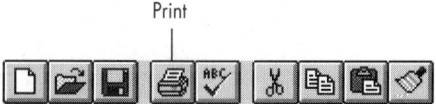

Figure 22. The Standard toolbar

Printing a Presentation

1. Select File/Print. Figure 21 shows the Print dialog box.
2. In the Print What list box, make sure Slides is selected.
3. To print all slides in the presentation, make sure All is selected for the Slide Range.
4. To print certain slides, choose Slides and then enter the range of slides you want to print. Put a dash between the numbers in a range (as in 1-5), and commas between each number or range (as in 1-5, 7, 10).
5. Click OK.

■ Tips

✓ The keyboard shortcut for printing is Ctrl+P.

✓ You can also print by choosing the Print button in the toolbar (Figure 22). However, this button does not display the Print dialog box—it prints the slide range last specified in the Print dialog box. It doesn't give you a chance to specify a slide range.

See pages 186–187 for more information about printing a presentation.

25

CHAPTER 2

Outline View

Outline view (Figure 23) displays an outline of your presentation: the slide titles and any main text, such as bulleted items. Optionally, you can hide or *collapse* part of the outline so that you see only the slide titles. Outline view is ideal for seeing the structure of your presentation and for reordering slides.

1. Click the Outline View button (Figure 24).
2. To display only the slide titles, click the Show Titles button in the Outlining toolbar (Figure 25). To redisplay the entire outline, click the Show All button.
3. To display or hide text formatting, click the Show Formatting button. Compare Figures 23 and 26. Figure 23 displays the formatting; Figure 26 does not.

■ Tip

✓ To move a slide, first click the icon in front of the slide title. Then click the Move Up or Move Down button until the slide is in its new position.

See Chapter 12, starting on page 155, for more information about Outline view.

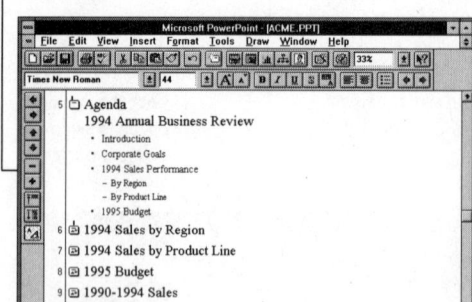

Figure 23. Outline view

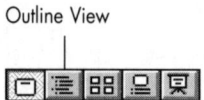

Figure 24. The view buttons

Figure 25. The Outlining toolbar

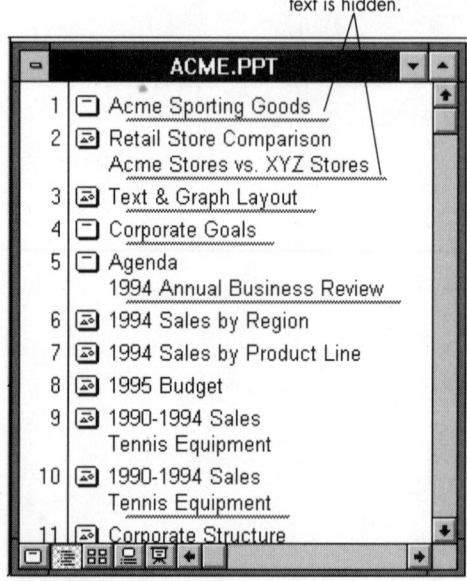

Figure 26. This outline shows only the titles (no body text) and does not display the text formatting.

A QUICK TOUR OF POWERPOINT

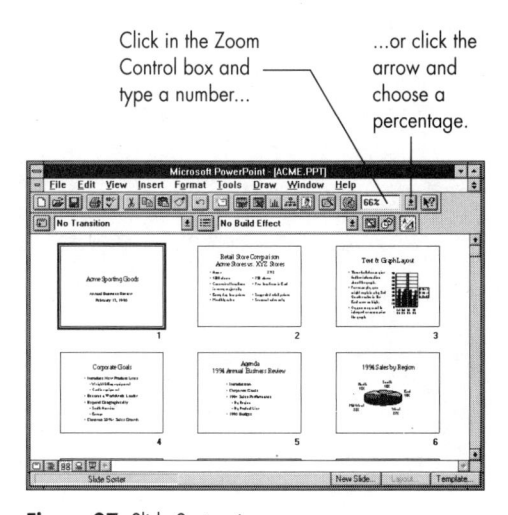

Click in the Zoom Control box and type a number...

...or click the arrow and choose a percentage.

Figure 27. Slide Sorter view

Slide Sorter View

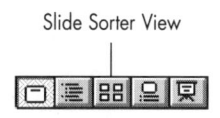

Figure 28. The view buttons

Slide Sorter View

Slide Sorter view (Figure 27) gives you the best of both worlds. As in Outline view, you can see the big picture of your presentation, and you can reorder the slides. As in Slide view, you can actually see the charts on the slides, albeit in miniature form. The size of the slides in Slide Sorter view can be controlled in the Zoom Control field, pointed out in Figure 27.

1. Click the Slide Sorter View button (Figure 28).
2. To see more (but smaller) slides, choose a smaller zoom percentage in the Zoom Control field. The slides in Figure 29 are zoomed out to 50%.
3. To see more detail on the slides, choose a higher zoom percentage in the Zoom Control field. The slides in Figure 30 are zoomed in to 150%.

■ Tip

✓ To move a slide, first select the slide by clicking on it, and then drag the slide to the new location. When the pointer is between two slides, a vertical line indicates where the slide will be inserted.

See Chapter 13, starting on page 165, for more information on Slide Sorter view.

Zoom percentage

Zoom percentage

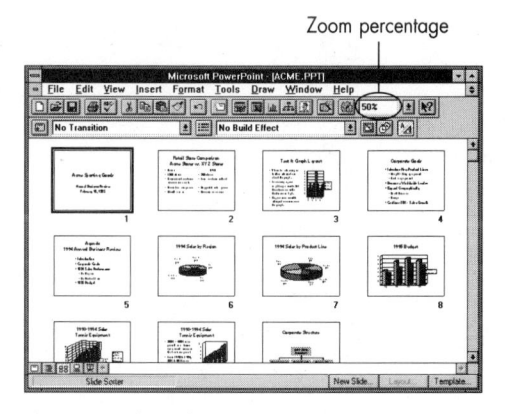

Figure 29. These slides are zoomed out so that more slides are displayed.

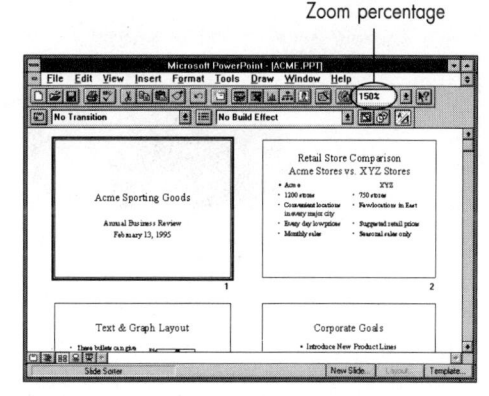

Figure 30. These slides are zoomed in so that more detail is displayed on each slide.

27

CHAPTER 2

Viewing a Slide Show

A *slide show* displays each of the slides in the presentation, one at time, full screen (Figure 33). To show slides to a large audience, you can project the slide show onto a large screen, saving you the time, cost, and trouble of producing 35mm slides.

1. Go to the slide you want to display first in the slide show. (To view the slide show from the beginning of the presentation, press Ctrl+Home to go to the first slide.)
2. Click the Slide Show button (Figure 32). The current slide displays full screen.
3. To view the next slide, click the left mouse button.

See Chapter 14, starting on page 173, for additional information on slide shows.

■ Tips

✓ To view the previous slide in a slide show, click the right mouse button.

✓ To cancel the slide show, press Esc.

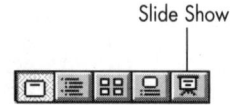

Figure 32. The view buttons

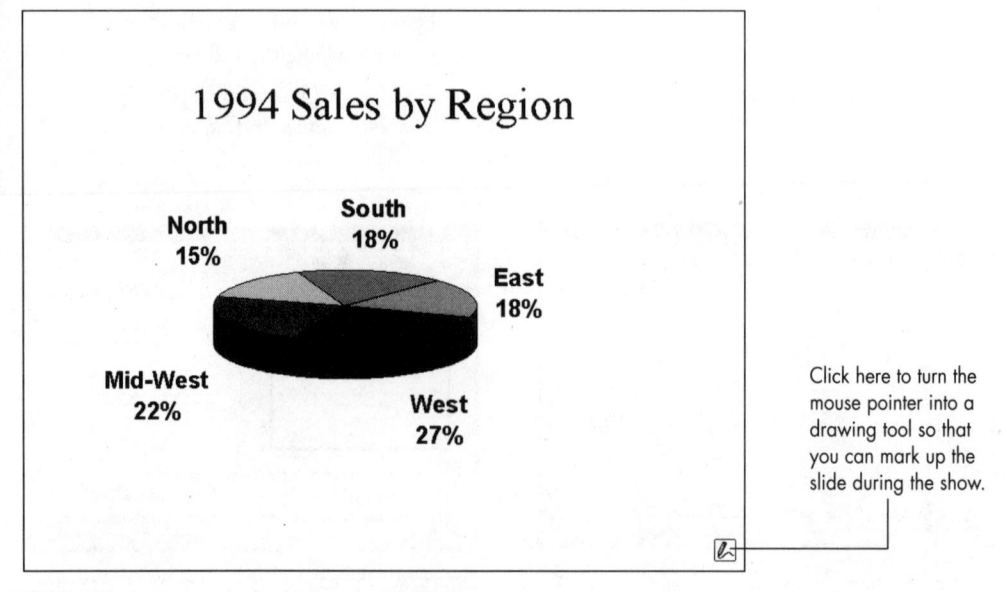

Figure 33. A pie chart displayed during a slide show.

Click here to turn the mouse pointer into a drawing tool so that you can mark up the slide during the show.

CREATING TEXT SLIDES 3

About Text Slides

In this chapter you'll learn how to create slides that contain text, and how to edit and format the text. The types of slides that consist primarily of text are Title slides (Figure 1), Bulleted Lists (Figure 2), and Two-Column Lists (Figure 3).

Slides can also combine text with a graph or with a piece of clip art. The slide in Figure 4 has both text and a graph.

Figure 1. A Title slide

Figure 2. A Bulleted List slide

Figure 3. A Two-Column List slide

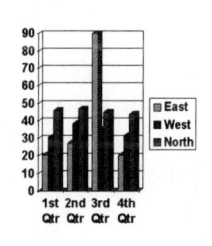

Figure 4. A slide that combines text with a graph

29

CHAPTER 3

Choosing a Text Layout

When you insert a slide into the presentation, you are given the opportunity to choose a layout for the new slide. You choose a layout that is appropriate for the slide you want to create. Of the 22 layouts for new slides, most have a text placeholder. (A *text placeholder* is simply a container for text.) Figure 5 points out the layouts that have text placeholders.

1. In Slide view, click the New Slide button. The New Slide dialog box (Figure 6) shows the first set of AutoLayouts.
2. Use the scroll bar to see additional layouts, if necessary.
3. Click the desired layout.
4. Click OK.

See also Choosing a Layout on page 19.

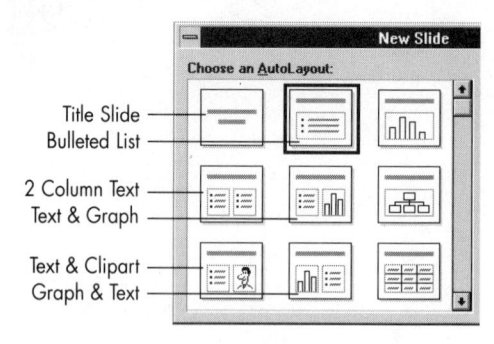

Figure 5. In the first set of layouts, the indicated layouts have main text placeholders.

■ Tips

✓ If you don't find an AutoLayout that fits your needs perfectly, don't dispair; you can add, move, or eliminate placeholders.

See Manipulating Text Placeholders on page 33.

✓ Outline view does not display the New Slide dialog box when you insert a slide. This view automatically inserts a slide with the Bulleted List layout.

See page 158 for information on creating bullet slides in Outline view.

✓ To create a new slide with the same layout as the current slide, hold down Shift as you click the New Slide button. This action bypasses the New Slide dialog box.

✓ To choose a different layout for an existing slide, click the Layout button at the bottom of the PowerPoint window or choose Format/Slide Layout.

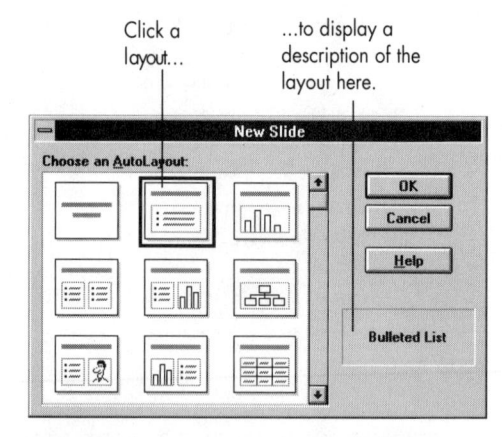

Figure 6. Choose a layout in the New Slide dialog box.

CREATING TEXT SLIDES

Dotted lines surround empty AutoLayout text placeholders; these lines disappear as soon as you enter text into the placeholder.

Click to add title

• Click to add text

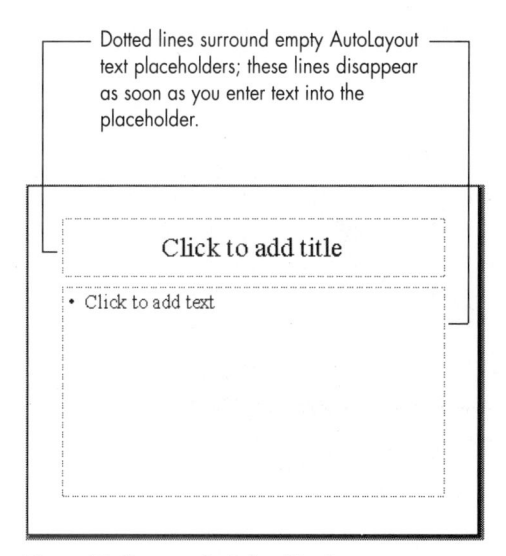

Figure 7. Choosing the Bulleted List layout creates two text placeholders: one for the title and one for the bulleted text.

Entering Text into a Placeholder

Text placeholders that were created with an AutoLayout have a dotted-line boundary around them (Figure 7). They also tell you exactly what to do to enter text in them: *Click to add title* or *Click to add text*. Thus, entering text into a text placeholder is easy:

1. Click inside the placeholder.
2. Start typing. Refer to the table below for ways to edit your text.

■ Tip

✓ To replace existing text with something new, it's not necessary to delete the unwanted text and then insert the new text. Instead, select the unwanted text and start typing—the new text will replace the existing text.

Moving the Cursor Within a Text Placeholder

To move cursor to...	*Do this...*
Beginning of line	Press Home
End of line	Press End
Next word	Press Ctrl+right arrow
Previous word	Press Ctrl+left arrow

Deleting Text

To delete...	*Do this...*
Character to the right	Press Delete
Character to the left	Press Backspace
Any amount of text	Select the text and press Delete

Selecting Text

To select...	*Do this...*
Word	Double-click word
Paragraph	Triple-click paragraph
All text in placeholder	Click placeholder and press Ctrl+A
Any amount of text	Click and drag

CHAPTER 3

Creating a Text Placeholder

Sometimes you'll need to add your own text placeholders—for example, to annotate a graph (Figure 8) or to insert a footnote on a Title slide (Figure 9).

1. Click the Text tool (Figure 10).
2. Place the pointer on the slide where you want to insert the placeholder.
3. To insert a one-line label, just click and start typing. Figure 11 shows a placeholder that was inserted this way.
4. To create a word-wrapped text box, drag a box to the desired size. When you type, text will word-wrap inside the box. The placeholder in Figure 12 was created with this technique.

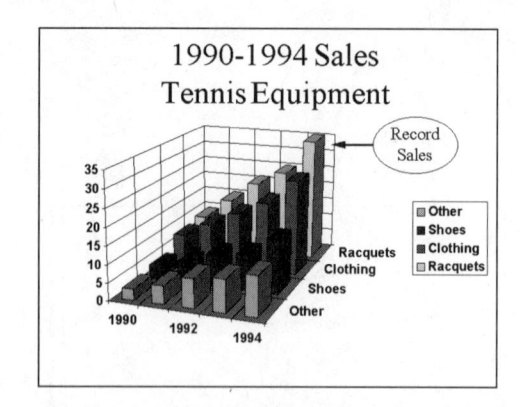

Figure 8. The *Record Sales* annotation is inside a text placeholder that was inserted.

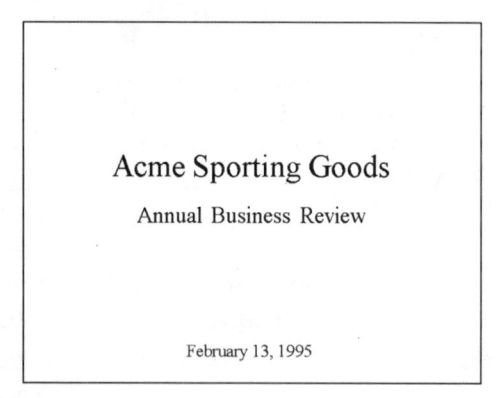

Figure 9. The date at the bottom of the slide is in an added text placeholder.

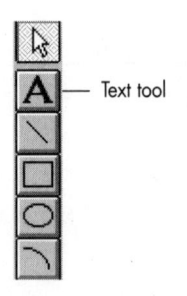

Figure 10. The Drawing toolbar

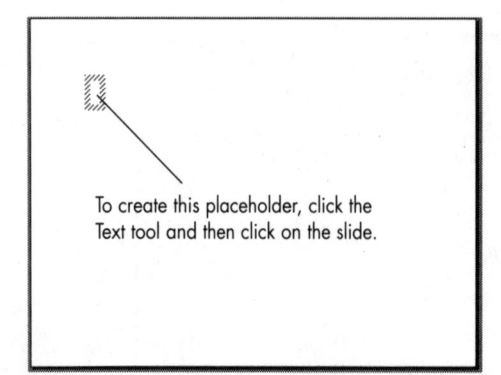

Figure 11. This type of placeholder is ideal for single-line labels. The box grows as you type.

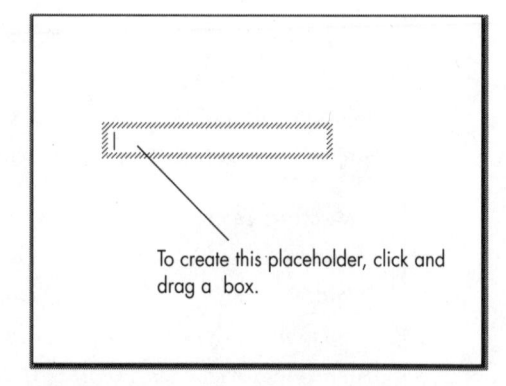

Figure 12. This type of placeholder will word-wrap text within the box.

CREATING TEXT SLIDES

Manipulating Text Placeholders

Text placeholders can be moved, copied, resized, and deleted.

Moving a Text Placeholder

1. Click inside the placeholder. You will see a selection box around the placeholder (Figure 13).
2. Place the mouse pointer on the selection box. The mouse pointer becomes an arrow.
3. Drag the placeholder to the desired location on the slide.

Copying a Text Placeholder

1. Click inside the text placeholder.
2. Place the mouse pointer on the selection box.
3. Hold down Ctrl as you drag to the desired location on the slide.

Resizing a Text Placeholder

1. Click inside the text placeholder.
2. Click the selection box to display selection handles (Figure 14).
3. Drag one of the selection handles until the placeholder is the desired size (Figure 15).

Deleting a Text Placeholder

1. Click inside the placeholder.
2. Click the selection box. Selection handles appear.
3. Press Delete. If you delete a title or main text placeholder, an empty text placeholder from the AutoLayout will appear.
4. If desired, press Delete again to delete the AutoLayout text placeholder.

Drag the selection box to move the placeholder. To copy the placeholder, hold down Ctrl as you drag.

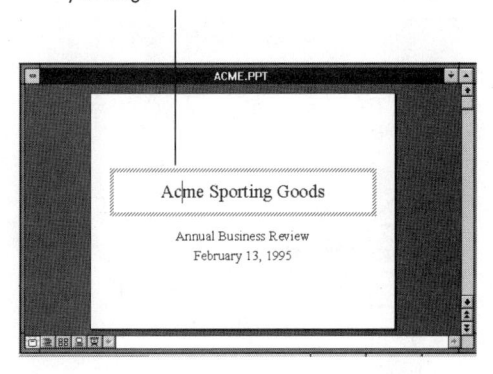

Figure 13. A selection box appears around the text placeholder when you click inside.

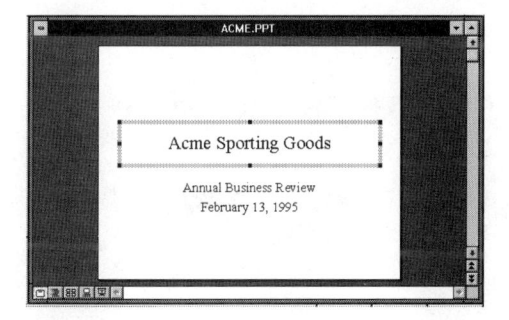

Figure 14. When you click the selection box, selection handles appear.

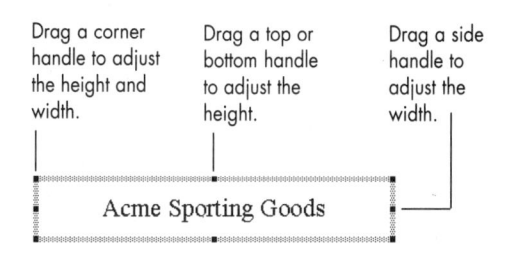

Drag a corner handle to adjust the height and width.

Drag a top or bottom handle to adjust the height.

Drag a side handle to adjust the width.

Figure 15. Using selection handles to resize a text block

33

CHAPTER 3

Moving Text

The standard way of moving text in a Windows application is using the *cut-and-paste* technique (Figure 16). PowerPoint offers an alternate method called *drag-and-drop* (Figure 17).

Cut-and-Paste

1. Select the text to be moved (Figure 18).
2. Select Edit/Cut.
3. Place the cursor where you want to insert the text.
4. Select Edit/Paste.

Drag-and-Drop

1. Select the text to be moved.
2. Place the pointer in the selection.
3. Hold down the mouse button and begin dragging. You will see a box under the pointer that indicates you are in the middle of moving text, and a vertical line that indicates the insertion point.
4. Release the mouse button when the vertical line is positioned where you want to insert the text. The text will then drop into place.

■ Tips

✓ To select a bullet item and all its sub-bullets, click the main bullet.

✓ When moving bullet items, you can place the cursor at the end of a paragraph (and the text will be inserted after that paragraph) or at the beginning of a paragraph (and the text will be inserted before that paragraph).

✓ You can also press Ctrl+X to cut and Ctrl+V to paste.

✓ The Standard toolbar contains buttons for cutting, copying, and pasting (Figure 19).

See page 158 for information on moving bullet items in Outline view.

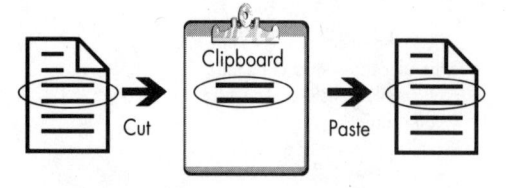

Figure 16. The cut-and-paste technique is a way of moving text. The Clipboard is a temporary storage area for objects that are cut or copied.

Figure 17. The drag-and-drop technique is another way to move text.

Notice that the bullets themselves are not highlighted (although they will be moved along with the text).

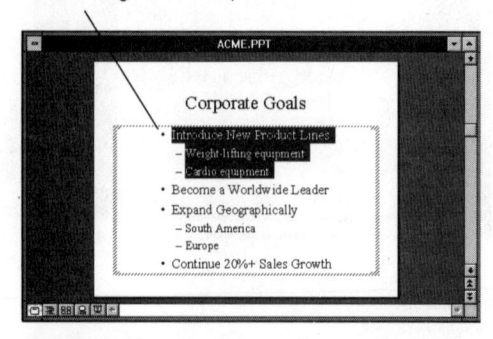

Figure 18. The selected text can be moved by using either cut and paste or drag and drop.

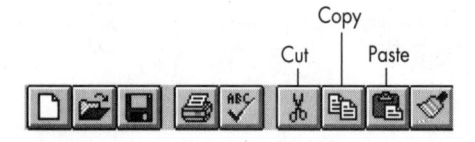

Figure 19. The Standard toolbar

CREATING TEXT SLIDES

Using the Spelling Checker

The spelling checker searches all text placeholders in the presentation and stops at words that aren't in PowerPoint's dictionary.

1. Select Tools/Spelling. The Spelling dialog box appears (Figure 20).
2. If the word is spelled correctly, choose Ignore or Ignore All.

   or

   If you'll use the word frequently, choose Add to add it to the custom dictionary.
3. For misspelled words, choose the correct spelling from the Suggestions list.

   or

   Edit the Change To field and then choose Change or Change All.
4. Repeat steps 2 and 3 for all "suspect" words.

■ Tips

✓ The keyboard shortcut for running the spelling checker is F7.

✓ The Spelling button is available in the Standard toolbar (Figure 21).

✓ The spelling checker doesn't find all misspellings. If the mistyped word is an actual word, the spelling checker isn't smart enough to consider the word suspect. Therefore, it's important that you still proofread the text yourself.

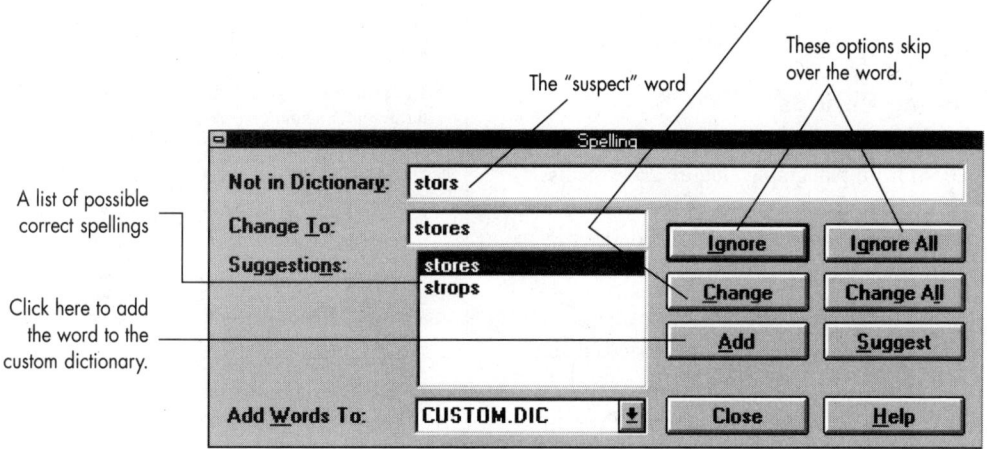

Figure 20. Select Tools/Spelling to display the Spelling dialog box.

Figure 21. The Standard toolbar

35

CHAPTER 3

Changing Case

The Change Case command lets you choose different combinations of upper- and lowercase for selected text.

1. Select the text you want to change.
2. Select F*o*rmat/Change Cas*e*.
3. Choose one of the case options (Figure 22).
4. Click OK.

■ **Tips**

✓ Toggle case is handy when you have mistakenly typed text with Caps Lock on—it turns lowercase letters into uppercase and vice versa.

✓ Title case capitalizes each word in the selected text, except for small words such as *the, and, or, of, at*.

✓ For some reason, you can't go directly from title case to sentence case. Here's a workaround: Go from title case to lowercase and then to sentence case.

Adding Periods

The Periods command lets you add or remove periods from paragraphs. Figure 23 explains the rules about which types of text placeholders are affected by the Periods command.

1. Select the text you want to change.
2. Select F*o*rmat/Periods. The Periods dialog box is shown in Figure 24.
3. Choose *A*dd Periods or *R*emove Periods.
4. Click OK.

■ **Tip**

✓ If the paragraph has multiple sentences, only the period at the end of the paragraph will be affected.

Study the upper- and lowercase used in the button names—they show you how that option will format the selected text. For example, the UPPERCASE option will capitalize every letter in the selected text.

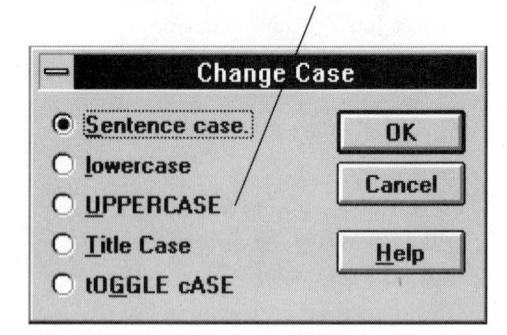

Figure 22. The Change Case dialog box

You can add or remove periods in the main text placeholder.

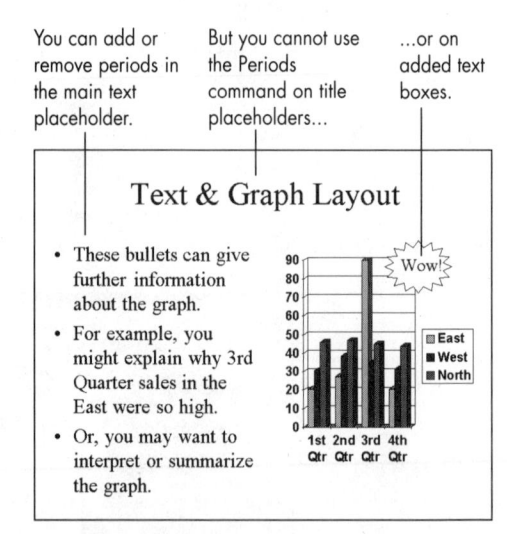

But you cannot use the Periods command on title placeholders...

...or on added text boxes.

Figure 23. All text placeholders are not created equal when it comes to the Periods command.

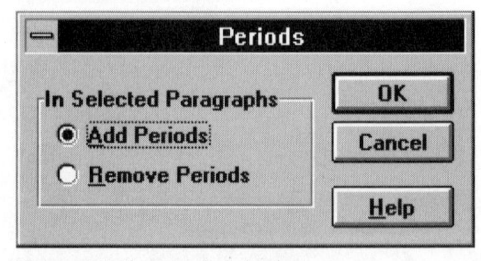

Figure 24. The Periods dialog box

36

CREATING TEXT SLIDES

> **Agenda**
> **1994 Annual Business Review**
>
> - Introduction
> - Corporate Goals
> - 1994 Sales Performance
>   – By Region
>   – By Product Line
> - 1995 Budget

Figure 25. The default bullet shapes

> **Agenda**
> **1994 Annual Business Review**
>
> ❏ Introduction
> ❏ Corporate Goals
> ❏ 1994 Sales Performance
>   ➢ By Region
>   ➢ By Product Line
> ❏ 1995 Budget

Figure 26. Modified bullet shapes

To decrease the size of the bullet, enter a number less than 100. To increase, enter a number greater than 100.

After you select a typeface, this area displays all the symbols in that typeface.

Clicking a symbol zooms in on it.

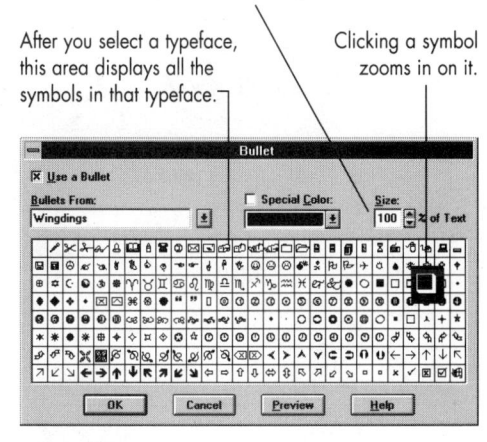

Figure 27. Choose a different bullet shape in the Bullet dialog box.

Changing the Bullet Shape

Figure 25 shows a Bulleted List slide that uses the default bullet shapes. Figure 26 shows this same list with different shapes selected for the two levels.

1. Click anywhere on the line whose bullet shape you want to change. To change the shape of bullets in several consecutive lines, select them by clicking and dragging.

2. Select F_ormat/_Bullet. The Bullet dialog box is shown in Figure 27.
   or
   Press the right mouse button to display the shortcut menu, and choose Bullet.

3. In the _Bullets From field, click the arrow to display a list of typefaces.

4. Choose the desired typeface. Wingdings and Zapf Dingbats are two typefaces that contain many symbols appropriate for bullet shapes.

5. Click the desired symbol.

6. Click OK.

See also Creating a Bulleted List on page 20.

■ Tips

✓ To remove a bullet from a line, click the Bullet On/Off button (Figure 28).

✓ To see the slide with the new bullet shapes, click the _P_review button. (You may need to drag the Bullet dialog box out of the way.)

✓ To change the bullet shapes for all bulleted lists, edit the Slide Master.

See Changing the Default Format for Text on page 149.

Bullet On/Off

Figure 28. The Formatting toolbar

37

CHAPTER 3

Adjusting the Bullet Placement

To change the horizontal spacing between the bullet and the text that follows it, you need to display the rulers (Figure 29) and drag the appropriate markers. Figure 30 shows a Bulleted List slide before any spacing change; Figure 31 shows the same list after a bit of space has been added between the bullet and text.

1. Select <u>V</u>iew/<u>R</u>uler.
2. Click anywhere inside the text placeholder. For each bullet level, the ruler shows a set of indent markers that can be individually adjusted. For example, if there are two bullet levels, the ruler displays two sets of indent markers.
3. To change the spacing between the bullet and the text, drag the left-indent marker in the ruler (Figure 32).
4. To adjust the position of the bullet, drag the first-line indent marker in the ruler.

   or

   To adjust the position of the bullet *without* changing the spacing between the bullet and the text, drag the square marker in the ruler. (Both markers will move together.)

■ Tips

✓ You don't need to select all the text in the placeholder before adjusting the indents—the ruler automatically controls the entire placeholder.

✓ To remove the ruler, choose <u>V</u>iew/<u>R</u>uler again.

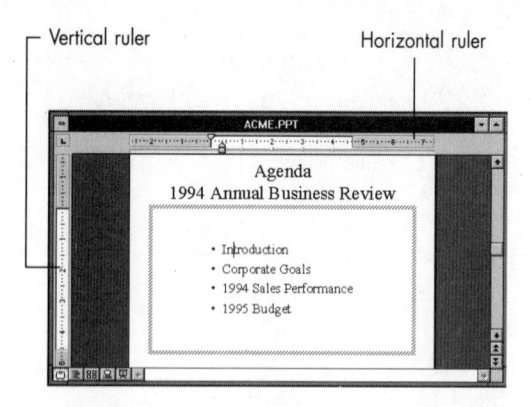

Figure 29. To display the rulers, select View/Ruler.

Figure 30. A Bulleted List slide before any adjustment of indents

Figure 31. The same list after the indents have been increased slightly

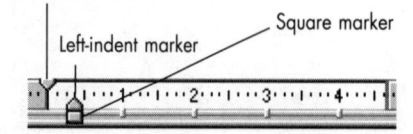

Figure 32. The indent markers in the horizontal ruler

CREATING TEXT SLIDES

Figure 33. The Formatting toolbar

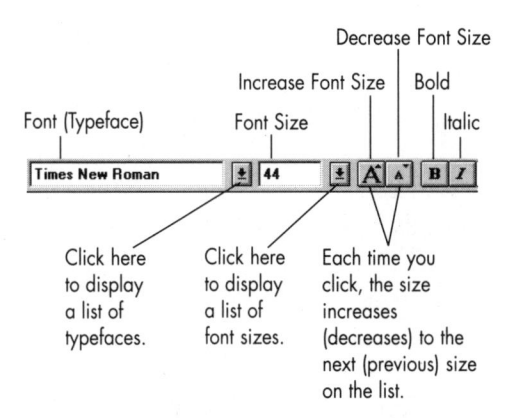

Font (Typeface) — Font Size — Increase Font Size — Decrease Font Size — Bold — Italic

Click here to display a list of typefaces.
Click here to display a list of font sizes.
Each time you click, the size increases (decreases) to the next (previous) size on the list.

Changing the Font

1. Select the text by clicking and dragging.

    or

    To select an entire text placeholder, click the text and then the selection box.

2. In the Formatting toolbar, use the Font and Font Size fields to change the font. Turn on the Bold and Italic buttons, if desired (Figure 33).

    or

    Select Format/Font. In the Font dialog box (Figure 34), choose a Font, Font Style, and Size and click OK.

    See the next page for more information on the Font dialog box.

■ Tip

✓ Another way to display the Font dialog box is with the shortcut menu: Press the right mouse button, and choose Font.

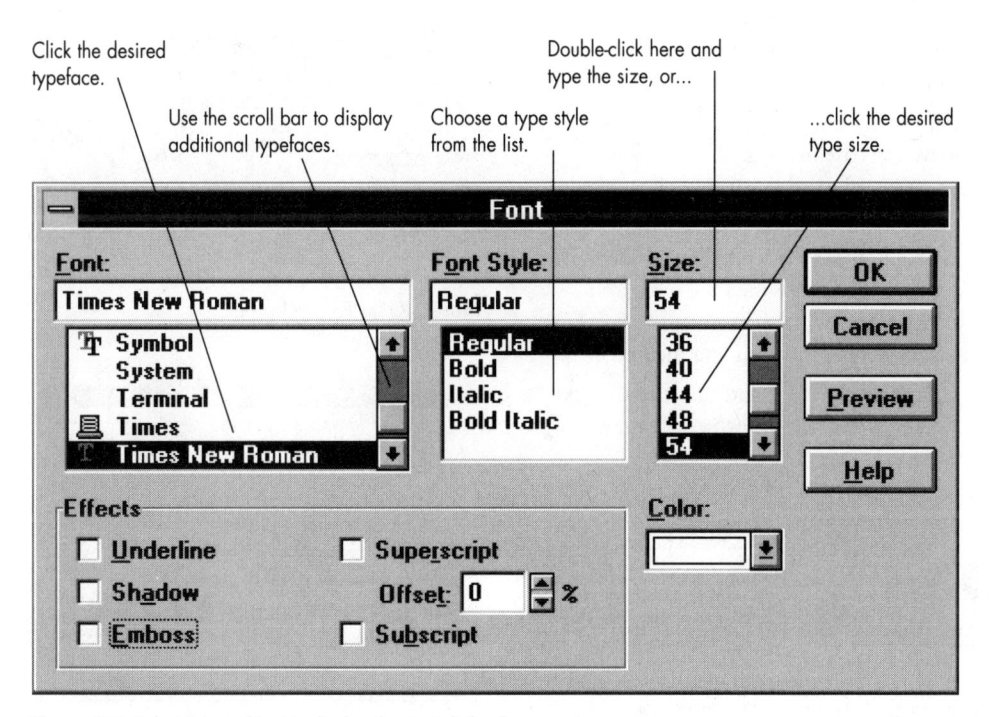

Click the desired typeface.
Use the scroll bar to display additional typefaces.
Choose a type style from the list.
Double-click here and type the size, or...
...click the desired type size.

Figure 34. Select Format/Font to display the Font dialog box.

CHAPTER 3

Adding Text Effects and Color

In addition to options for typeface, size, and style of text, the Font dialog box has options for special effects (such as Underline, Shadow, and Emboss) and Color. Figure 35 shows examples of these special text effects.

1. Select the text by clicking and dragging.

   or

   To select an entire text placeholder, click the text and then the selection box.

2. In the Formatting toolbar, turn on the Underline or Shadow buttons, if desired (Figure 36).

   or

   Select Format/Font. In the Font dialog box (Figure 37), choose an effect. Figures 37 through 39 explain how to choose a color. Click OK.

■ **Tips**

✓ Another way to display the Font dialog box is with the shortcut menu: press the right mouse button, and choose Font.

✓ Use the Superscript effect to raise text above the baseline (e.g., x^2). Use the Subscript effect to lower text below the baseline (e.g., H_2O).

✓ Instead of using the Underline effect, you can draw a line with the Line tool. (You might choose to do this to control the spacing between the text and the line.)

✓ To control the color and offset of the text shadow effect, select Format/Shadow.

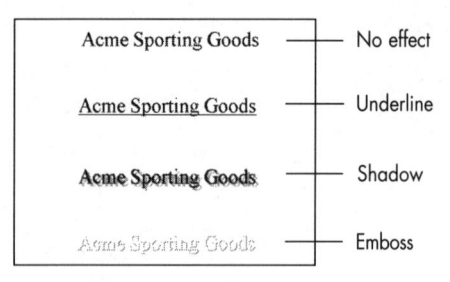

Figure 35. Special text effects

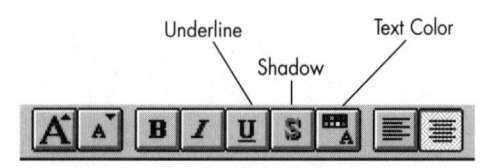

Figure 36. The Formatting toolbar

Figure 37. The Font dialog box

Choose a color, or...

...click here to display a large palette of colors.

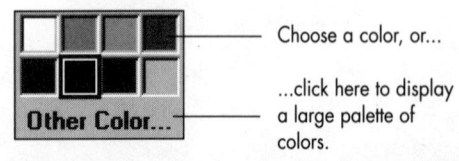

Figure 38. The small color palette that displays when you click the Color field in the Font dialog box or when you click the Text Color button on the toolbar.

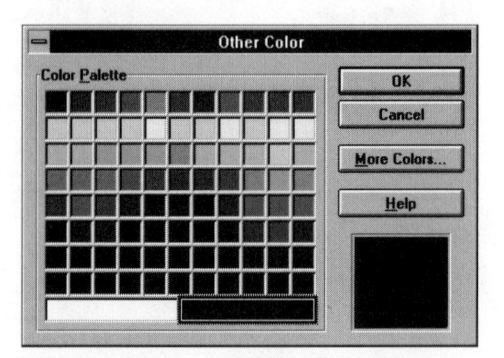

Figure 39. The large color palette

Creating Text Slides

40

CREATING TEXT SLIDES

This paragraph is **left-aligned** within the text placeholder. This alignment is used for single-line labels, titles, and for bulleted paragraphs.
This paragraph is **justified** within the text placeholder. This alignment is useful for long, wide paragraphs of text.
This paragraph is **centered** within the text placeholder. This alignment is useful for titles and multiple-line labels.
This paragraph is **right-aligned** within the text placeholder. This alignment is useful for special formatting situations.

Figure 40. The four types of paragraph alignment

Figure 41. The Alignment submenu

Aligning Paragraphs

Figure 40 shows examples of the four types of paragraph alignment.

1. Select the paragraphs to be aligned.
2. Select F_ormat/_Alignment (Figure 41).
   or
   Press the right mouse button to display the shortcut menu, and choose Alignment.
3. Choose _Left, _Center, _Right, or _Justify.

■ Tips

✓ The Formatting toolbar contains buttons for left-aligning and centering text (Figure 42).

✓ To align a single paragraph, just click on it—you don't need to select any text.

✓ To select all the text in the placeholder, click the text and then the selection box. Then, when you give an alignment command, all text will be aligned.

✓ Text is aligned within the text placeholder. If the text isn't positioned quite where you want it, try adjusting the size or position of the placeholder.

See the next page to see how to center a list inside a placeholder.

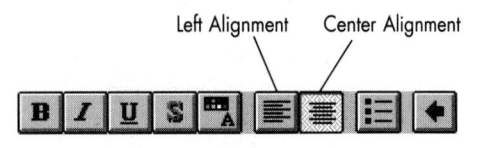

Figure 42. The Formatting toolbar

Setting Anchor Points in a Text Placeholder

Compare Figures 43 and 44. In Figure 43, the list is aligned on the left side of the placeholder; in Figure 44, the list is centered. To center the list, you don't use the Alignment command, because this would center each line separately. Instead, use the Text Anchor command to control the positioning of the text as a whole.

1. Click anywhere in the text placeholder.
2. Select Format/Text Anchor. The Text Anchor dialog box is shown in Figure 45.
3. Click in the Anchor Point field, and choose where you want the text anchored in the placeholder:
    Top
    Middle
    Bottom
    Top Centered
    Middle Centered
    Bottom Centered
4. Click OK.

■ Tips

✓ If the title has center alignment, bulleted lists usually look best when you choose one of the centered text anchor points. Otherwise, the list won't be centered under the title.

✓ The Top, Middle, and Bottom anchor points are all anchored to the left side of the placeholder.

✓ To add extra space between the placeholder boundary and the text, adjust the Box Margins settings.

✓ To make a text placeholder the same size as the text inside it, turn on the Adjust Object Size to Fit Text check box. That way, it doesn't matter which centering anchor point you choose (Top Centered, Middle Centered, or Bottom Centered).

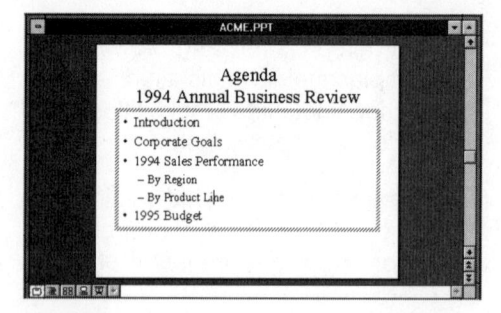

Figure 43. The list is anchored to the left side of the placeholder.

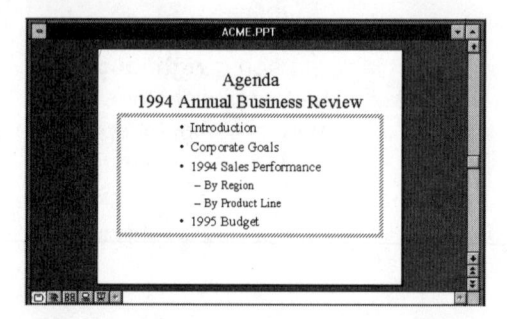

Figure 44. The list is anchored in the center of the placeholder.

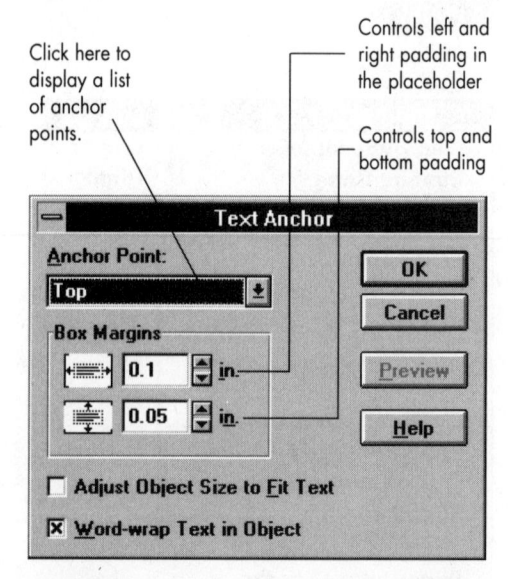

Figure 45. Use the Text Anchor dialog box to control the horizontal and vertical positioning of all the text in a placeholder.

CREATING TEXT SLIDES

Controlling Line and Paragraph Spacing

PowerPoint helps you control spacing between lines in a paragraph as well as between each paragraph. Figure 46 illustrates these two types of spacing.

1. Select the paragraphs to be formatted.
2. Select Format/Line Spacing. Figure 47 shows the Line Spacing dialog box.
3. Enter the new values for Line Spacing, Before Paragraph, and/or After Paragraph.
4. Click OK.

■ Tips

✓ You won't usually want to choose both Before Paragraph and After Paragraph spacing. If you choose both, the two spacing values will be added together.

✓ Do not use the Enter key to get extra space between paragraphs. The Line Spacing command gives you more precise control over the spacing.

✓ To select a single paragraph, just click on it—you don't need to select any text.

✓ To select all the text in the placeholder, click the text and then the selection box. Then, when you give a spacing command, all text will be formatted.

✓ If you choose the points measuring system for line or paragraph spacing, it's helpful to know that there are about 72 points to an inch.

Spacing before a paragraph

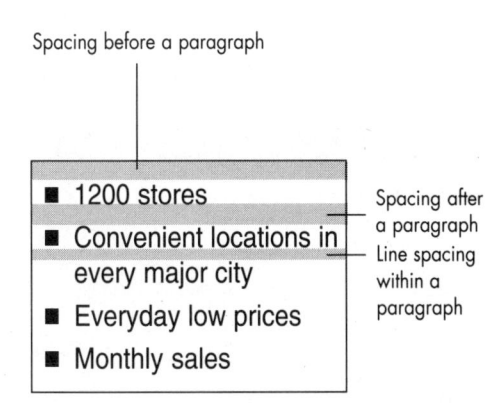

- 1200 stores
- Convenient locations in every major city
- Everyday low prices
- Monthly sales

Spacing after a paragraph
Line spacing within a paragraph

Figure 46. The three types of spacing.

Double-click in the box and enter a new value, or...

...click the arrows to increase (or decrease) the value in 0.05 increments.

Click here to choose a measuring system (lines or points).

Line Spacing

Line Spacing: 1 Lines
Before Paragraph: 0.2 Lines
After Paragraph: 0 Lines

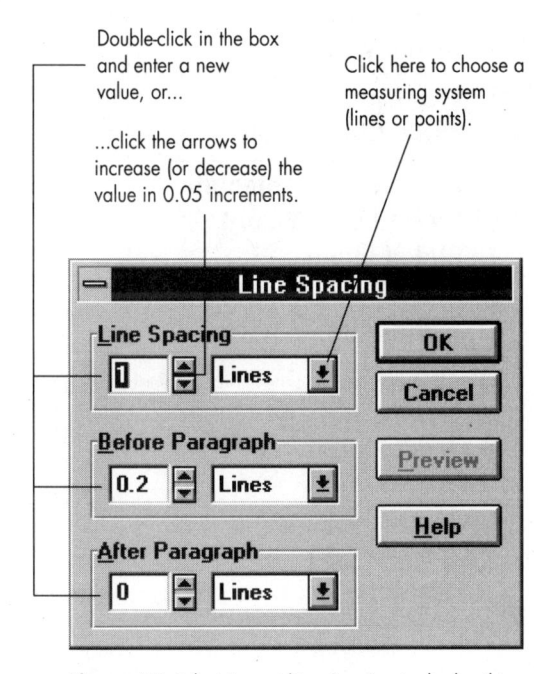

OK | Cancel | Preview | Help

Figure 47. Select Format/Line Spacing to display this dialog box.

43

CHAPTER 3

Copying Formatting Attributes

If you want the text in one placeholder to be formatted exactly like another, you can do so by "painting" the format.

1. Click the text whose format you want to copy, and then click the selection box.
2. Click the Format Painter button (Figure 48).
3. Place the pointer (which now includes a paintbrush) on the text placeholder to which you want to apply the format, and then click.

Or, using the Format menu (Figure 49)...

1. Click the text whose format you want to copy and then click the selection box.
2. Select Format/Pick Up Object Style.
3. Click the text to which you want to apply the format.
4. Select Format/Apply Object Style.

■ Tips

✓ You can use the Format Painter to "paint" the format of other types of objects (such as boxes, circles, and arrows).

✓ You can also copy formatting attributes using the shortcut menu: press the right mouse button, and choose Pick Up Object Style or Apply Object Style.

Figure 48. The Standard toolbar

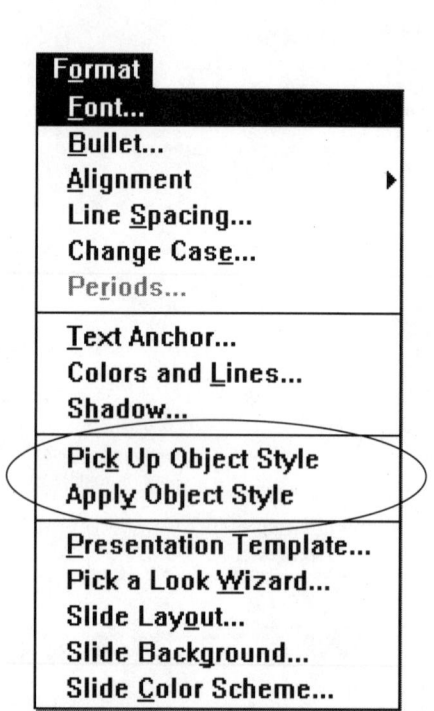

Figure 49. Instead of using the Format Painter button, you can use options on the Format menu.

Types of Formatting You Can "Paint" or Apply

Font
Style
Size
Effects
Color
Alignment
Line spacing
Paragraph spacing
Bullets

INSERTING GRAPHS 4

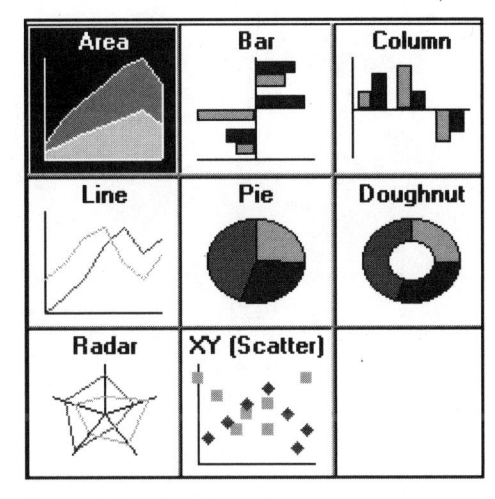

Figure 1. Two-dimensional chart types

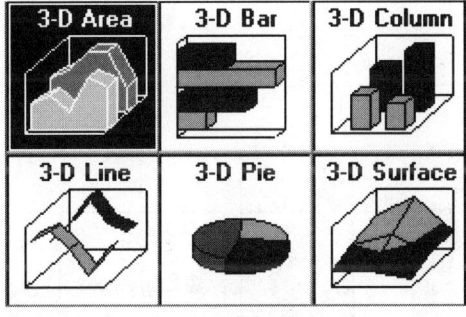

Figure 2. Three-dimensional chart types

About Graphs

You can create a wide variety of two- and three-dimensional graphs in PowerPoint: Area, Bar, Column, Line, Pie, Doughnut, Radar, XY, and Surface (Figures 1 and 2). This chapter concentrates on the types that have x- and y-axes. Chapter 6 covers pie and doughnut charts.

When you create graphs in PowerPoint, you actually use the *Microsoft Graph* program (Figure 3). When you're in Graph, you'll notice that the toolbar offers tools specific to graphing, and the menu bar contains Data instead of Draw—otherwise, you won't be able to tell that another program is running. (The title bar even says PowerPoint.)

To launch Graph, double-click a graph placeholder or an embedded graph; you'll see a thick border around the graph (Figure 3) when you're in Graph. To return to PowerPoint, click anywhere on the slide outside of this border.

Graph offers its own toolbar.

This border around the graph indicates you're in Graph.

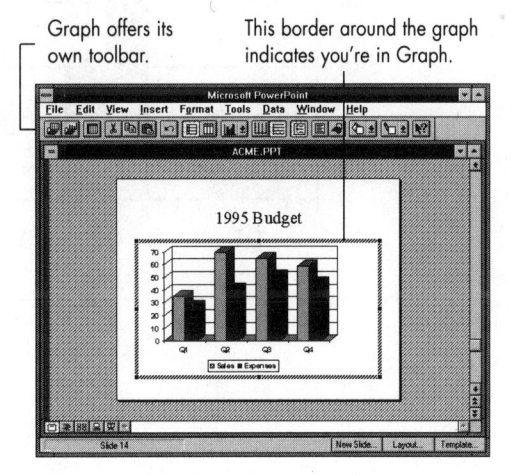

Figure 3. Working in Microsoft Graph

Inserting Graphs

45

CHAPTER 4

Graph Terminology

Figure 4 points out the key areas of a column chart; many chart types have these same areas.

The *y-axis* is also known as the value axis since it always displays numbers on its scale. The *x-axis* is also known as the category axis because it displays categories of data (quarters, months, years, names, and so forth).

Tick marks appear next to each value on the y-axis and between categories on the x-axis. *Gridlines* extend from the tickmarks to help you interpret the values at each *data point*.

When a graph has more than one *data series* (Figure 3 has two—Sales and Expenses), a *legend* identifies each series.

■ Tip

✓ On a 3-D chart, the value axis is called a *z-axis*.

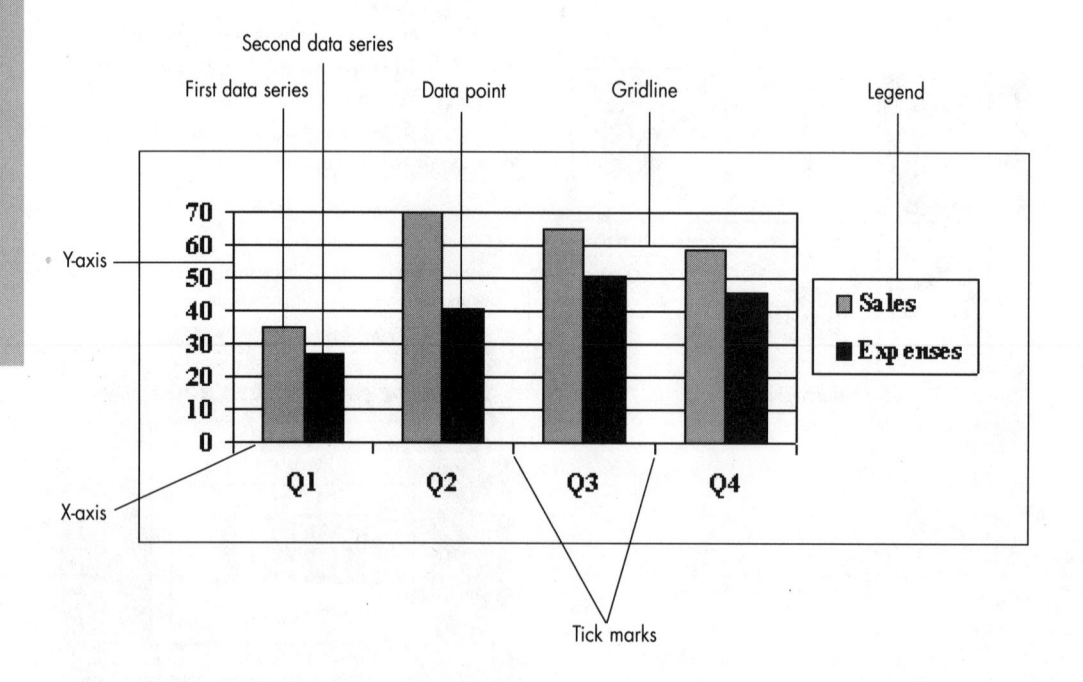

Figure 4. Key areas of a column chart

46

INSERTING GRAPHS

Layouts that combine text and graphs
Graph-only layout

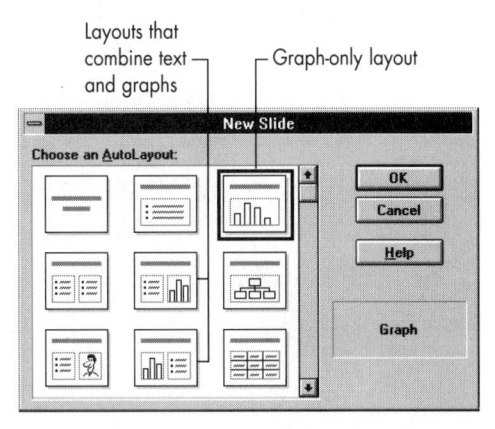

Figure 5. Choose a graph layout in the New Slide dialog box.

Figure 6. The Text & Graph AutoLayout

Title placeholder

Graph placeholder

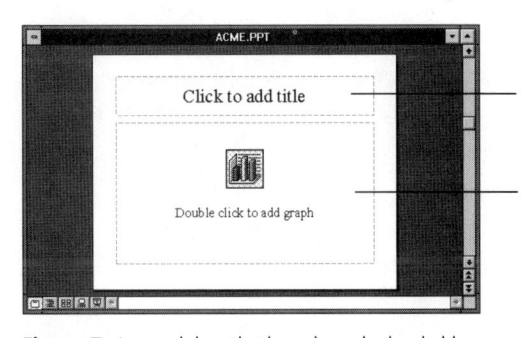

Figure 7. A new slide with title and graph placeholders in the Graph layout

Inserting a Graph Slide

PowerPoint offers three AutoLayouts that include graphs (Figure 5). An example of a slide that combines a bulleted list with a graph is shown in Figure 6.

1. Click the New Slide button at the bottom of the PowerPoint window.
2. In the New Slide dialog box, choose one of the graph layouts (Figure 5).
3. Click OK. The slide appears with title, graph, and perhaps text placeholders (Figure 7).
4. Click the title placeholder and type the title of your graph.
5. If the slide has a text placeholder, click it and type the text.
6. Double-click the graph placeholder to create your graph.

■ Tip

✓ In the text placeholder of a Text & Graph or Graph & Text layout, you can provide details about the graph, such as an interpretation of the data or a conclusion that can be drawn.

For information on creating multiple graphs on a slide, see Creating Two Graphs on a Slide on page 55.

Inserting Graphs

47

CHAPTER 4

Entering Data

You enter your chart data in the datasheet window (Figure 8). The datasheet initially appears with sample data. Be sure to erase it before entering your own data. Each box in the datasheet is called a *cell*.

1. If you haven't already done so, double-click the graph placeholder to launch Microsoft Graph.
2. If the datasheet window isn't already displayed, click the View Datasheet button (Figure 9).
3. To erase the sample data, click the Select All button (Figure 8) and press Delete.
4. Enter the graph data (Figure 10).
5. To view the graph, move the datasheet aside (by dragging the window's title bar) or close the datasheet window (by clicking the View Datasheet button).

■ Tips

✓ Be sure to use the Select All button when deleting the sample data. If you don't and your data consumes fewer rows and columns than the sample data, Microsoft Graph still reserves space for this data on the graph (Figure 11). To fix this problem, use the Exclude Row/Col command on the Data menu.

✓ If you accidentally enter data in a row or column and then erase it, Graph reserves space for this erased data, anyway. Again, you can fix this problem by using the Exclude Row/Col command on the Data menu.

✓ Feel free to enter legend labels in the top row and x-axis labels in the leftmost column. But if you do this, you must let Graph know that the data series are entered into columns instead of rows. Use the Series in Columns command on the Data menu, or click the By Column button on the Graph toolbar (Figure 9).

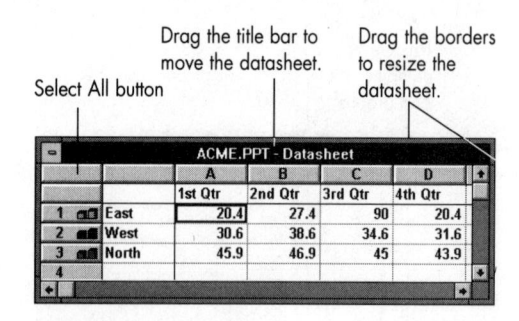

Figure 8. The sample data in the datasheet

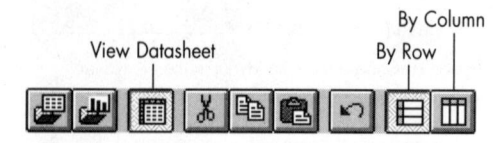

Figure 9. When you see the Graph toolbar, you know you're in Microsoft Graph.

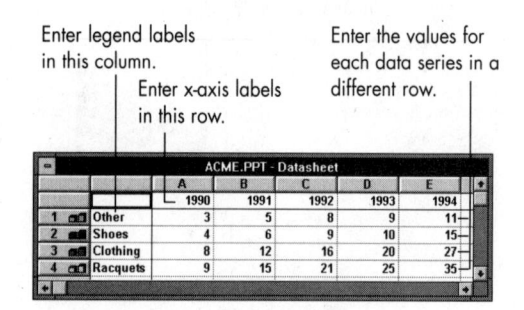

Figure 10. How to enter data in the datasheet

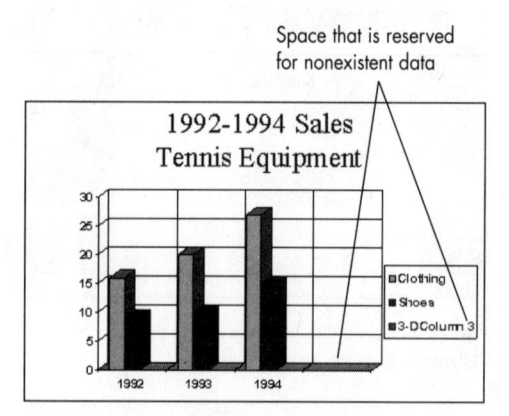

Figure 11. The Exclude Row/Col command on the Data menu will fix the problems on this graph.

48

INSERTING GRAPHS

Choose the file type first.

Don't forget to specify to import the entire file or a range.

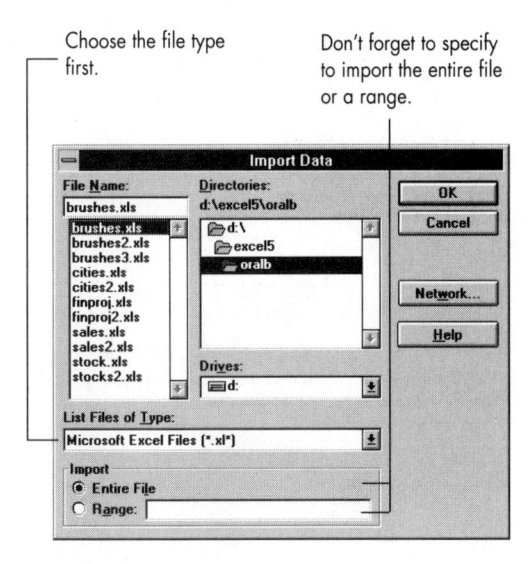

Figure 12. The Import Data dialog box

Import Data

Figure 13. The Graph toolbar

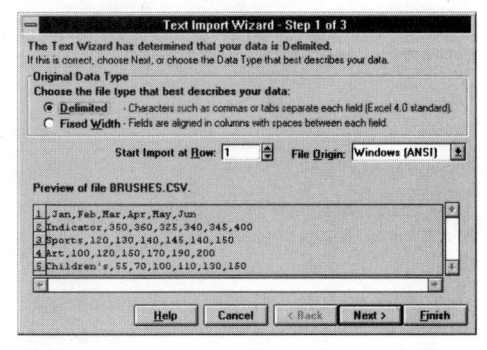

Figure 14. The Text Import Wizard steps you through the process of importing a text file.

Importing Data

If the chart data already exists in Microsoft Excel, Lotus 1-2-3, or in a text file, you don't need to retype it in the datasheet—you can *import* the data.

1. Delete the sample data in the datasheet (see previous page).
2. Click the first cell of the datasheet.
3. Select Edit/Import Data. The Import Data dialog box appears (Figure 12).
4. Click the List Files of Type field to display a list of file types, and choose the desired type (such as Microsoft Excel or Lotus 1-2-3).
5. Choose Entire File.

    or

    Choose Range and then type the range to be imported.
6. Choose the appropriate drive letter in the Drives list.
7. In the Directories list, navigate to the directory that contains the file.
8. In the File Name list, click the file name.
9. Click OK.

■ Tips

✓ You can also import data by clicking the Import Data button (Figure 13).

✓ The range can be specified either with cell coordinates (such as A5:H10) or with a range name.

✓ If you aren't sure of the range, import the entire file and then use Edit/Delete (not the Delete key) to remove rows and columns you don't need.

✓ When importing a text file, you are prompted for information on how the file is delimited—*delimiters* are the characters between fields, such as commas, spaces, and tabs (Figure 14).

Inserting Graphs

49

CHAPTER 4

Linking Data

Another way to import data is to *link* it to the source data file. When data is linked, changes to the source file are automatically reflected in the PowerPoint datasheet and graph.

1. Launch the application that created the source file, and open the file (Figure 15).
2. Select the data to be linked, and select Edit/Copy.
3. Switch back to PowerPoint.
4. Create a new graph slide, double-click the graph placeholder, and then delete the sample data in the datasheet.
5. Click the first cell of the datasheet.
6. Select Edit/Paste Link, and click OK to continue.
7. Look at the sample chart in the ChartWizard dialog box (Figure 16), and change any options if necessary.
8. Click OK.
9. Move or close the datasheet to see your new slide.

■ Tips

✓ By default, data is updated automatically. In other words, if you change a number in the source file, the datasheet and graph instantly reflect the new value. To update the links yourself, select Edit/Link to display the Link dialog box (Figure 17). Then, choose Manual.

✓ In the Link dialog box, you can also change the source file, break links, and update manual links.

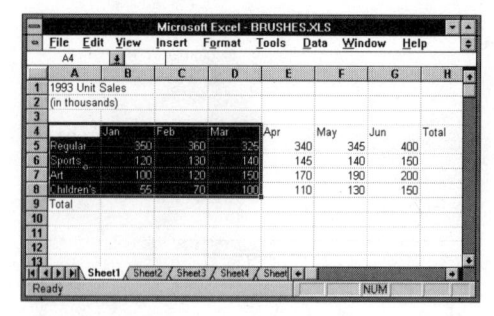

Figure 15. The selected range in a Microsoft Excel spreadsheet will be copied and then paste-linked in a PowerPoint datasheet.

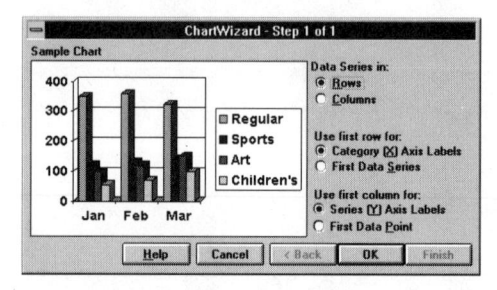

Figure 16. The ChartWizard dialog box. Feel free to change any options if the sample graph is not laid out properly.

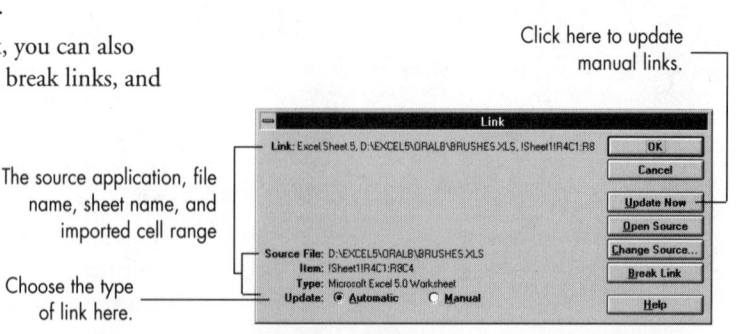

Figure 17. While in the datasheet, select Edit/Link to display the Link dialog box.

INSERTING GRAPHS

Choose a chart dimension first.　　Then, click a chart type.　　Finally, click here to choose a subtype.

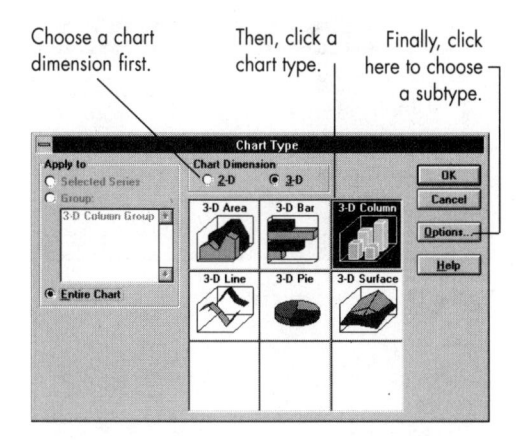

Figure 18. The Chart Type dialog box

A preview of the selected subtype　　Redisplays Chart Type dialog box

Subtype tab

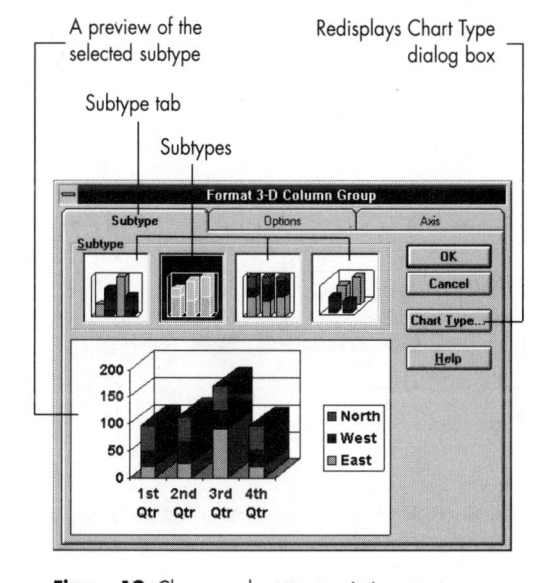

Subtypes

Figure 19. Choose a chart type variation.

Click here to display a palette of chart types.

Chart Type

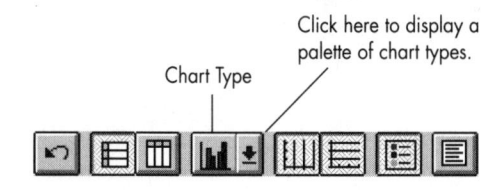

Figure 20. The Graph toolbar

Choosing a Chart Type

The default chart type is 3-D column. You can choose a different chart type before or after you enter data in the datasheet. In addition to choosing a chart type, you can choose a *subtype*. Subtypes are variations of the selected chart type. For example, a 3-D column graph has subtypes for clustered bars, stacked bars, 100% bars, and so forth.

1. If necessary, double-click the embedded graph to go into Microsoft Graph.
2. Select Format/Chart Type. The Chart Type dialog box appears (Figure 18).
3. For the Chart Dimension, choose 2-D or 3-D.
4. Click one of the chart types.
5. Click Options and then click the Subtype tab (Figure 19).
6. Click the desired subtype. Watch the preview box to see how your graph looks.
7. Click OK.

■ Tip

✓ Another way to change the chart type is with the Chart Type button (Figure 20). By clicking the arrow next to the button, you will see a palette of 14 chart types. However, you cannot choose subtypes here.

Inserting Graphs

51

CHAPTER 4

Inserting Titles

You can insert titles at the top of the chart, on the x-axis, on the y-axis, and on the z-axis (the equivalent of the y-axis on a 3-D graph).

1. Select Insert/Titles. The Titles dialog box appears (Figure 21).
2. Select one or more of the titles.
3. Click OK. For each title, a placeholder containing dummy text is inserted (Figure 22).
4. With the placeholder selected, type the title text. (The dummy text automatically disappears.)

Figure 21. Choose one or more titles.

Rotating an Axis Title

Frequently, you will want the y- or z-axis title rotated 90 degrees (Figure 23).

1. Select the axis title—make sure the placeholder has selection handles around it. If you see the text cursor, click elsewhere on the graph and then again on the title.
2. Select Format/Selected Axis Title.

    or

    Press the right mouse button to display the shortcut menu, and choose Format Axis Title.
3. Click the Alignment tab (Figure 24).
4. Choose one of the Orientation options.
5. Click OK.

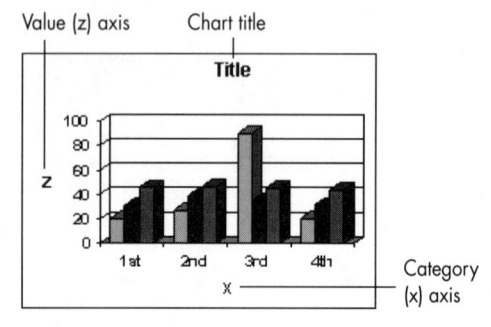

Figure 22. Chart and axis title placeholders

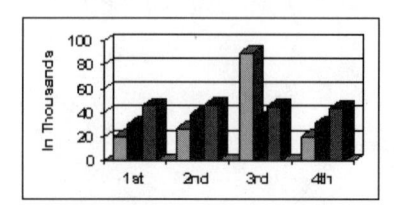

Figure 23. The z-axis title is rotated 90 degrees.

■ **Tip**

✓ The Titles command is not available when the datasheet is open. Just click the chart to close the datasheet.

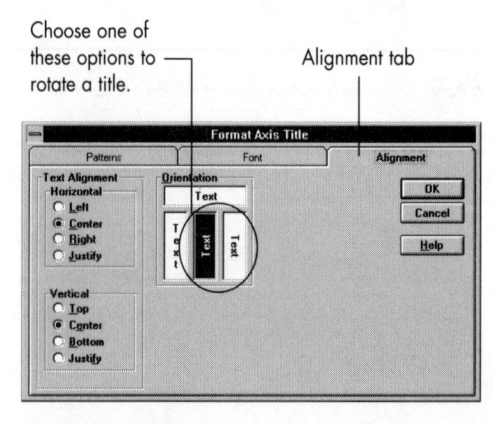

Figure 24. Use this dialog to rotate an axis title.

52

INSERTING GRAPHS

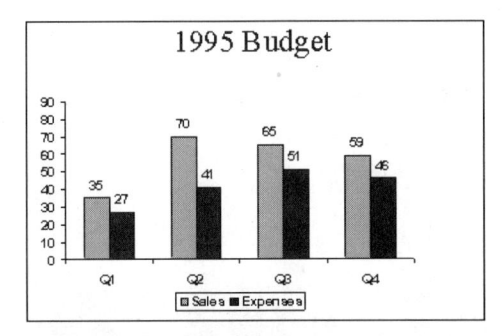

Figure 25. Data labels appear above each column.

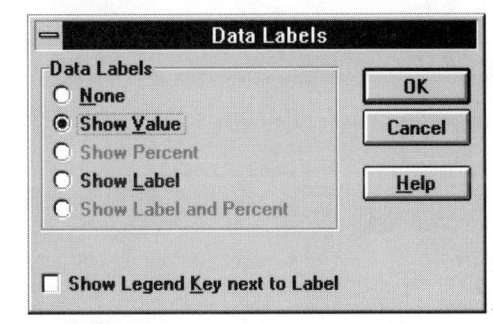

Figure 26. Select Insert/Data Labels to display the Data Labels dialog box.

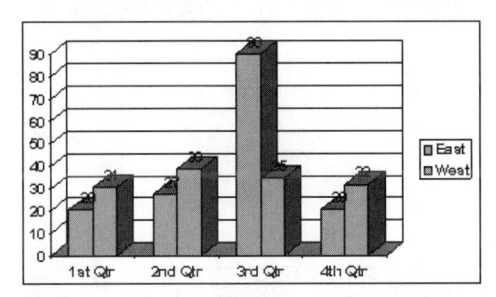

Figure 27. With the data labels in the default positions, the values are difficult to read.

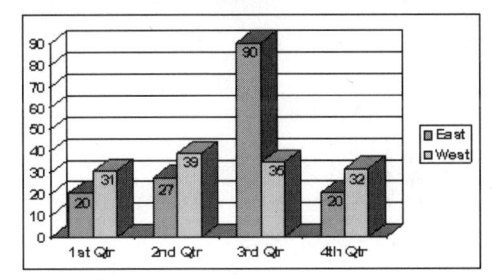

Figure 28. After the data labels are moved inside the bars, the values become easier to see.

Inserting Data Labels

By placing *data labels* on the graph, you can see the exact value of each data point (Figure 25).

1. Select Insert/Data Labels. The Data Labels dialog box appears (Figure 26).
2. Choose Show Value.
3. Click OK.

Repositioning Data Labels

Graph inserts the data labels near the data point but sometimes the labels from one series will overlap the labels from another, or the label may be unreadable in its current position (Figure 27). Fortunately, you can position the data labels exactly where you want them (Figure 28).

1. *Slowly* click the data label until selection handles appear around the label. (Don't click fast or you will double-click and bring up the Format dialog box.)
2. Place the mouse pointer on the selected label's border. Make sure that you see the arrow pointer, not the text cursor.
3. Drag the label to the desired positon.
4. Repeat steps 1–3 for each label to be repositioned.

■ Tips

✓ The Data Labels command is not available when the datasheet is open. Just click on the chart to close the datasheet.

✓ Data labels are not appropriate for all graphs. If the graph has many data points or many data series, the graph may look too busy with data labels.

✓ If a label appears above the plot area, you can either move the label or change the upper value on the y-axis scale.

See Scaling the Axis on page 65.

CHAPTER 4

Revising a Graph

To revise a graph you have previously created, you will need to reopen the graph in Microsoft Graph.

1. Double-click the embedded graph (Figures 29 and 30).
2. To display the datasheet, click the View Datasheet button (Figure 31).
3. To replace the contents of a cell, click the cell and type the new value. The graph instantly reflects the change to the datasheet.
4. To edit the contents of a cell, double-click the cell. A text cursor appears. Position the cursor where you want to make the change, and then insert or delete characters. Press Enter when you are finished.
5. Click the graph to close the datasheet.
6. Make any desired changes to the graph (insert titles, insert data labels, change the chart type, and so forth).
7. When you are finished making changes, click the slide outside of the graph.

Double-click the embedded graph.

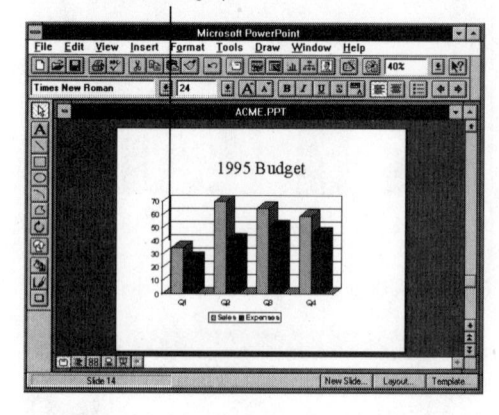

Figure 29. Opening the embedded graph in Microsoft Graph

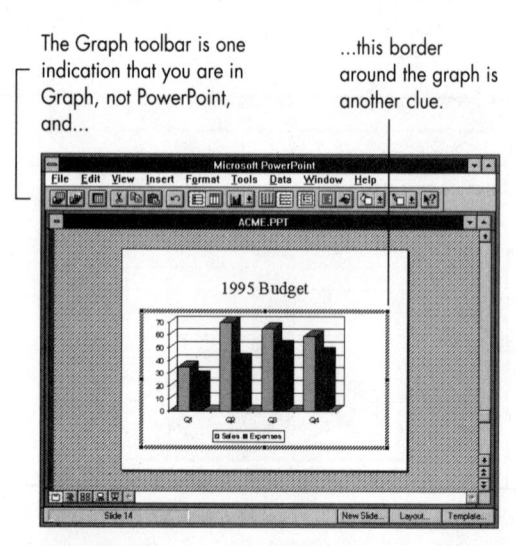

The Graph toolbar is one indication that you are in Graph, not PowerPoint, and...

...this border around the graph is another clue.

Figure 30. The graph after it is opened in Microsoft Graph

View Datasheet

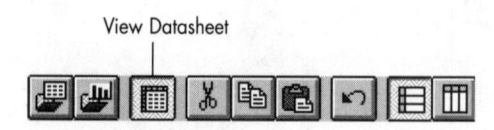

Figure 31. The Graph toolbar

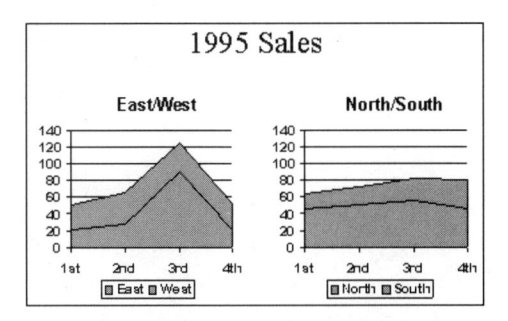

INSERTING GRAPHS

Figure 32. Two graphs on one slide

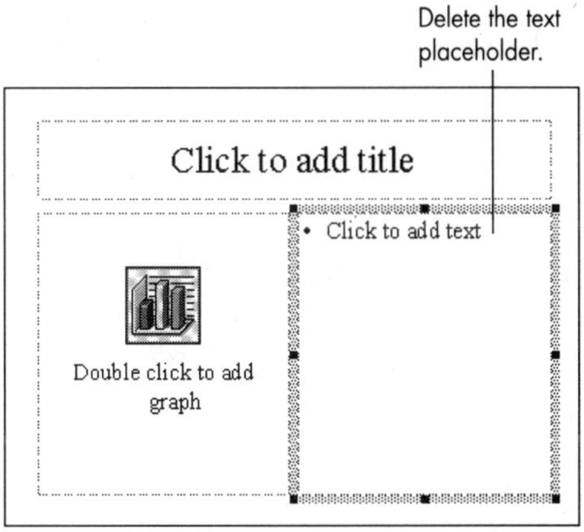

Figure 33. A slide with the Graph & Text layout

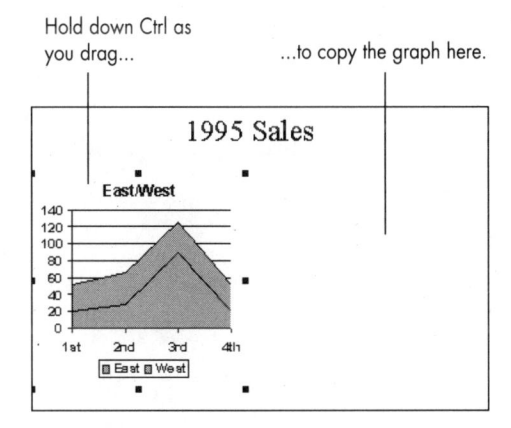

Figure 34. Creating a second graph on a slide

Creating Two Graphs on a Slide

Although PowerPoint doesn't offer a layout for two graphs, you can still create a slide with more than one graph (Figure 32).

1. Use the New Slide button to insert a new slide with the Graph & Text or Text & Graph layout.
2. Delete the text placeholder by clicking the selection box and pressing Delete (Figure 33).
3. Create the first graph: Double-click the graph placeholder, enter data, choose a chart type, and so forth.
4. Exit Graph by clicking the slide outside of the graph.
5. To copy the graph, place the mouse pointer on the embedded graph, and hold down Ctrl as you drag to the right side of the slide (Figure 34).
6. Revise the second graph by double-clicking it, entering data, choosing the chart type, and so on.
7. Exit Graph.

■ Tips

✓ To make sure the two graphs are aligned at the bottom, use the Draw/Align command.

See Aligning Objects on page 133.

✓ It's easier to compare data in the two graphs when the axes use the same scale.

See Scaling the Axis on page 65.

✓ Each graph should have its own title. You can either use the Insert/Titles command in Microsoft Graph or use the Text tool in PowerPoint.

See Inserting Titles on page 52 and Creating a Text Placeholder on page 32.

55

FORMATTING GRAPHS 5

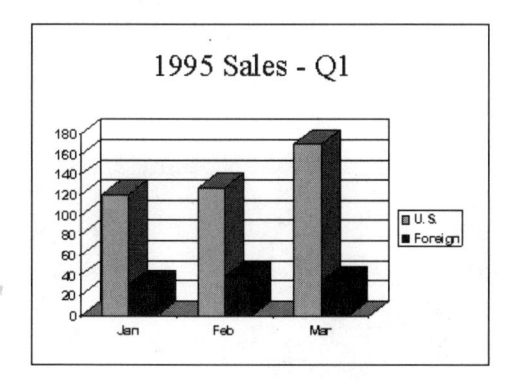

Figure 1. A 3-D column graph with the default settings

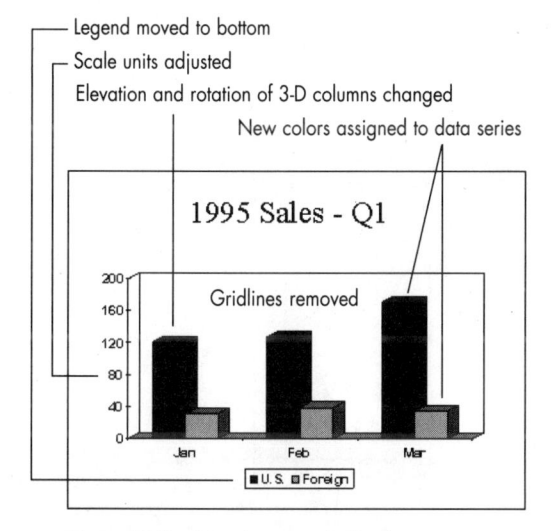

Legend moved to bottom
Scale units adjusted
Elevation and rotation of 3-D columns changed
New colors assigned to data series
Gridlines removed

Figure 2. The 3-D column graph after formatting

Figure 3. When the legend is selected, the Format menu offers the command Selected Legend.

Ways to Format Graphs

Microsoft Graph offers an abundance of ways to format your graphs. You can reposition the legend, add and remove gridlines, change the color of the data series, change the upper and lower limits on the value axis, and so forth. Figure 1 shows a graph with the default settings, and Figure 2 shows the same graph after formatting.

See Graph Terminology on page 46.

Follow this basic procedure for formatting a graph in Microsoft Graph:

1. Select the area of the graph you want to format—you may need to click more than once. For example, to format the legend, click the legend until you see selection handles around it.

2. Select Format/Selected *xxx*, where *xxx* is the name of the selected area. For example, if the legend is selected, the command will be Selected Legend (Figure 3).

Alternatively, you can point to the area you want to format and press the right mouse button to display the shortcut menu. Then click Format *xxx*, where *xxx* is the name of the selected area.

■ **Tips**

✓ Sometimes you'll think you have selected a certain area, but in fact have selected a different area. A clue that you have done this is when the Format menu shows Selected *xxx* and *xxx* is not the area you want to format. If this happens, cancel the menu and reselect the area.

✓ Another way to display the appropriate Format dialog box is to double-click the area you want to format.

Formatting Graphs

57

CHAPTER 5

Formatting the Legend

By default, the legend has a thin border around it. If you like, you can thicken the border, add a drop shadow, remove it altogether, or shade the background. Figure 4 shows a legend with the default border. In Figure 5 the legend is formatted with a thicker line and a drop shadow.

1. Select the legend.
2. Select F*o*rmat/S*e*lected Legend. The Format Legend dialog box appears.

   or

   Press the right mouse button to display the shortcut menu. Then choose Format Legend.
3. Click the Patterns tab (Figure 6).
4. To choose a different line style (such as dashed lines), display the *S*tyle list (Figure 7) and choose one of the styles.
5. To choose a different line thickness, display the *W*eight list (Figure 8) and choose one of the weights.
6. To add a drop shadow, turn on the Sha*d*ow check box.
7. To shade the background of the legend, click one of the colors in the palette (Figure 6).
8. To remove the border, choose *N*one in the Border section.
9. Click OK.

■ **Tip**

✓ To enlarge the legend, drag the selection handles.

To format the legend text, see Formatting Graph Text on page 67.

To reposition the legend, see the opposite page.

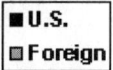

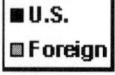

Figure 4. The default legend border

Figure 5. The formatted legend border

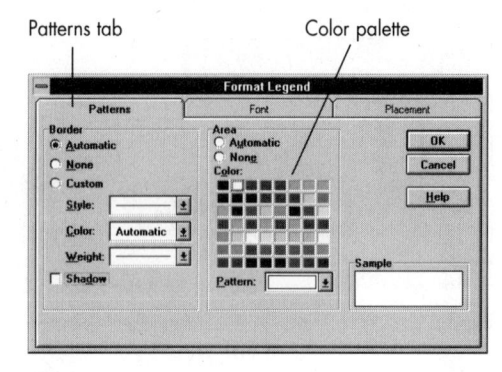

Figure 6. Formatting the legend

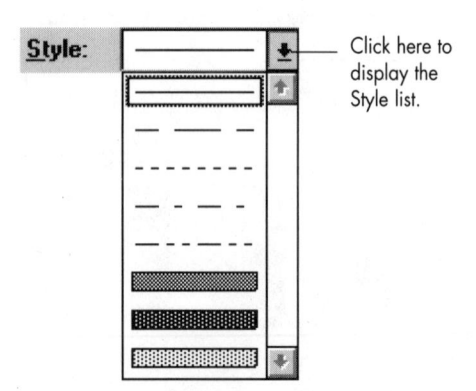

Figure 7. The Style list

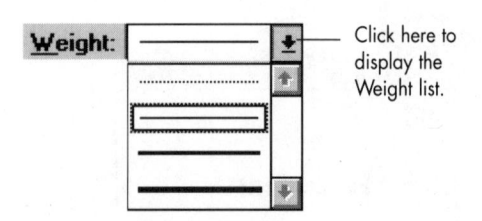

Figure 8. The Weight list

FORMATTING GRAPHS

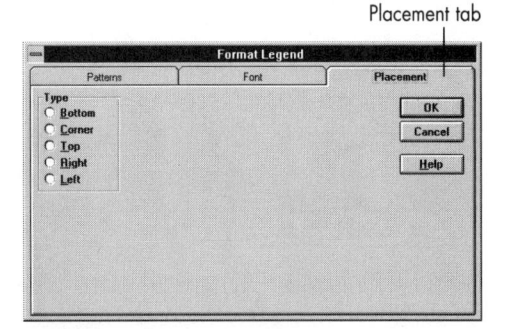

Figure 9. Choosing a legend position

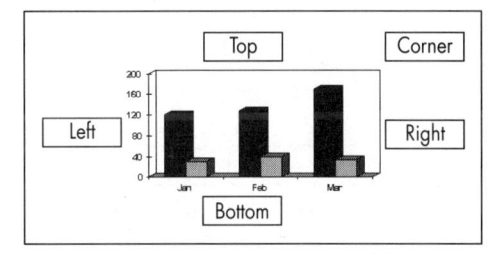

Figure 10. Legend placements

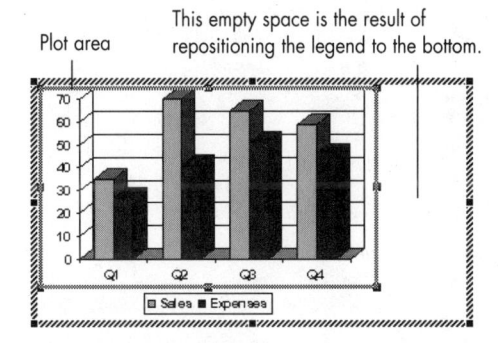

Figure 11. You may want to resize the plot area after repositioning the legend.

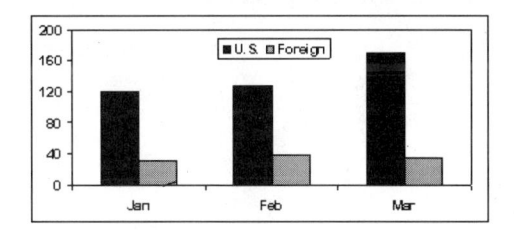

Figure 12. The legend was positioned inside the plot area by dragging it manually.

Repositioning the Legend

You can place the legend in a variety of standard positions on the graph.

1. Select the legend.
2. Select Format/Selected Legend.

   or

   Press the right mouse button to display the shortcut menu. Then choose Format Legend.

3. Click the Placement tab (Figure 9).
4. Choose one of the placement positions illustrated in Figure 10.
5. Click OK.

■ Tips

✓ When you reposition a legend using the Format Legend dialog box, the plot area resizes to allow room for the legend in its new location. However, Microsoft Graph still allows room for the legend in its former location, as well (Figure 11). To solve this problem, resize the plot area yourself: Select the plot area and drag the selection handles.

   For more information on selecting plot areas, see page 69.

✓ Another way to reposition the legend is to drag it to the desired location (Figure 12). Depending on where you position the legend, you may need to manually resize the plot area.

CHAPTER 5

Changing the Color or Pattern of a Data Series

1. Click one of the data series (a line, bar, column, area, and so forth). There should be selection handles around the series as shown in Figures 13 and 14.
2. Select Format/Selected Data Series.

   or

   Press the right mouse button to display the shortcut menu. Then choose Format Data Series.
3. Click the Patterns tab (Figures 15 and 16).
4. Choose a color in the Color palette.
5. Click OK.

■ Tip

✓ Bars, columns, areas, and surfaces can have patterns (Figure 17). Click the arrow in the Pattern field (Figure 15) to display the pattern palette, and then choose a pattern. To choose a different color for the pattern, display the pattern palette again and choose a color. The pattern background will use whatevever color is selected in the color palette.

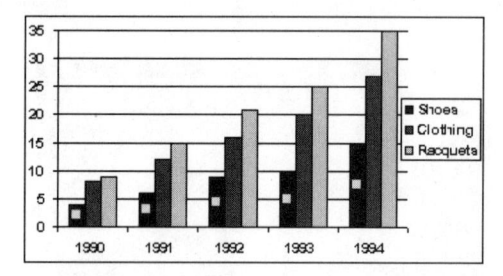

Figure 13. The first data series is selected in this column graph.

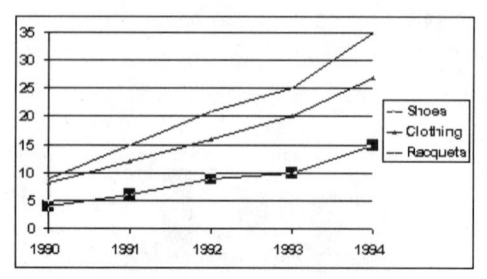

Figure 14. The last data series is selected in this line graph.

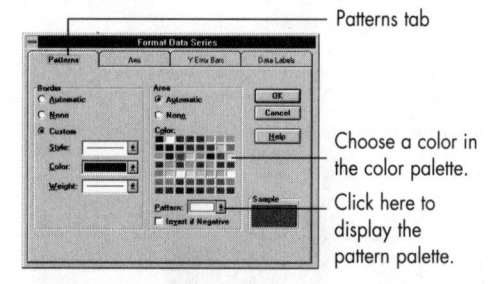

Figure 15. The Patterns tab for bar, column, area, and surface graphs (for a 2-D graph)

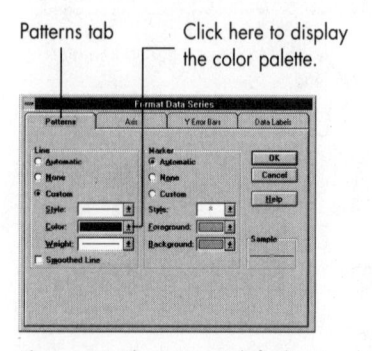

Figure 16. The Patterns tab for line graphs offers options specific to this graph type.

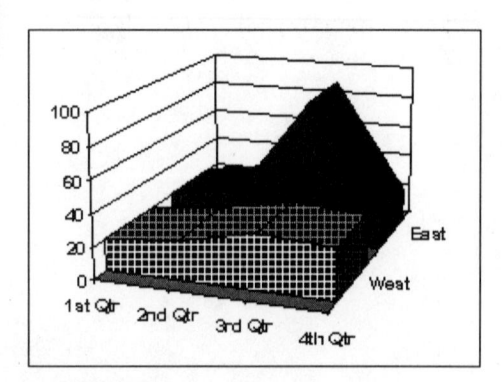

Figure 17. The West data series has a criss-cross pattern.

FORMATTING GRAPHS

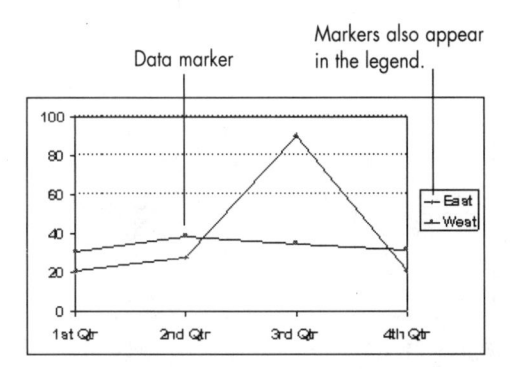

Figure 18. A line graph with data markers

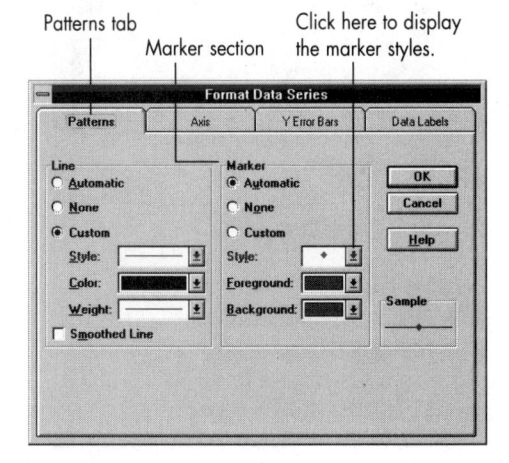

Figure 19. Choosing a marker style

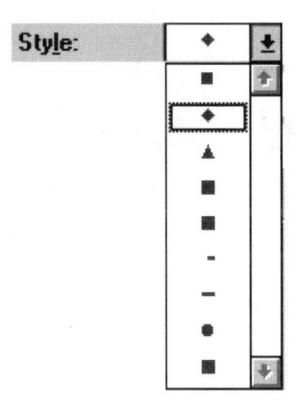

Figure 20. The list of marker styles

Formatting Data Markers

Data markers are symbols, such as circles or squares, that appear at data points on line, XY, and radar graphs. The markers also appear in the legend to help you identify each data series (Figure 18).

1. Click one of the data series. There should be selection handles at each data point.
2. Select Format/Selected Data Series.

    or

    Press the right mouse button to display the shortcut menu. Then choose Format Data Series.
3. Click the Patterns tab (Figure 19).
4. In the Marker section, display the Style list and choose a marker style (Figure 20).
5. Click OK.
6. Repeat steps 1–5 for other data series, if desired.

■ Tips

✓ In the Marker section, choose None if you don't want any markers on the line. Make sure, though, that each line is a different color so you have some way of differentiating the series.

✓ The markers appear quite small in Microsoft Graph and in PowerPoint (Figure 18). However, the markers will be easily discernable when you print the slide or show it in a Slide Show.

61

CHAPTER 5

Inserting/Removing Gridlines

Gridlines are the lines that extend from the tick marks on the axes (Figure 21). They are useful for interpreting the actual values of the data points. A graph can have horizontal and/or vertical gridlines.

1. Select Insert/Gridlines. The Gridlines dialog box appears (Figure 22).
2. To insert/remove vertical gridlines, turn on/off the Major Gridlines check box under the Category Axis heading.
3. To insert/remove horizontal gridlines, turn on/off the Major Gridlines check box under the Value Axis heading.
4. Click OK.

■ Tips

✓ You can also insert and remove gridlines with the Vertical Gridlines and Horizontal Gridlines buttons (Figure 23). These buttons are toggles—they will insert or remove gridlines each time you click them.

✓ *Minor gridlines* extend from the minor tick marks (ticks between the scale increments). You will not usually want minor gridlines because the graph would then contain too many lines (Figure 24).

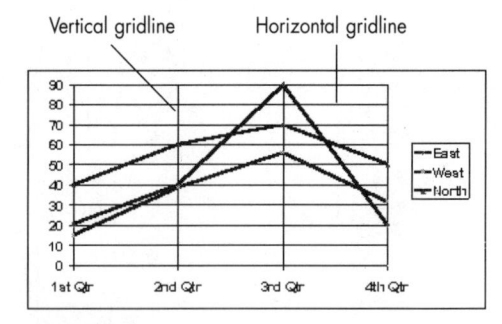

Figure 21. A line graph with horizontal and vertical gridlines

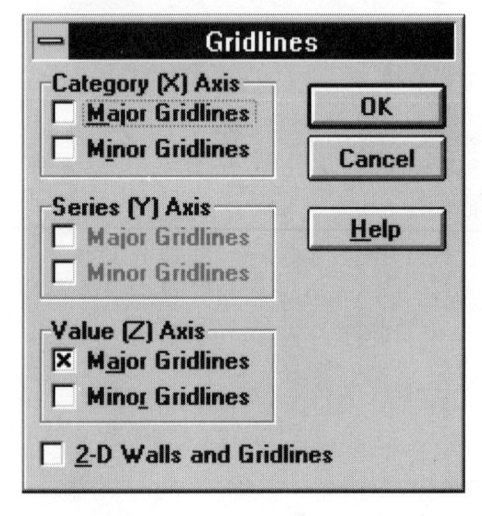

Figure 22. The Gridlines dialog box (for a 3-D graph)

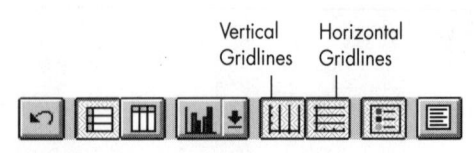

Figure 23. The Graph toolbar

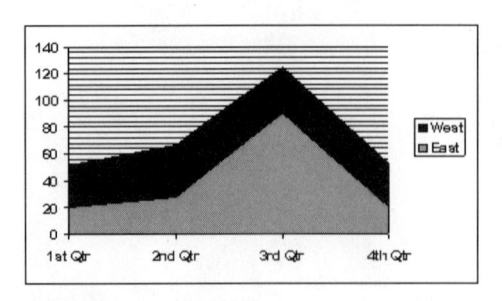

Figure 24. Minor gridlines

FORMATTING GRAPHS

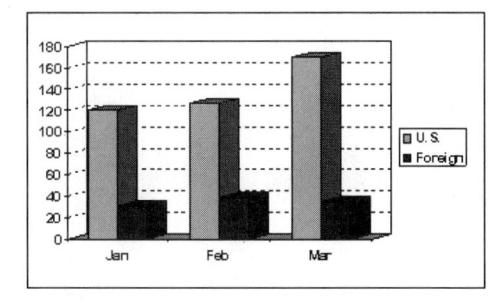

Figure 25. Gridlines with a dotted style

Patterns tab

Figure 26. Choosing a different format for the gridlines

Formatting Gridlines

You can change both the thickness and the style of the gridlines (Figure 25).

1. Select one of the gridlines.
2. Select Format/Selected Gridlines.

   or

   Press the right mouse button to display the shortcut menu. Then choose Format Gridlines.

3. Choose the Patterns tab (Figure 26).
4. To choose a different line style (such as dashed lines), display the Style list and choose one of the styles.
5. To choose a different color, display the Color palette and choose a color.
6. To choose a different line thickness, display the Weight list and choose one of the weights.
7. Click OK.

■ Tip

✓ It's difficult to see the line weights when you are in Microsoft Graph (Figure 27). To get a better idea of how the gridline looks with a certain line weight, go to PowerPoint (Figure 28) by clicking on the slide outside of the graph.

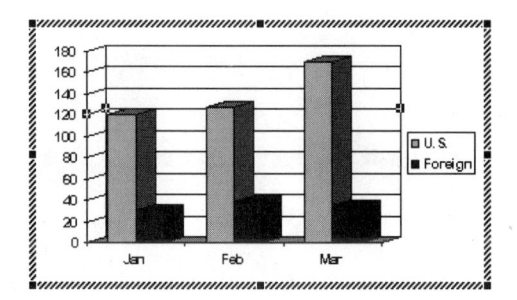

Figure 27. The heaviest weight of gridlines does not look very heavy in Microsoft Graph.

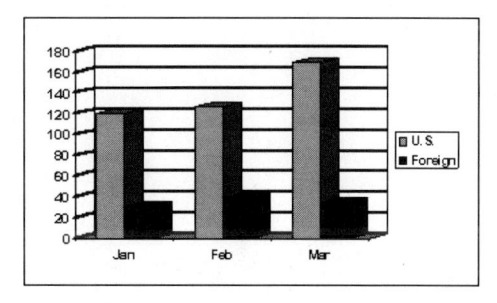

Figure 28. PowerPoint shows a better representation of gridline weights.

Formatting Graphs

63

CHAPTER 5

Formatting the Tick Marks

A *tick mark* is a tiny line next to each label on an axis. You can place tick marks inside, outside, or crossing the axis (Figures 29 and 30). You can also choose to have *minor tick-marks* between the major marks (Figure 31).

1. Select the axis whose tick marks you want to format.
2. Select Format/Selected Axis.

   or

   Press the right mouse button to display the shortcut menu. Then choose Format Axis.
3. Click the Patterns tab (Figure 32).
4. In the Tick Mark Type section, select the type of Major mark: None, Inside, Outside, or Cross.
5. Select the type of Minor mark: None, Inside, Outside, or Cross.
6. Click OK.

■ **Tip**

✓ The frequency of the tick marks depends on the major and minor units.

   See Scaling the Axis on the opposite page for information on specifying the major and minor units.

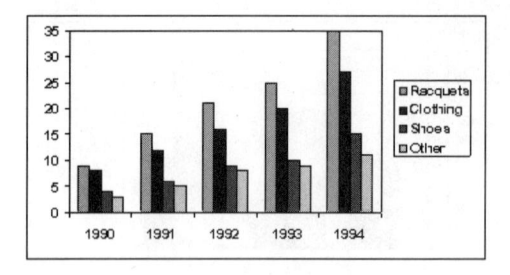

Figure 29. The x- and y-axes have outside tick-marks.

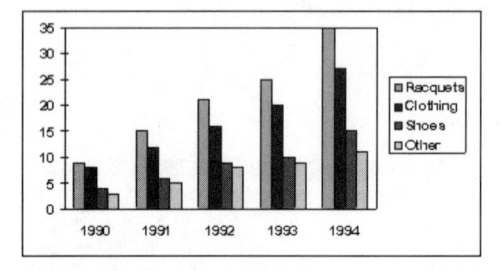

Figure 30. On this graph, the tick marks cross the y-axis; no marks appear on the x-axis.

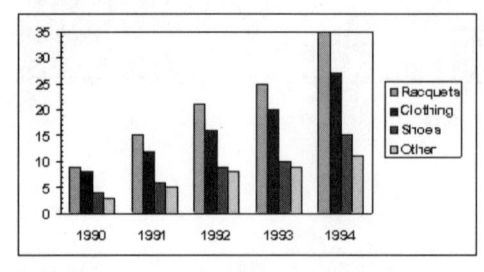

Figure 31. The y-axis has major tick marks on the outside, and minor tick marks on the inside.

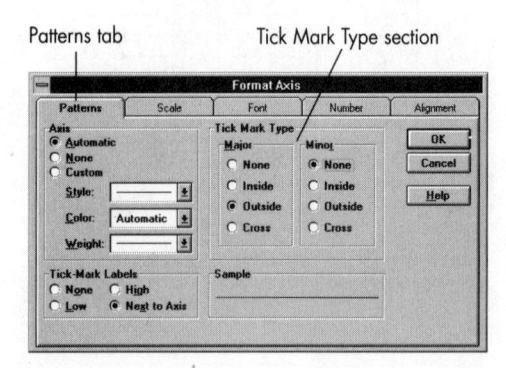

Figure 32. Choosing types of tick marks

FORMATTING GRAPHS

Minimum value is 0.
Major Unit is 10.
Maximum value is 90.
Number of categories between tick-mark labels is 1.

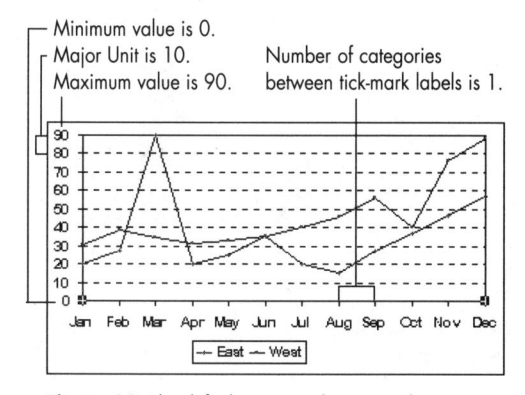

Figure 33. The default y-axis and x-axis scales

Minimum value is 0.
Major Unit is 20.
Maximum value is 100.
Number of categories between tick-mark labels is 2.

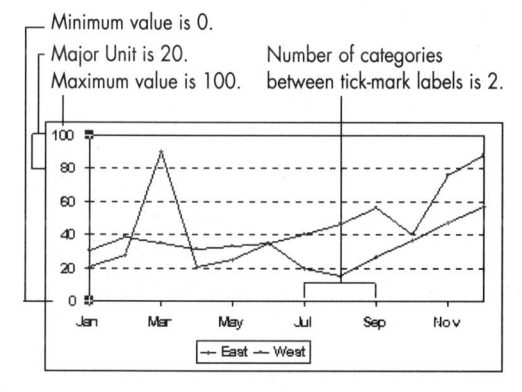

Figure 34. Scaling has been adjusted on this line graph.

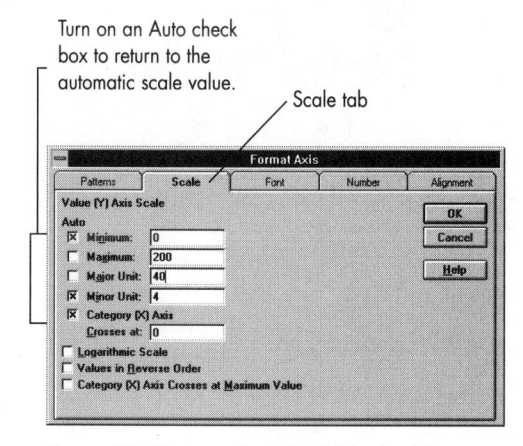

Turn on an Auto check box to return to the automatic scale value.
Scale tab

Figure 35. Changing the scale of the value (Y) axis

Scaling the Axis

On the *value axis* (such as the y-axis in Figure 33), Microsoft Graph lets you adjust the maximum value, minimum value, and major unit (increments between labels). On the *category axis* (such as the x-axis in Figure 33), you can adjust the number of categories between labels and tick marks. Figure 34 shows the line graph after adjusting the scales.

1. Select the axis to be scaled. Selection handles appear at both ends of the axis.
2. Select Format/Selected Axis.

   or

   Press the right mouse button and choose Format Axis.
3. Click the Scale tab (Figures 35 and 36).
4. For the value axis, enter new values for the Minimum, Maximum, Major Unit, and/or Minor Unit. (The X disappears in the Auto column when you change a value.)

   or

   For the category axis, enter new values for Number of Categories between Tick-Mark Labels and/or Number of Categories between Tick Marks.
6. Click OK.

■ Tip

✓ To return to the default scale values, turn on the check box in the Auto column, next to the appropriate item (Figure 35).

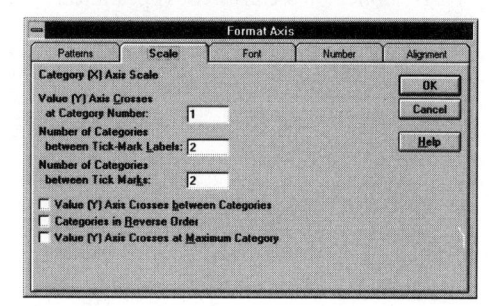

Figure 36. Changing the scale of the category (X) axis

Formatting Graphs

65

CHAPTER 5

Formatting the Axis Numbers

Figure 37 shows a value axis in which the numbers have been formatted to display dollar signs.

1. Select the axis whose numbers you want to format.
2. Select Format/Selected Axis.

   or

   Press the right mouse button to display the shortcut menu. Then choose Format Axis.
3. Choose the Number tab (Figure 38).
4. From the Category list, choose the appropriate formatting category (such as Number, Percentage, or Currency).
5. In the list of Format Codes, choose the code with the appropriate formatting.
6. Click OK.

■ Tips

✓ After clicking a format code, look at the Sample (circled in Figure 38) to preview what the number will look like.

✓ Instead of formatting all the numbers to currency, you can insert an axis title that explains that the values are in dollars (Figure 39).

   See Inserting Titles on page 52.

✓ Data label values can also be formatted. Suppose some of the numbers in the datasheet have 1 decimal place and others have none. For a consistent appearance, you may want to format all the data labels on the graph to 0 decimal places.

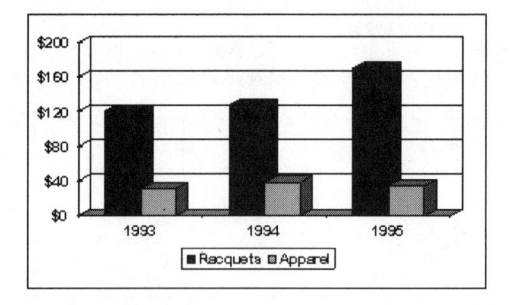

Figure 37. The numbers on the value axis have been given a Currency format.

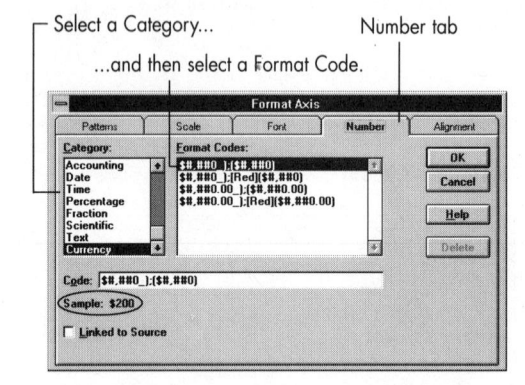

Figure 38. Formatting axis numbers

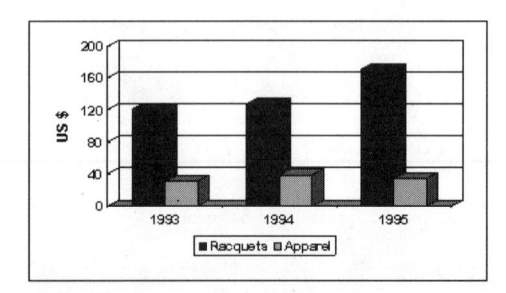

Figure 39. In this 3-D column graph, the value axis has a title that explains the scale is in U.S. dollars.

FORMATTING GRAPHS

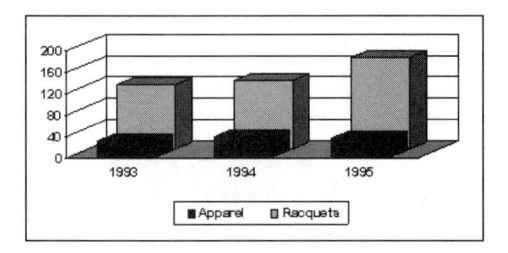

Figure 40. The text in this graph uses the default typeface (Arial) and size (18 points).

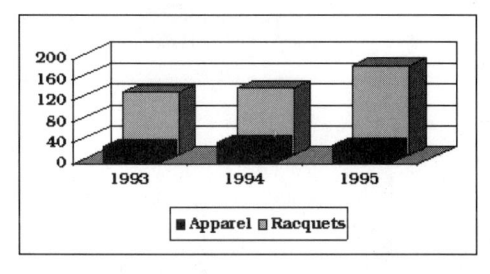

Figure 41. The text in this graph has been formatted to 22-point Bookman.

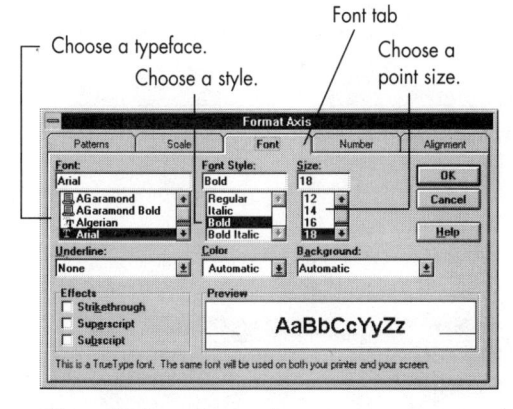

Figure 42. Formatting graph text

Click just inside this border to select the chart area.

Selection handles here indicate the chart area is selected.

Formatting Graph Text

You can format the text in each graph area (legend, titles, and so forth) with a particular typeface, size, and style (Figures 40 and 41).

1. Select the area whose text you want to format.

   or

   Within a selected title, drag across the individual characters you want to format.

2. Select Format/Selected *xxx* where *xxx* is the area you selected.

   or

   Press the right mouse button to display the shortcut menu. Then choose Format *xxx*.

3. Click the Font tab (Figure 42).
4. In the Font list, choose the desired typeface (use the scroll bar if necessary).
5. Select the desired Font Style (Regular, Italic, Bold, Bold Italic).
6. In the Size list, choose the desired point size (use the scroll bar if necessary).
7. Click OK.

■ Tips

✓ To format all the chart text to the same font, select the entire chart area (Figure 43).

✓ To avoid the "ransom note" look, use only one typeface on a graph.

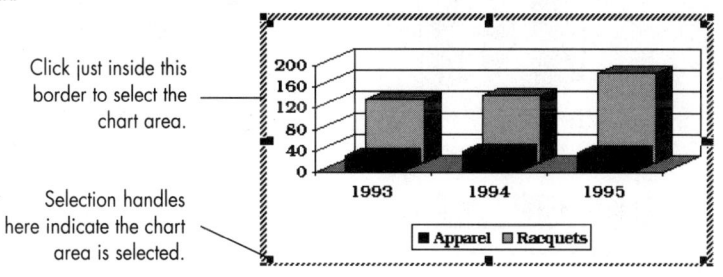

Figure 43. Select the chart area to format all the text at once.

Formatting Graphs

67

CHAPTER 5

Adjusting 3-D Effects

You can adjust the three-dimensionality of your 3-D graphs—their chart depth, gap depth, and gap width. Figure 44 shows a 3-D column graph with the default 3-D settings and Figure 45 shows the same graph after formatting.

You can see in Figures 44 and 45 that the *chart depth* is the depth of the graph's base, the *gap depth* is the vertical distance between each data point, and the *gap width* is the horizontal distance between each data point.

1. Select Format/1 3-D *xxx* Group where *xxx* is the type of graph, such as Column or Line.
2. Click the Options tab (Figure 46).
3. Click the arrows to adjust each 3-D setting. Watch the preview in the dialog box to see how the new values affect the three-dimensionality of the graph.
4. Click OK.

■ Tip

✓ You can also adjust the 3-D view of a graph. Figure 47 shows a graph after adjusting the elevation, rotation, and perspective, using the Format/3-D View command.

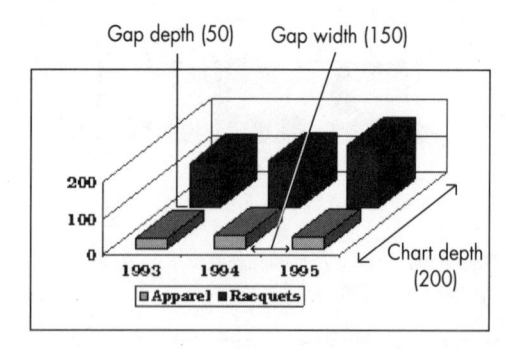

Figure 44. A 3-D column graph with the default 3-D settings

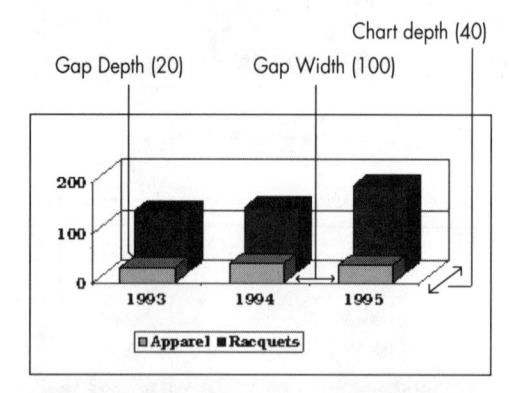

Figure 45. A 3-D column graph with altered 3-D settings

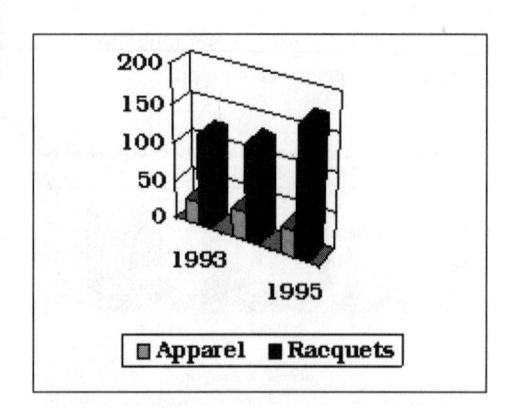

Figure 47. This 3-D column graph has a different perspective.

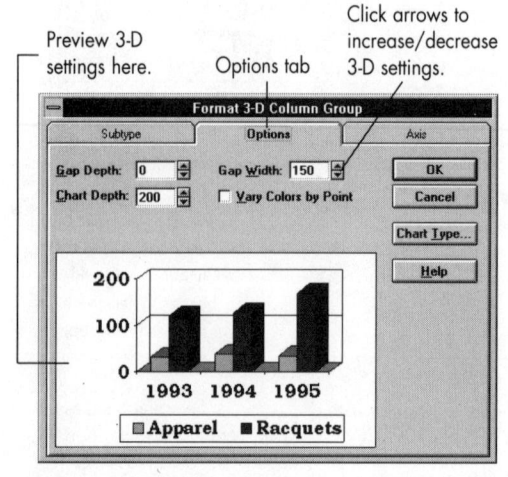

Figure 46. Adjusting 3-D settings for a 3-D column graph.

FORMATTING GRAPHS

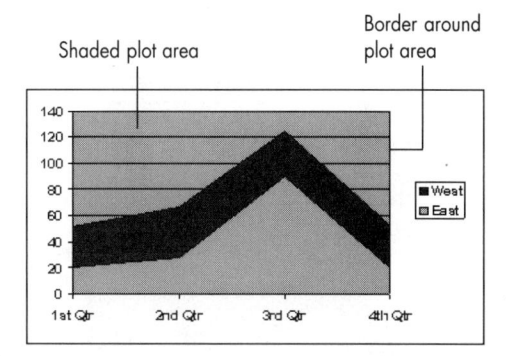

Shaded plot area
Border around plot area

Figure 48. An area graph with a formatted plot area

Places a border around the plot area
Shades the plot area

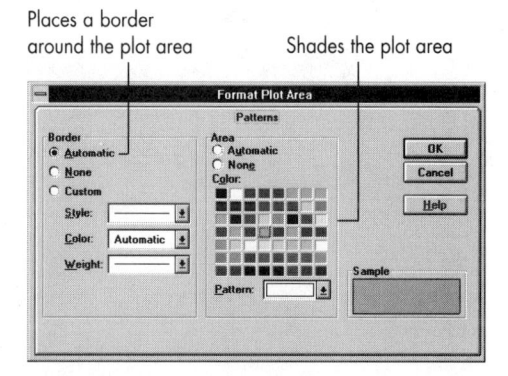

Figure 49. Formatting the plot area

Formatting the Plot Area

The *plot area* is the box formed by the horizontal and vertical axes. Figure 48 shows a graph with a formatted plot area.

1. Select the plot area (see first tip below).
2. Select Format/Selected Plot Area. The Format Plot Area dialog box appears (Figure 49).

   or

   Press the right mouse button and choose Format Plot Area.
3. To place a border around the plot area, turn on Automatic in the Border section.
4. To shade the plot area, choose a color from the palette in the Area section.
5. Click OK.

■ Tips

✓ The plot area can be tricky to select because there are so many other items inside or near this area. On 2-D graphs, either click inside the plot area in an area not occupied by any other item (Figure 50). On 3-D graphs, click between numbers on the value axis.

✓ In the Format Plot Area dialog box, you can also adjust the line style, weight, and color of the border.

For information on resizing the plot area, see page 59.

On 3-D graphs, click here to select the plot area.

On 2-D graphs, click in here to select the plot area.

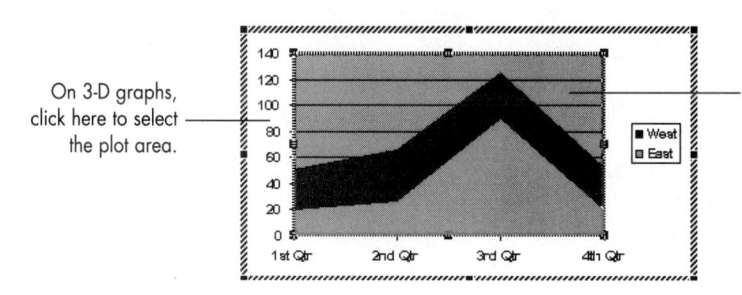

Figure 50. Selecting the plot area

69

CHAPTER 5

Formatting a Graph Automatically

With Microsoft Graph's *autoformatting* feature, you can quickly choose a chart type and apply formatting. Figures 51 and 52 show a graph before and after autoformatting.

1. Select Format/AutoFormat. The AutoFormat dialog box appears (Figure 53).
2. In the Galleries list, choose a chart type. The Formats area then displays subtypes with different formatting options.
3. Click one of the formats.
4. Click OK.

See opposite page for information on creating your own custom formats.

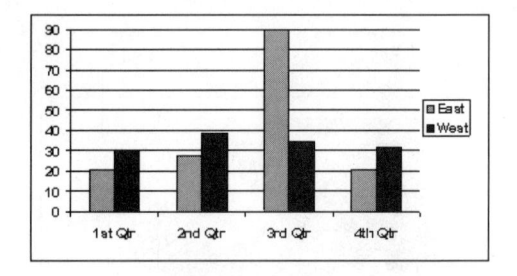

Figure 51. A column graph before autoformatting

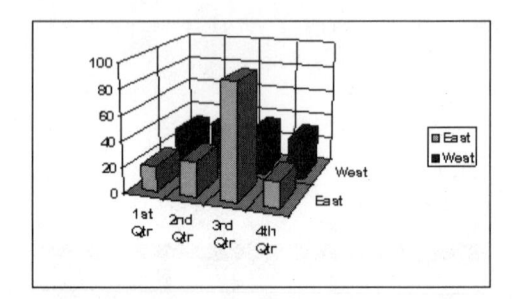

Figure 52. The same graph after autoformatting

First, choose a chart type...

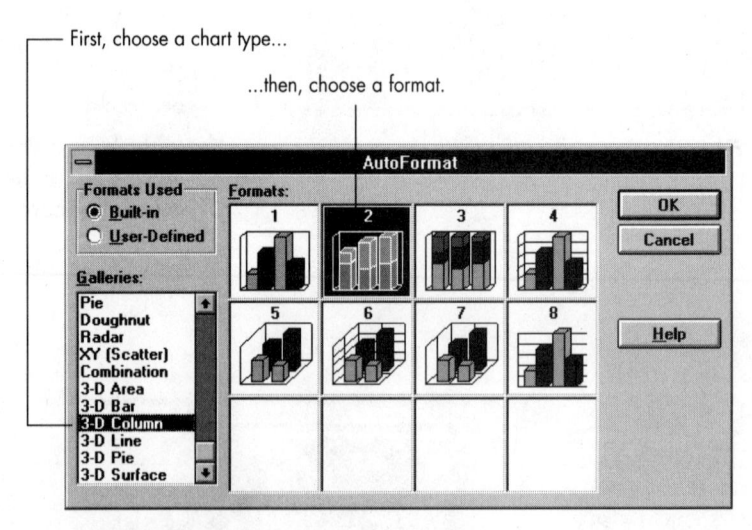

...then, choose a format.

Figure 53. Choosing an AutoFormat

Formatting Graphs

70

FORMATTING GRAPHS

Click here first...

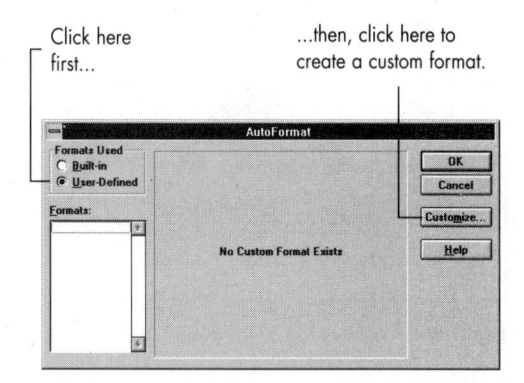

...then, click here to create a custom format.

Figure 54. Creating a custom format

Click here to add a custom format.

Figure 55. This dialog box lists the custom formats that have already been defined and lets you add and delete formats.

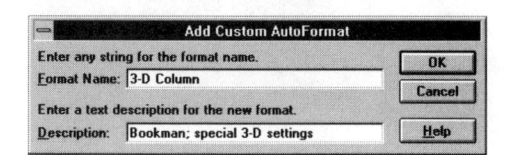

Figure 56. Enter the name and description for the custom format.

Defining a Custom AutoFormat

Suppose you want to format a series of graphs with the same settings. You can create your own AutoFormat and then apply it to any graph; these are called *user-defined* AutoFormats (as opposed to *built-in* AutoFormats).

1. Format a graph with the exact settings you want to duplicate in other graphs. This graph should be the active graph.
2. Select Format/AutoFormat.
3. In the Formats Used section, select User-Defined (Figure 54).
4. Click the Customize button. The User-Defined AutoFormats dialog box appears (Figure 55).
5. Click the Add button. The Add Custom AutoFormat dialog box appears (Figure 56).
6. In the Format Name field, type a name for the format (up to 31 characters).
7. In the Description field, describe the format in more detail (up to 32 characters).
8. Click OK.
9. Click Close.
10. Click OK.

■ Tip

✓ It's best to keep the format name under 15 characters. (Although the name can be up to 31 characters long, only the first 15 characters or so will show in the Formats list.)

CHAPTER 5

Applying a Custom AutoFormat

Figures 57 and 58 show a graph before and after applying a custom format.

1. Display the graph you want to format.
2. Select Format/AutoFormat.
3. In the Formats Used section, select User-Defined (Figure 59).
4. In the Formats list, click the name you want to use.
5. Click OK.

■ **Tip**

✓ The preview box (Figure 59) shows you how the active graph looks with the selected custom format. Because the preview box is so small in comparison to the actual graph, the labels may wrap or overlap. For example, in Figure 59, the x-axis labels (1990, 1991, etc.) wrap onto two lines. This does not mean that the labels will wrap on the actual graph.

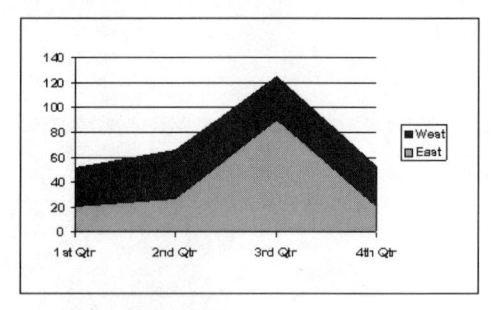

Figure 57. A chart before applying a custom format

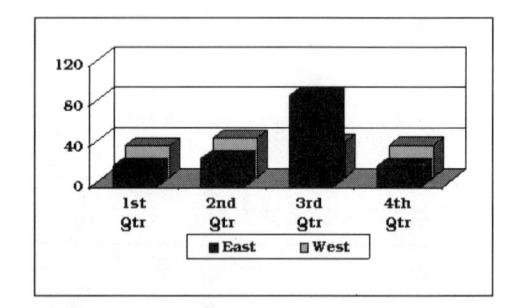

Figure 58. The same chart after applying a custom format

To apply a custom format, click here first...

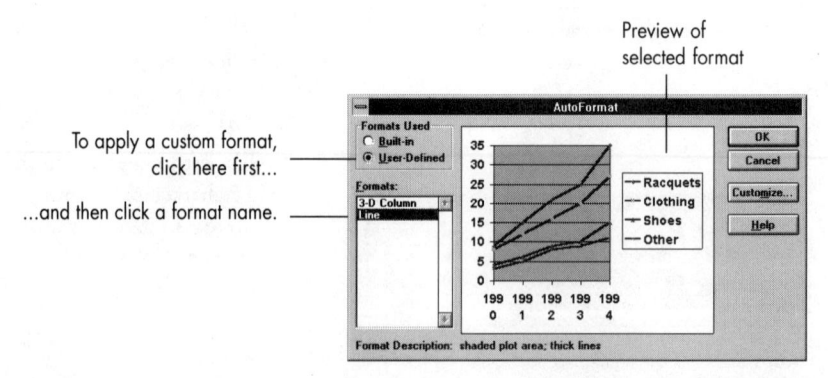

...and then click a format name.

Preview of selected format

Figure 59. Use Format/AutoFormat to apply a custom format.

CREATING PIE CHARTS 6

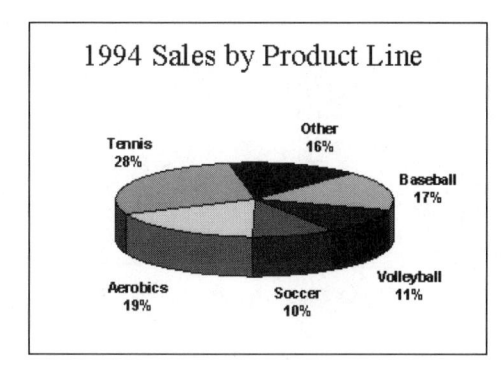

Figure 1. A 3-D pie chart

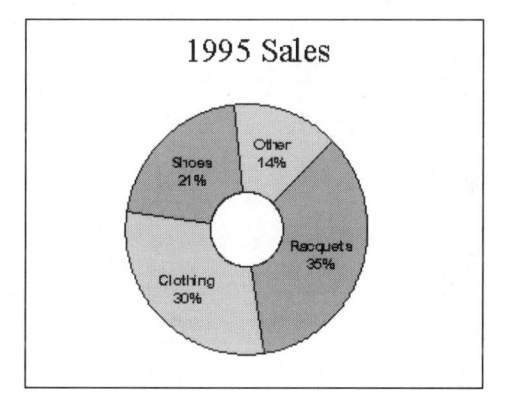

Figure 2. A doughnut chart

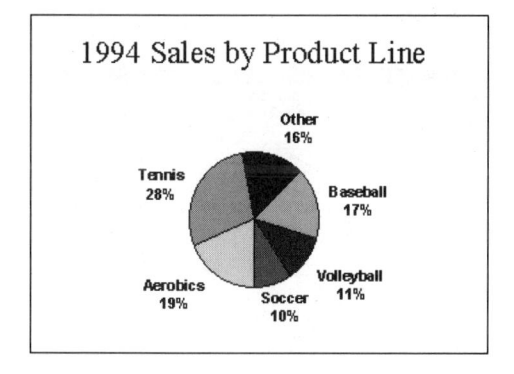

Figure 3. A 2-D pie chart

About Pie Charts

A pie chart shows the relative proportions of several items. By looking at the relative size of the pie slices and their accompanying percentage figures, you can clearly see the relationship between the items (Figure 1).

Unlike column and line graphs, which typically show different values over time, pie charts show values at a particular point in time (such as 1994 sales). Pie charts are one of the simplest types of graphs to create because they have only one data series.

Microsoft Graph offers a number of ways to enhance your pie charts. For instance, you can explode a slice, assign new colors or patterns to the slices, and rotate the pie.

■ Tips

✓ Another chart type similar to a pie is a doughnut (Figure 2). Like pie charts, doughnut charts show the breakdown of a total at a certain point in time.

✓ Microsoft Graph offers pie chart types in 2-D (Figure 3) and 3-D (Figure 1).

Creating Pie Charts

73

CHAPTER 6

Inserting a Pie Slide

Pie charts use the graph AutoLayouts, just as the other types of graphs do.

1. Click the New Slide button at the bottom of the PowerPoint window.
2. In the New Slide dialog box, choose one of the graph AutoLayouts (Figure 4).
3. Click OK. The slide appears with title and graph placeholders (Figure 5).
4. Click the title placeholder and type the title of your graph.
5. Double-click the graph placeholder to create your graph.
6. Select Format/Chart Type. The Chart Type dialog box appears (Figure 6).
7. For the Chart Dimension, choose 2-D or 3-D.
8. Click the pie chart type.
9. Click OK. You are now ready to fill in the datasheet.

See Entering Pie Data on the next page.

■ Tips

✓ Another way to choose the pie chart type is with the Format/AutoFormat command (Figure 7).

   See Formatting a Graph Automatically on page 70.

✓ Later in this chapter (page 84) you'll learn how to create two pie graphs on a slide.

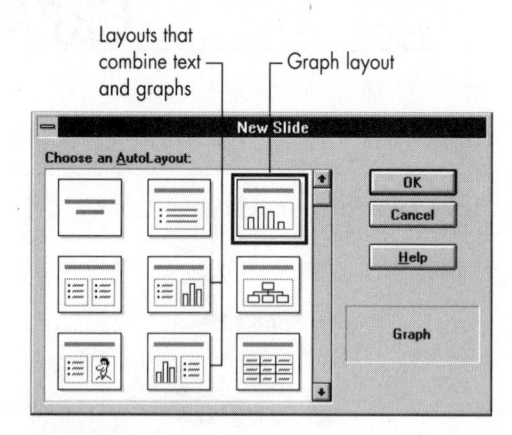

Figure 4. Choose a graph layout in the New Slide dialog box.

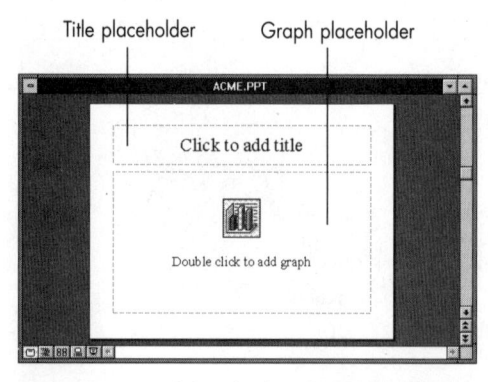

Figure 5. A new slide with title and graph placeholders

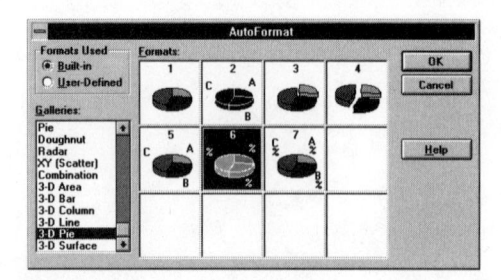

Figure 7. Choosing an AutoFormat for a pie chart

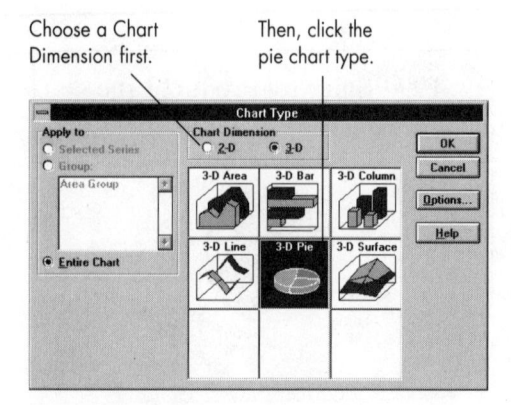

Figure 6. Choosing the pie chart type

CREATING PIE CHARTS

Double-click here to close the datasheet.
Drag the title bar to move the datasheet.
Drag the borders to resize the datasheet.
Select All button

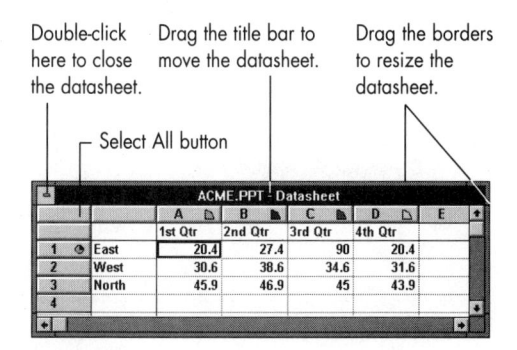

Figure 8. The sample data in the datasheet

View Datasheet
By Column
By Row

Figure 9. The Graph toolbar

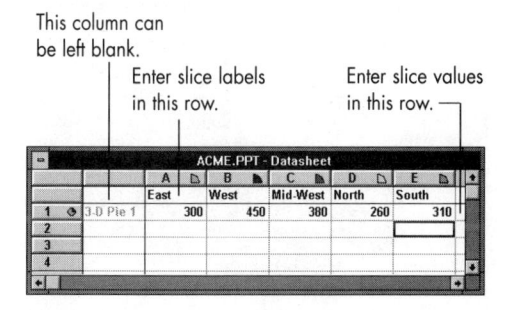

This column can be left blank.
Enter slice labels in this row.
Enter slice values in this row.

Figure 10. How to enter pie data in the datasheet

Figure 11. Another way to enter pie data

Entering Pie Data

You enter your chart data in the datasheet window (Figure 8). The datasheet contains sample data that you erase before entering your own data.

1. If you haven't already done so, double-click the graph placeholder to launch Microsoft Graph.
2. If the datasheet window isn't already displayed, click the View Datasheet button (Figure 9).
3. To erase the sample data, click the Select All button (Figure 8) and press Delete.
4. Enter the graph data (Figure 10).
5. To view the graph, move or close the datasheet.

■ Tips

✓ Be sure to use the Select All button when deleting the sample data. If you delete a range of cells and your data consumes fewer columns than the sample data, Microsoft Graph will still insert a slice label for this data on the chart. To fix this problem, use the Exclude Row/Col command on the Data menu or the Delete command on the Edit menu.

✓ If you accidentally enter data in a column and then erase it, Graph will still reserve space for this data. Again, you can fix this problem by using the Exclude Row/Col command on the Data menu or the Delete command on the Edit menu.

✓ Feel free to enter slice labels in the first column and values in the second column (Figure 11). If you do this, you must let Graph know that the data series are entered into columns instead of rows. Use the Series in Columns command on the Data menu or click the By Column button on the Graph toolbar (Figure 9).

Creating Pie Charts

75

CHAPTER 6

Showing Labels, Values, and Percents

By default, a pie chart doesn't have any identifying labels next to its slices—there is only a legend. Figures 12 through 15 show the different types of data (slice) labels you can place on a pie chart.

1. Select Insert/Data Labels.
2. Choose one of the options in the Data Labels dialog box (Figure 16).
3. Click OK.

■ Tips

✓ The Data Labels command is not available if the datasheet is open. Just click on the chart to close the datasheet.

✓ When you display only values or percents, you will need a legend to identify the slices, like the one in Figures 12 and 13.

✓ To remove the legend, select it and press Delete. You will then need to reize the graph.

See Resizing and Repositioning a Pie on page 82.

✓ Another way to insert data labels is with the Format/AutoFormat command.

See Formatting a Graph Automatically on page 70.

✓ You can position the data labels exactly where you want them.

See Repositioning Data Labels on page 53.

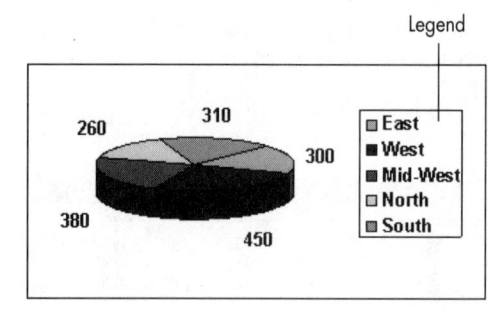

Figure 12. This chart has values next to each slice.

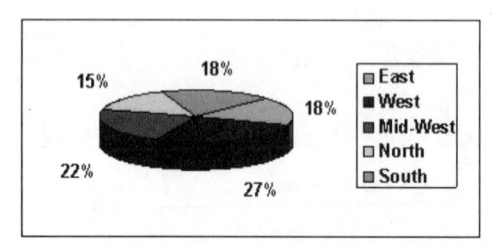

Figure 13. This chart has percentages next to each slice.

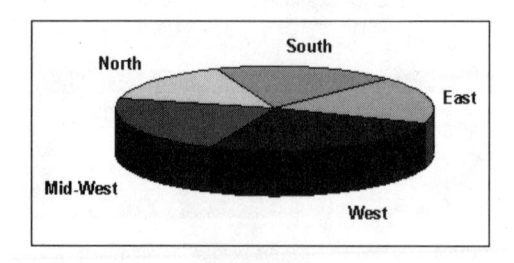

Figure 14. This chart has labels next to each slice.

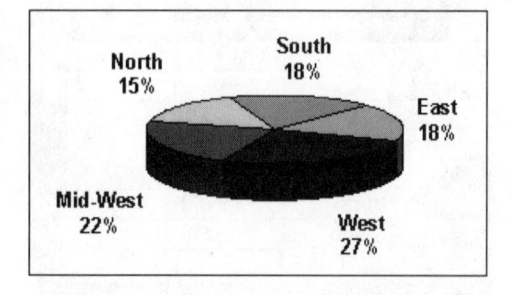

Figure 15. This chart has labels and percentages next to each slice.

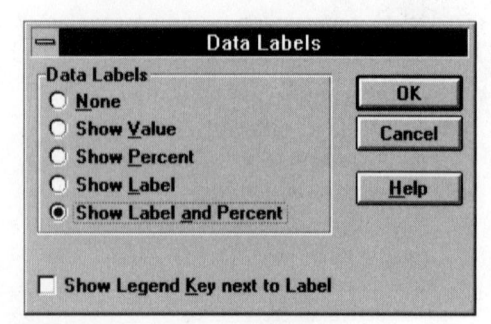

Figure 16. Inserting data labels on a pie chart

CREATING PIE CHARTS

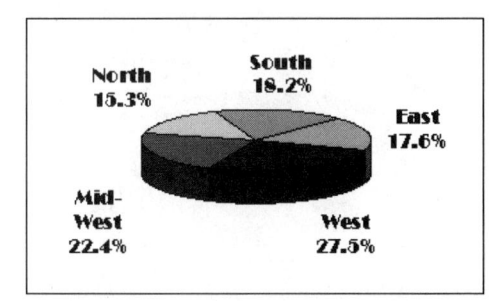

Figure 17. These labels have been formatted to 20-point Broadway; the percentages have been formatted to display one decimal place.

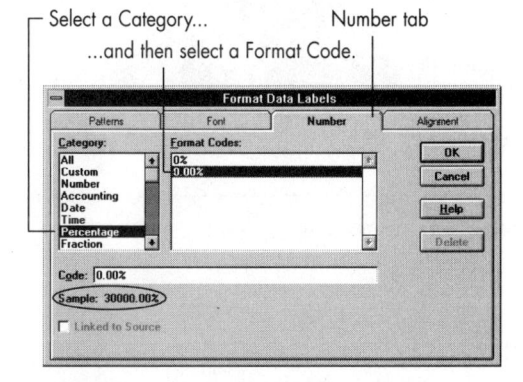

Figure 18. Formatting numbers in data labels

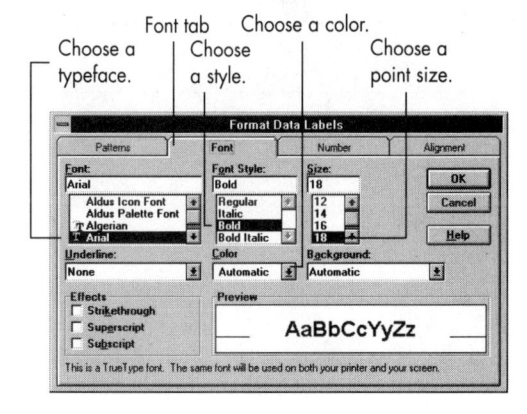

Figure 19. Formatting text in data labels

Formatting Slice Labels

You can format the numbers (percents or values) and the text in the slice labels (Figure 17).

1. Select the slice labels.
2. Select F_ormat/Se_lected Data Labels.

   or

   Press the right mouse button to display the shortcut menu. Then choose Format Data Labels.

3. To format numbers:
   - Choose the Number tab (Figure 18).
   - From the C_ategory list, choose the appropriate formatting category (such as Number, Percentage, or Currency).
   - In the list of F_ormat Codes, choose the code with the appropriate number of decimal places.

4. To format text:
   - Choose the Font tab (Figure 19).
   - In the F_ont list, choose the desired typeface (use the scroll bar if necessary).
   - Select the desired F_ont Style (Regular, Italic, Bold, Bold Italic).
   - In the S_ize list, choose the desired point size (use the scroll bar if necessary).
   - Choose a color.

5. Click OK.

See also Formatting the Axis Numbers on page 66 and Formatting Graph Text on page 67.

■ Tips

✓ After clicking a format code, look at the Sample (circled in Figure 18) to preview what the number will look like.

✓ If you want to display one decimal place in your percentages, you can create a custom format code: First, choose 0.00% from the F_ormat Codes list and then edit the C_ode field to read 0.0%.

77

CHAPTER 6

Exploding a Slice

To emphasize one of the pie slices, you can *explode* it as shown in Figure 20.

1. Click the pie to select it.
2. Click the slice you want to explode. You'll see selection handles around it (Figure 21).
3. Place the mouse pointer inside the slice, and drag away from the pie center until the slice is the desired distance from the rest of the pie.

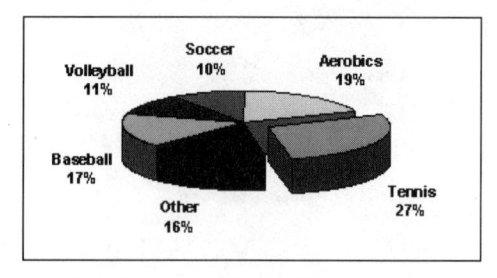

Figure 20. The Tennis slice is exploded from the pie to emphasize that it has the greatest portion of sales.

■ Tips

✓ You can explode 2-D and 3-D pie charts.
✓ To unexplode a slice, select it and drag it back toward the pie center.
✓ To explode all the slices (Figure 22), select the entire pie and drag any slice—all slices will explode.
✓ If you want the exploded slice to be in a particular position (for instance, at the 5:00 position on the pie), rotate the pie until the slice is in the desired place.

See Rotating a Pie on page 80.

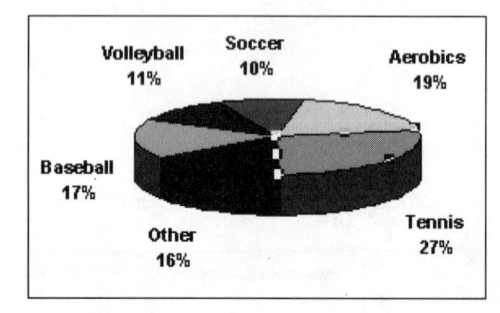

Figure 21. The Tennis slice is selected.

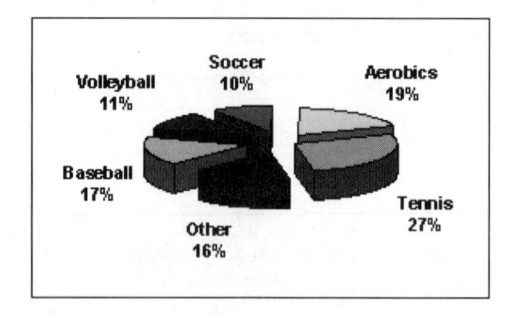

Figure 22. All slices are exploded in this pie chart.

CREATING PIE CHARTS

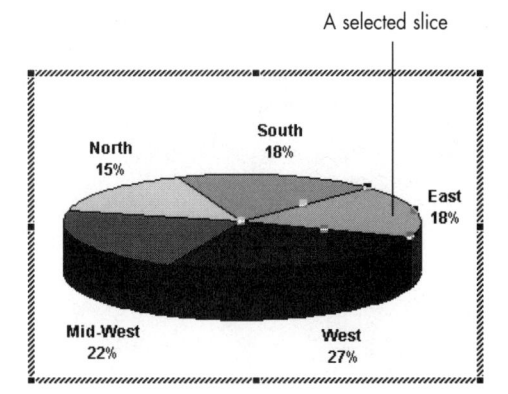

Figure 23. The East slice is selected.

A selected slice

Coloring the Slices

1. Click the pie to select it.
2. Click the slice you want to explode. You'll see selection handles around it (Figure 23).
3. Select Format/Selected Data Series.

   or

   Press the right mouse button to display the shortcut menu. Then choose Format Data Series.
4. Choose the Patterns tab (Figure 24).
5. Choose a color in the Area Color palette.
6. Click OK.
7. Repeat steps 2 through 6 for each slice.

■ Tip

✓ Slices can also have distinguishing patterns (Figure 25). Click the arrow in the Pattern field to display the pattern palette (Figure 26) and then choose a pattern. The colors in the pattern palette affect the pattern's *foreground* (lines, dots, etc.). The colors in the Area color palette affect the pattern's *background*.

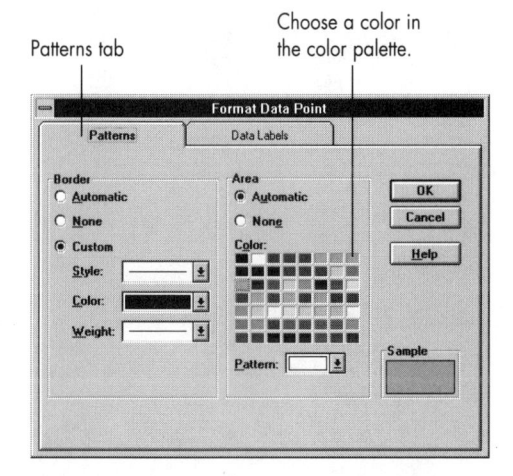

Figure 24. Changing the color of a slice

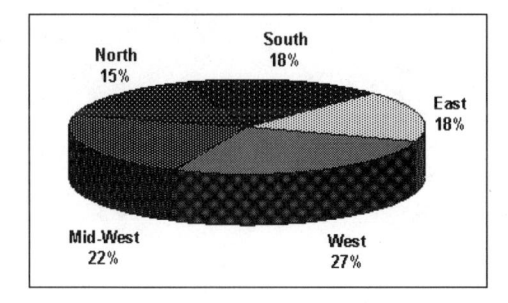

Figure 25. Each slice has a different pattern.

Figure 26. The pattern palette

Creating Pie Charts

79

CHAPTER 6

Rotating a Pie

To control the positioning of the slices, you can rotate the pie (Figures 27 and 28).

1. Select F_ormat/_1 3-D Pie Group.

    or

    Select F_ormat/_1 Pie Group.

2. Choose the Options tab (Figure 29).
3. In the _A_ngle of First Slice field, click the up arrow to rotate the pie clockwise in 10-degree increments, or click the down arrow to rotate the pie counterclockwise.
4. Click OK.

■ Tips

✓ The angle is measured from the 12:00 position on the pie.

✓ Watch the preview box (Figure 29) as you click the arrows in the _A_ngle of First Slice field—the pie rotates with each click.

✓ After rotating the pie, you may want to reposition some of the data labels.

   See Repositioning Data Labels on page 53.

✓ After rotating the pie, you may end up with too much space on one side of the chart. To solve this problem, you may want to increase the size of the plot area.

   For information on resizing the plot area, see Resizing and Repositioning a Pie on page 82.

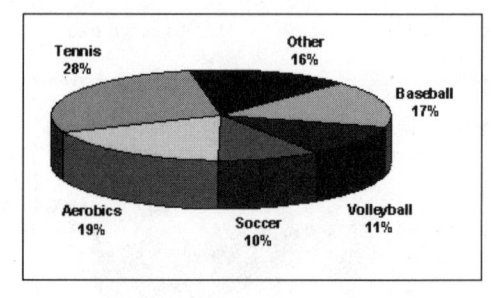

Figure 27. Before rotating the pie (angle=45)

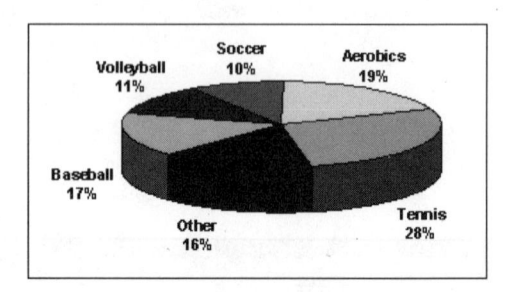

Figure 28. After rotating the pie (angle=225)

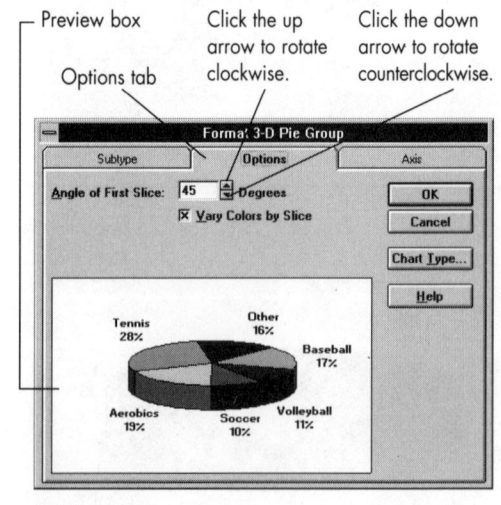

Figure 29. Rotating a pie

CREATING PIE CHARTS

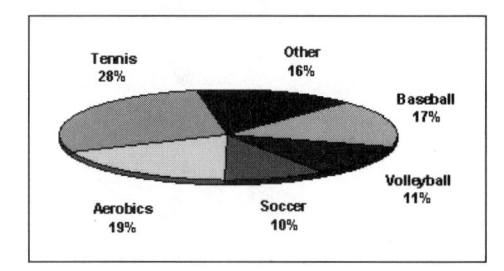

Figure 30. This pie chart has a height of 10%.

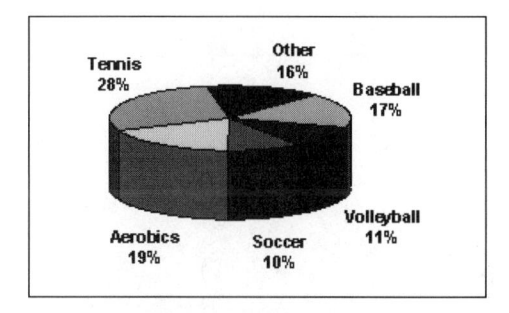

Figure 31. This pie chart has a height of 200%.

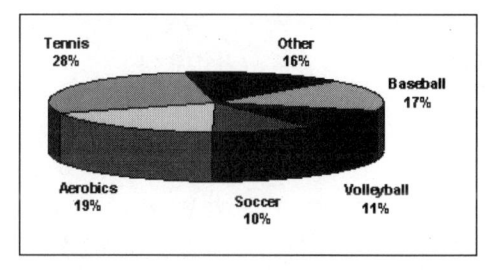

Figure 32. This pie chart has an elevation of 10 (the minimum).

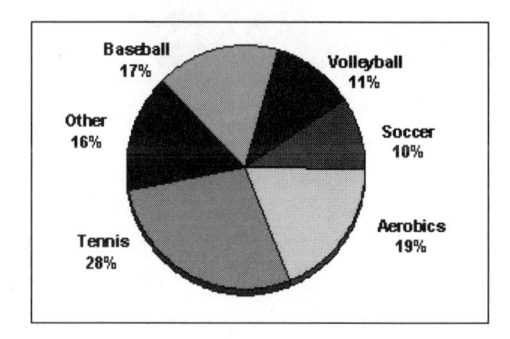

Figure 33. This pie chart has an elevation of 80 (the maximum).

Formatting 3-D Effects

For 3-D pies, you can control the height of the pie (Figures 30 and 31) and the elevation angle at which you are viewing the pie (Figures 32 and 33).

1. Select Format/3-D View. The Format 3-D View dialog box appears (Figure 34).
2. Click the large up or down arrows to increase or decrease the Elevation angle.
3. Enter a percentage in the Height field. The Height value is a percentage of the default height (100%). For instance, 50% is half the default height and 200% is twice the default height.
4. Click Apply to see the result of your changes without closing the dialog box.
5. Repeat steps 2 through 4 until you are satisfied with the results.
6. Click OK.

■ Tips

✓ With a low Elevation value, it is as if you are standing next to the pie and looking at it from the side. With a high value, it is as if you are in an airplane and viewing the pie from up above.

✓ To return to the default settings, click Default in the Format 3-D View dialog box.

✓ Because you may need to rotate your pie after adjusting the Elevation and Height, the Format 3-D View dialog box has a Rotation field.

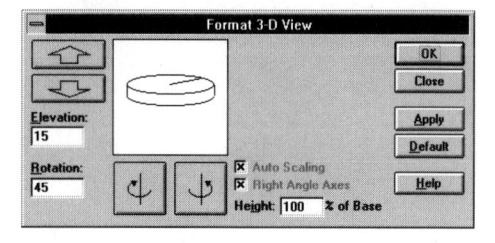

Figure 34. Changing the elevation and height of a 3-D pie chart

81

CHAPTER 6

Resizing and Repositioning a Pie

After you format and modify a pie chart, you may notice that it seems too small or that it is no longer centered in the chart area (Figure 35). You can solve these types of problems by manipulating the plot area. Figure 36 shows the results.

1. Select the plot area (Figure 37).
2. To enlarge the pie, drag a corner selection handle. You may also want to drag the handle on the opposite corner to finish enlarging the pie.
3. To reposition the pie, drag the border of the selected plot area.

■ Tips

✓ The plot area can be tricky to select because there are so many other items inside or near this area. Click just outside the edge of the pie, but not on a data label (Figure 37). Keep clicking in different places until you successfully select the plot area.

✓ When resizing or moving a pie, the data labels move with their respective slices. However, you may want to manually reposition some of them.

See Repositioning Data Labels on page 53.

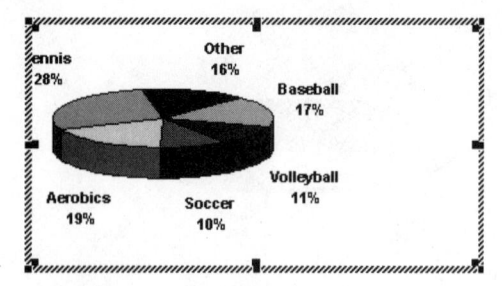

Figure 35. This pie chart is off center and smaller than it could be.

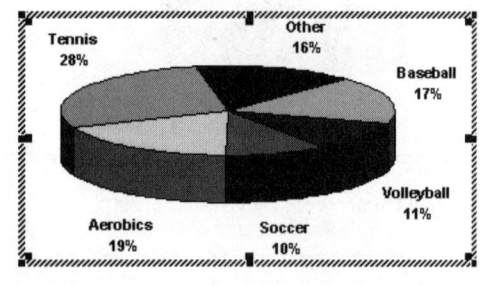

Figure 36. The pie chart has been resized and repositioned.

Click near, but not on, the pie to select the plot area.

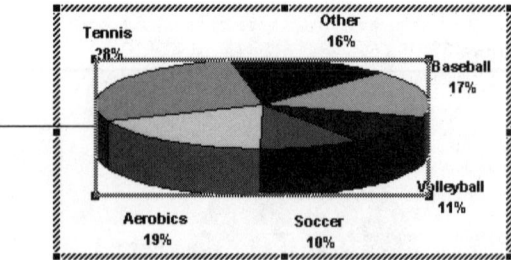

Figure 37. The selected plot area

CREATING PIE CHARTS

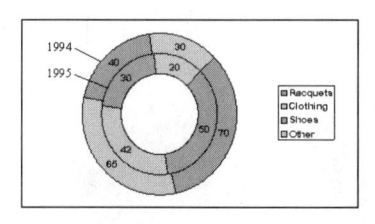

Figure 38. A doughnut chart with two data series

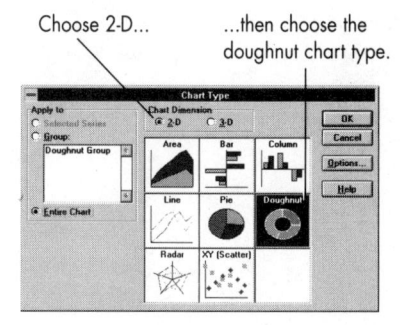

Figure 39. Choosing the doughnut chart type

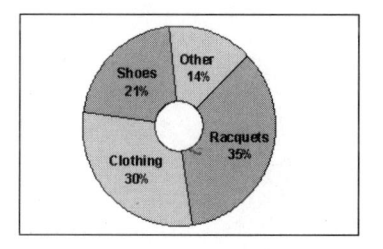

Figure 40. To fit the labels inside the doughnut pieces, the doughnut hole was reduced in size.

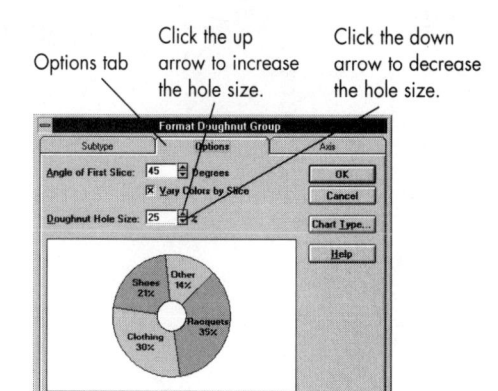

Figure 41. Changing the size of the doughnut hole

Creating a Doughnut

A doughnut chart is more than just a two-dimensional pie chart with a hole in the center: It can also display more than one data series (Figure 38).

1. Insert a graph slide and fill in the data sheet with each data series in a different row.

   See Inserting a Pie Slide on page 74 and Entering Pie Data on page 75.

2. Select Format/Chart Type. The Chart Type dialog box appears (Figure 39).
3. For the Chart Dimension, choose 2-D.
4. Click the doughnut chart type.
5. Click OK.

■ Tips

- ✓ Use Insert/Data Labels to label the doughnut pieces (Figure 40). Notice that the labels are inside the pieces.

   To move the labels outside the pieces, see Repositioning Data Labels on page 53.

- ✓ Because the legend identifies the doughnut pieces, not the data series, you need to identify the data series yourself. In Figure 38, this was accomplished by typing the labels 1994 and 1995 with PowerPoint's Text tool and drawing the pointers with the Line tool.

Sizing the Doughnut Hole

If there isn't enough room inside the doughnut pieces for the data labels, you can reduce the doughnut hole size.

1. Select Format/1 Doughnut Group.
2. Choose the Options tab (Figure 41).
3. Click the up or down arrows in the Doughnut Hole Size field to increase or decrease the size of the hole.
4. Click OK.

83

CHAPTER 6

Creating Two Pies on a Slide

For comparison purposes, it is sometimes useful to display two pie charts on a slide (Figure 42).

See *Creating Two Graphs on a Slide on page 55*.

■ Tip

✓ Because the pies are smaller when you have two to a slide, you will probably have to reduce the size of the data labels. (This was done in Figure 42.)

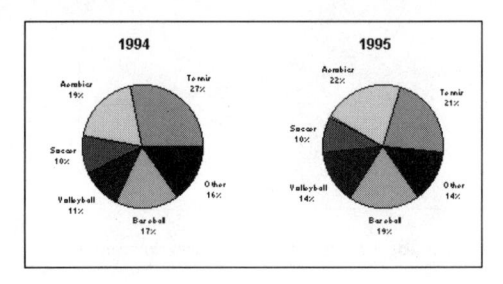

Figure 42. Two pie charts on a slide

BUILDING ORGANIZATION CHARTS   7

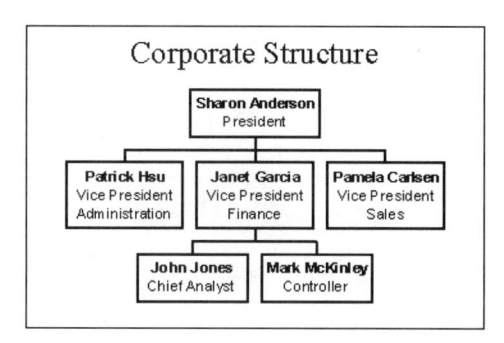

Figure 1. An organization chart

Organization Chart toolbar

Notice that the title bar indicates you are in a different program.

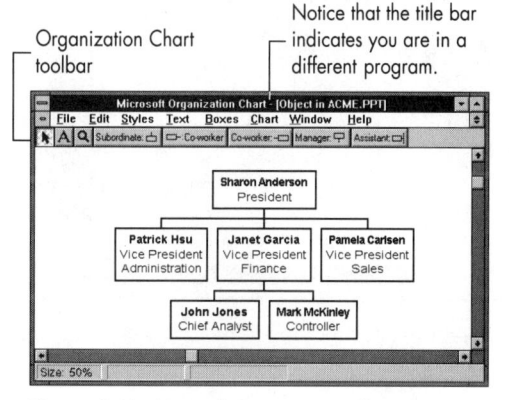

Figure 2. Use Microsoft Organization Chart to create your org charts.

About Organization Charts

The most common use for an organization chart is to illustrate a corporation's structure (Figure 1). This chart type, commonly referred to as an *org chart*, identifies the names and titles of the key people in a company or division. You can also use org charts to create a simplified flowchart, an outline of tasks in a project, a family tree, and a diagram of a hard disk's directory structure.

Org charts are actually created in a separate program called *Microsoft Organization Chart* (Figure 2). You launch Organization Chart by double-clicking the org chart placeholder or an embedded org chart. To return to PowerPoint, choose File/Exit and Return.

Organization charts are made up of managers, subordinates, co-workers, and assistants (Figure 3). A *manager* is someone who has other people—*subordinates*—reporting to him/her. *Co-workers* are subordinates who have the same manager. An *assistant* provides adminstrative assistance to a manager.

Assistant to Sharon Anderson

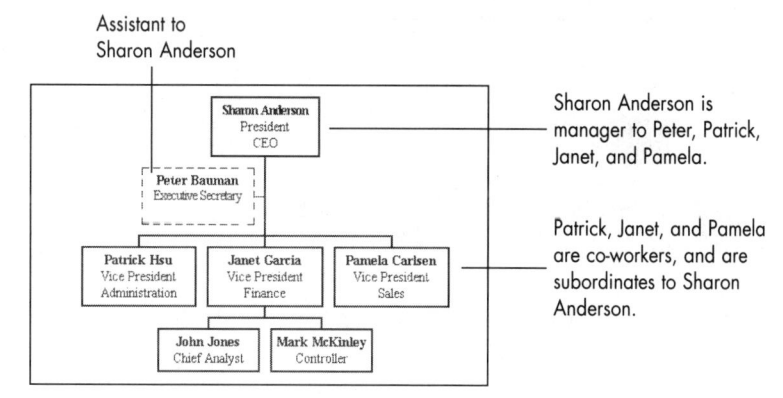

Sharon Anderson is manager to Peter, Patrick, Janet, and Pamela.

Patrick, Janet, and Pamela are co-workers, and are subordinates to Sharon Anderson.

Figure 3. The types of boxes in an org chart

Building Organization Charts

85

CHAPTER 7

Inserting an Org Chart Slide

1. Click the New Slide button at the bottom of the PowerPoint window.
2. In the New Slide dialog box, choose the Org Chart layout (Figure 4).
3. Click OK. The slide appears with title and org chart placeholders (Figure 5).
4. Click the title placeholder and type the title of your org chart.
5. Double-click the org chart placeholder to create your organization chart. This action launches Microsoft Organization Chart (Figure 6).

■ **Tip**

✓ When you are ready to return to PowerPoint, select File/Exit and Return to *xxx*.PPT, where *xxx*.PPT is the name of the presentation. Choose Yes to update the object.

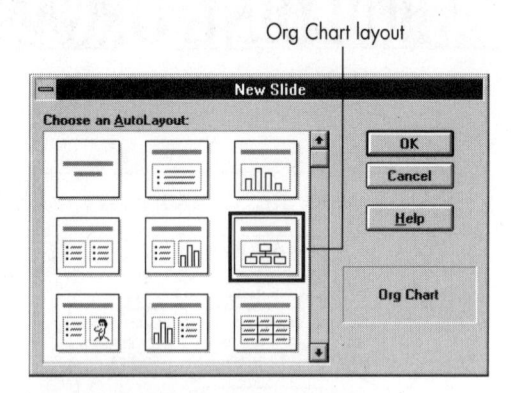

Figure 4. Choosing the Org Chart layout

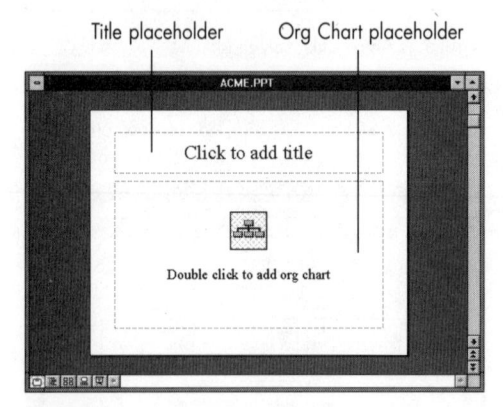

Figure 5. A new slide with title and org chart placeholders

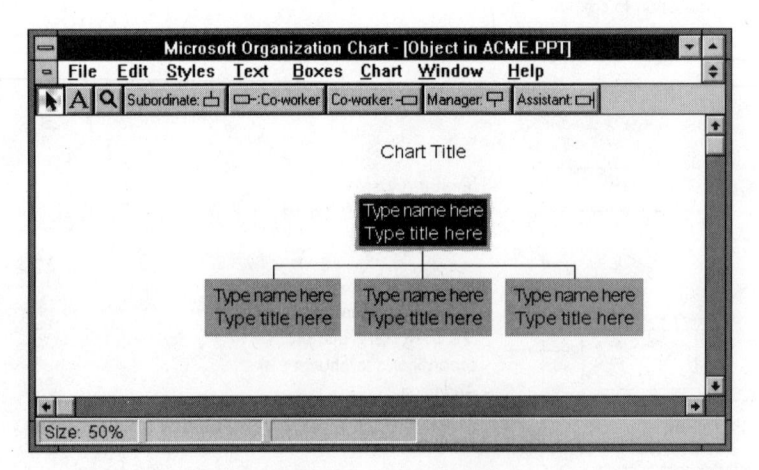

Figure 6. A new chart in Microsoft Organization Chart

BUILDING ORGANIZATION CHARTS

Figure 7. A box before any text is entered

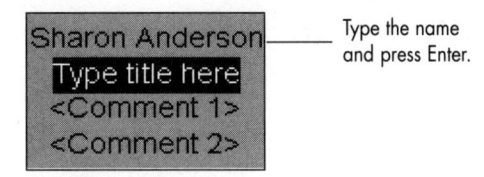

Figure 8. Entering the name
— Type the name and press Enter.

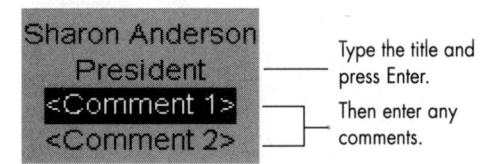

Figure 9. Entering the title and comments
— Type the title and press Enter.
— Then enter any comments.

Entering Text into Boxes

You can have up to four lines of text in a box: name, title, and two comment lines (Figure 7).

1. Click to select the box into which you want to enter text.
2. Type the name and press Enter (Figure 8). The next line is highlighted.
3. Type the title and press Enter (Figure 9). The next line is highlighted.
4. If needed, type a comment and press Enter.
5. Type an additional comment line, if desired.
6. To close the box, click on another box or click elsewhere in the window.

See next page for information on inserting additional boxes on the org chart.

■ Tips

✓ You can either press Enter or Tab to go to the next line in the box.

✓ To edit the text in a box, click the box to select it; then click again in the text to see the text cursor.

✓ Boxes automatically resize to fit the text you type inside. To make a box smaller, you must choose a smaller point size for the text.

See Formatting Box Text on page 93.

✓ When you are ready to return to PowerPoint, select File/Exit and Return to *xxx*.PPT, where *xxx*.PPT is the name of the presentation. Choose Yes to update the object.

87

CHAPTER 7

Inserting a Box

Since the default org chart has only four boxes, it is likely that you will want to insert additional boxes.

1. Click the appropriate Box tool (Figure 10) for the type of box you are inserting.
2. Click the existing box to which the new box should be attached (Figure 11).

Figure 12 shows the results.

Inserting Multiple Boxes

Using the following technique, the Box tool remains active so that you can easily insert multiple boxes of the same type.

1. Hold down Shift as you click the appropriate Box tool.
2. Click the existing box to which you want to attach the new box.
3. Repeat step 2 for each new box you want to insert.
4. Click the Selection Arrow tool (Figure 10) to deactivate the Box tool.

■ Tips

✓ Note that there are two Co-worker Box tools. The first one inserts the box to the left, and the second one inserts it to the right.

✓ To insert a box between subordinates and their manager (Figure 13), select the boxes for which you want to create a new manager. Then hold down the Ctrl key as you click the Manager Box tool.

✓ To delete a box, select it and press Delete.

✓ When you are ready to return to PowerPoint, select File/Exit and Return to xxx.PPT, where xxx.PPT is the name of the presentation. Choose Yes to update the object.

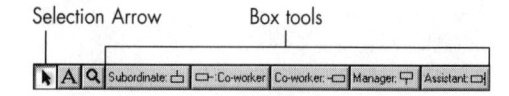

Figure 10. The Org Chart toolbar

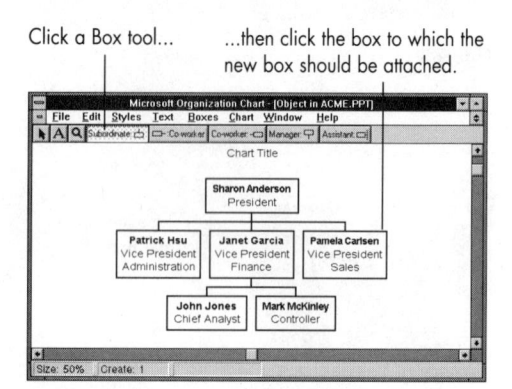

Figure 11. Inserting a subordinate box

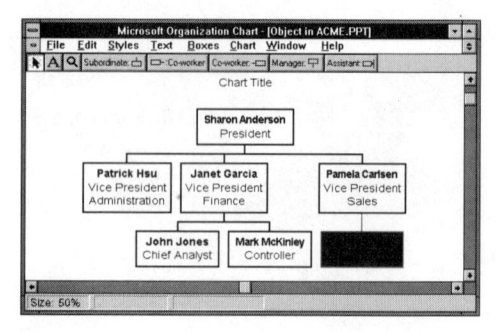

Figure 12. An inserted subordinate box

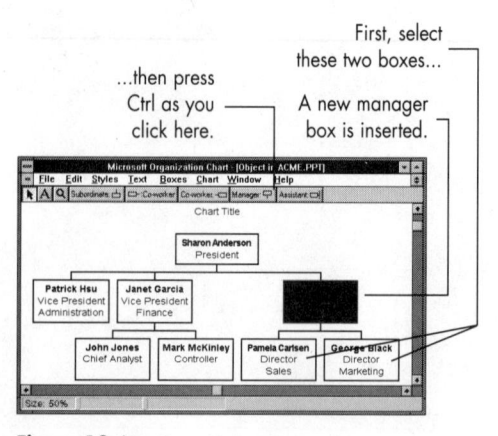

Figure 13. Inserting a new manager

BUILDING ORGANIZATION CHARTS

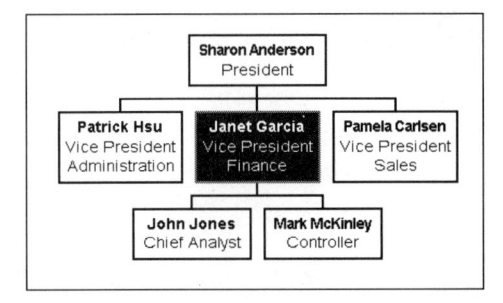

Figure 14. Before moving Janet Garcia

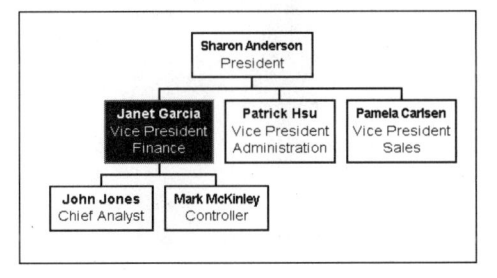

Figure 15. After moving the box to a new location

Rearranging Boxes

You can easily restructure an organization chart by dragging the boxes (Figures 14 and 15).

1. Select the box to be repositioned.
2. Place the mouse pointer on the box border—make sure you see the pointer and not the text cursor.
3. Drag the box over its new manager or co-worker.
4. Release the mouse button.

■ Tips

- ✓ As you drag one box over another, the pointer displays an icon to indicate the new positioning of the box:
  - ⇨ Box will be inserted as a co-worker to the right.
  - ⇦ Box will be inserted as a co-worker to the left.
  - ⊥ Box will be inserted as a subordinate.
- ✓ When you move a manager box, all its subordinates move along with it. (They don't need to be selected.)
- ✓ Another way to move a box is by cutting and pasting. Select the box and choose Edit/Cut. Then, select the box of the new manager and choose Edit/Paste Boxes.
- ✓ When you are ready to return to PowerPoint, select File/Exit and Return to *xxx*.PPT, where *xxx*.PPT is the name of the presentation. Choose Yes to update the object.

89

CHAPTER 7

Selecting Boxes

To format the boxes in an org chart, you must first select them. To select boxes:

    Shift+click each box.

or

Select Edit/Select and choose the item you wish to select (Figure 16).

or

Select Edit/Select Levels and enter a range of levels to select (Figures 17 and 18).

Here are a few terms you need to know when selecting boxes (Figure 19):

Group   All boxes with the same manager.

Branch   A box and all the boxes that report to it, all the way to the bottom of the chart.

Co-managers   Share responsibility for the same group of subordinates.

■ Tips

- ✓ The shortcut for selecting all boxes is Ctrl+A.
- ✓ The shortcut for selecting a group is Ctrl+G. (You must first select one box in the group.)
- ✓ The shortcut for selecting a branch is Ctrl+B. (You must first select one box in the branch.)

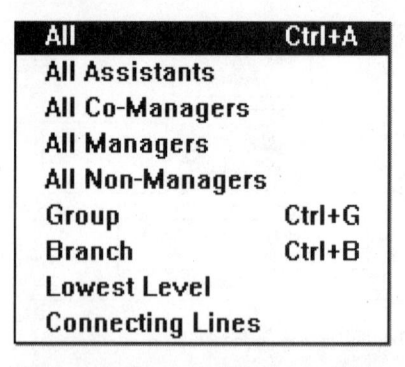

Figure 16. Choose Edit/Select to display this menu.

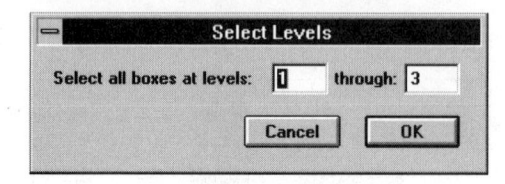

Figure 17. Choose Edit/Select Levels to display this dialog box.

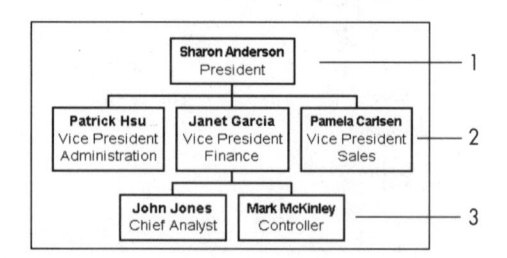

Figure 18. This organization chart has three levels.

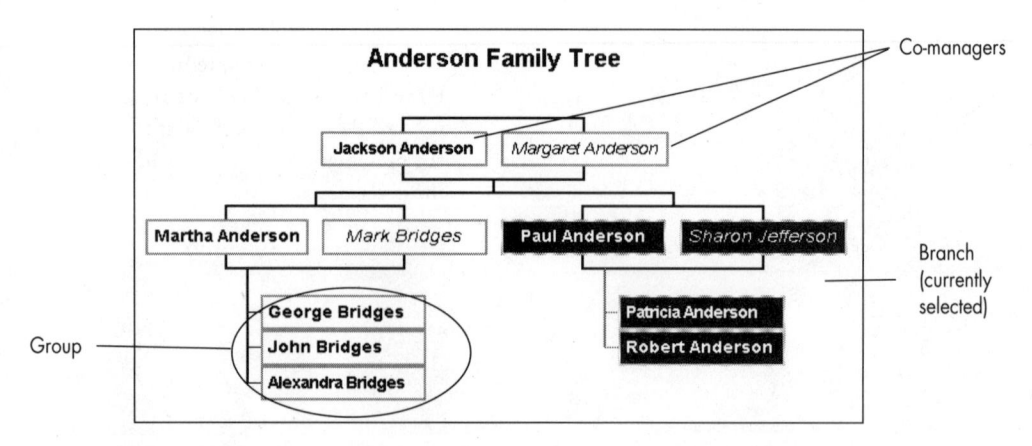

Figure 19. Elements of an organization chart

BUILDING ORGANIZATION CHARTS

Choosing a Style

You can choose from a variety of styles for your organization charts. Figures 20 through 22 show several of these styles.

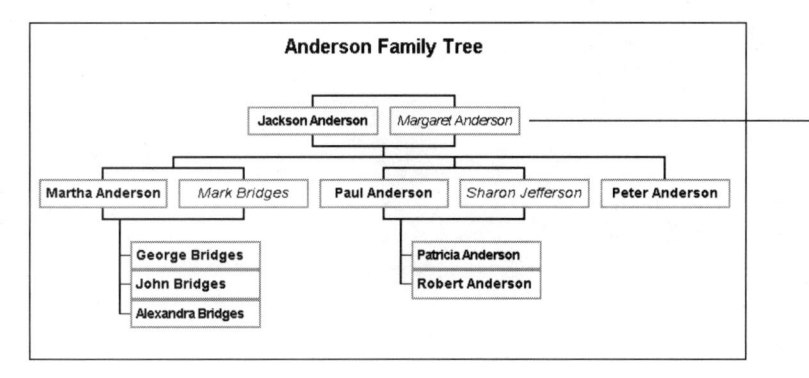

Each married couple was selected and then formatted with the Co-manager style.

Figure 20. The lowest level is vertically oriented; each name is in a box.

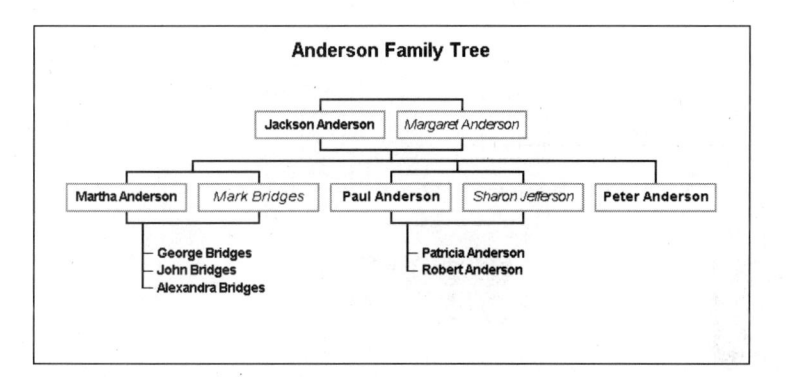

Figure 21. The lowest level is vertically oriented; the names are not boxed.

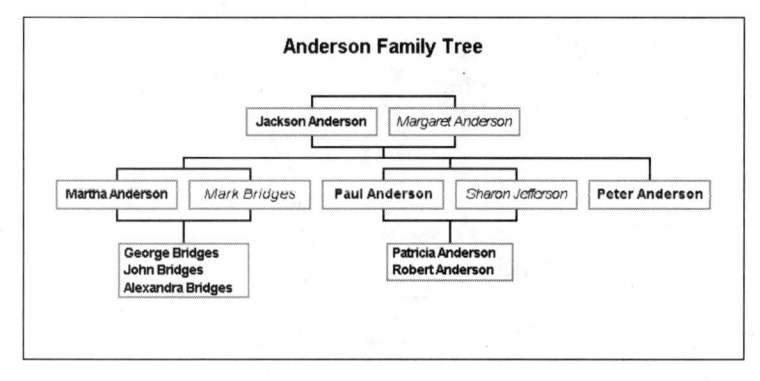

Figure 22. The lowest level is vertically oriented; all names in a group are in one box.

CHAPTER 7

Choosing a Style (cont'd)

1. Select the boxes (such as a level or a group) for which you want to choose a new style (Figure 23).

   See Selecting Boxes on page 90.

2. Select the Styles menu and choose the desired style (Figure 24).

■ Tips

✓ The styles with vertical orientation are typically used on the lowest level of an organization chart.

✓ Before choosing Group or Branch from the Select menu, click in one of the boxes of the group or branch.

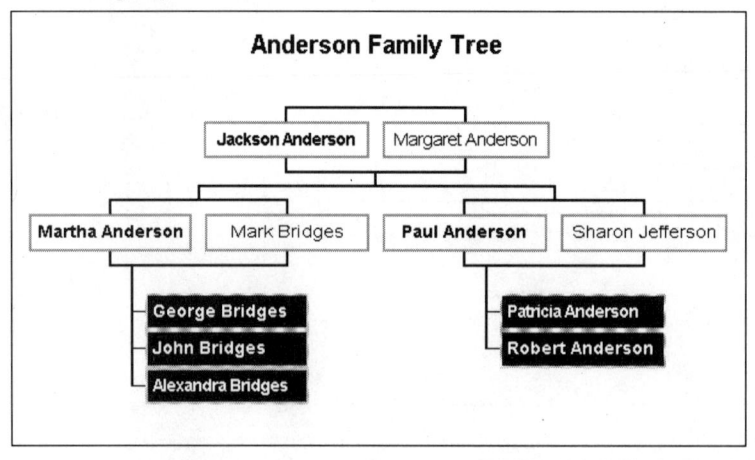

Figure 23. The lowest level of this organization chart is selected.

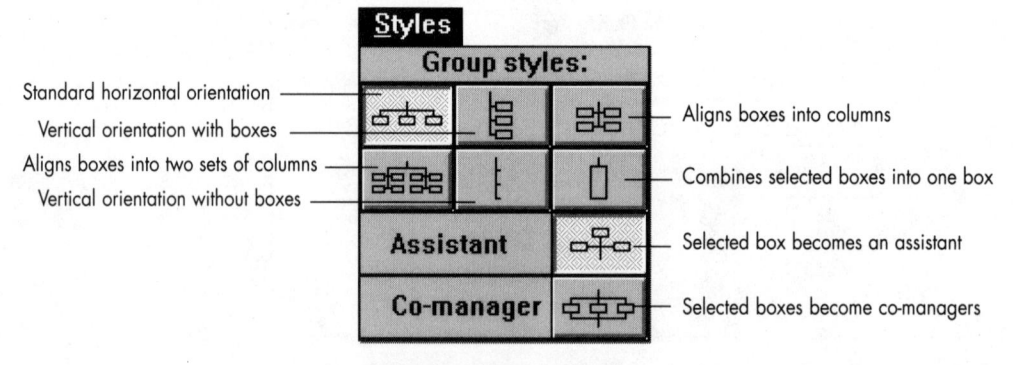

Figure 24. Choosing a style

Standard horizontal orientation — Aligns boxes into columns
Vertical orientation with boxes
Aligns boxes into two sets of columns — Combines selected boxes into one box
Vertical orientation without boxes
Assistant — Selected box becomes an assistant
Co-manager — Selected boxes become co-managers

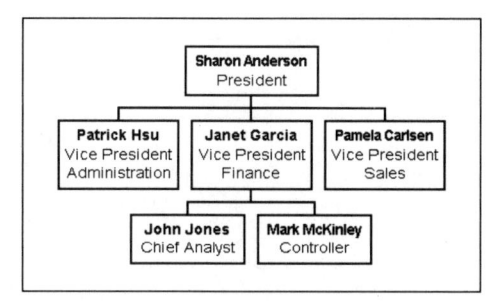

Figure 25. All the names are in bold.

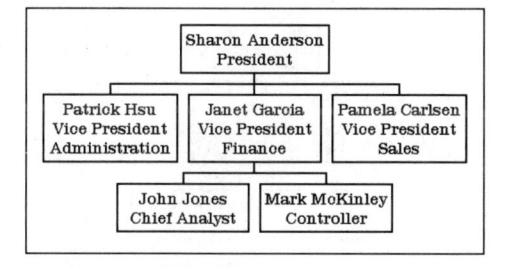

Figure 26. All the box text is formatted to 18-point Clarendon.

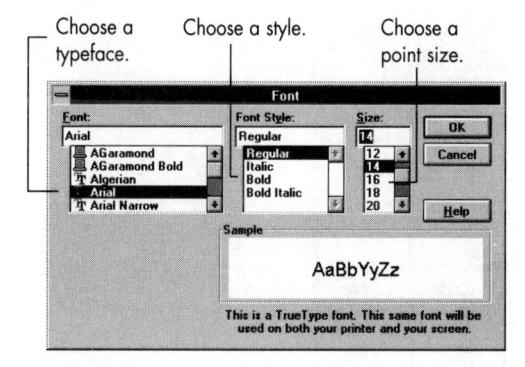

Figure 27. Formatting box text

Formatting Box Text

You can format all or any part of the text inside the boxes (Figures 25 and 26).

1. To format a selection of text, click in the box and then drag the text cursor over the characters you want to select.

    or

    To format all the text in one or more boxes, select the boxes.

    See Selecting Boxes on page 90.

2. Select Text/Font. The Font dialog box appears (Figure 27).

3. In the Font list, choose the desired typeface (use the scroll bar if necessary).

4. Select the desired Font Style (Regular, Italic, Bold, or Bold Italic).

5. In the Size list, choose the desired point size (use the scroll bar if necessary).

6. Click OK.

■ Tips

✓ You can also change the alignment of text within the boxes. On the Text menu, choose Left, Right, or Center. (Center is the default.)

✓ To avoid the "ransom note" look, use only one typeface on an organization chart.

✓ When you are ready to return to PowerPoint, select File/Exit and Return to *xxx*.PPT, where *xxx*.PPT is the name of the presentation. Choose Yes to update the object.

CHAPTER 7

Formatting the Boxes

You can choose a different border style (Figure 28), add a drop shadow (Figure 29), or change the color inside your boxes.

1. Select the boxes you want to format.

   See Selecting Boxes on page 90.

2. Use any of the following formatting commands found on the Boxes menu:
   - Select Box Border to change the border style (Figure 30).
   - Select Box Shadow to add a shadow effect (Figure 31).
   - Select Box Color to change the background color of the boxes.

■ **Tips**

✓ To format all the boxes, select them first with Ctrl+A.

✓ If you don't want any color inside the boxes, choose None at the bottom of the color palette.

✓ When you are ready to return to PowerPoint, select File/Exit and Return to *xxx*.PPT, where *xxx*.PPT is the name of the presentation. Choose Yes to update the object.

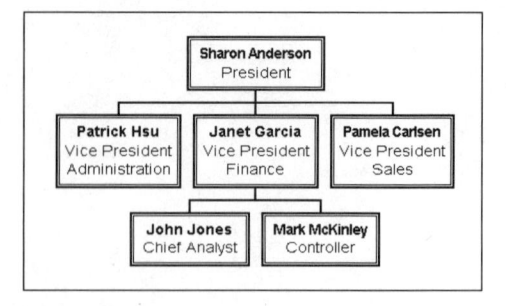

Figure 28. The boxes have a double-line border.

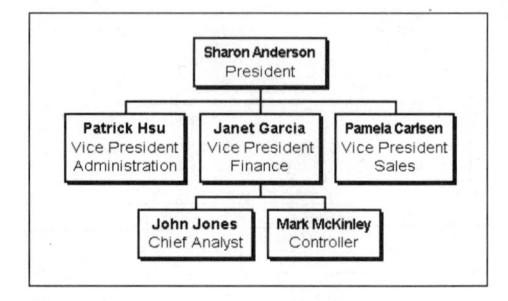

Figure 29. The boxes have drop shadows.

Figure 31. Box shadows

Figure 30. Box borders

94

BUILDING ORGANIZATION CHARTS

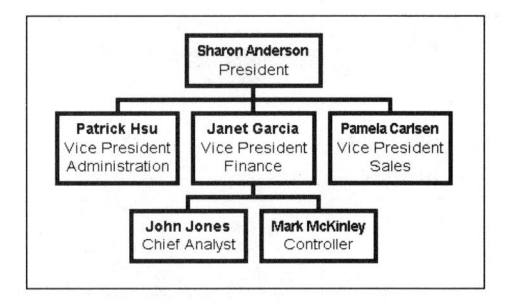

Figure 32. All the lines and borders have a 4-point thickness.

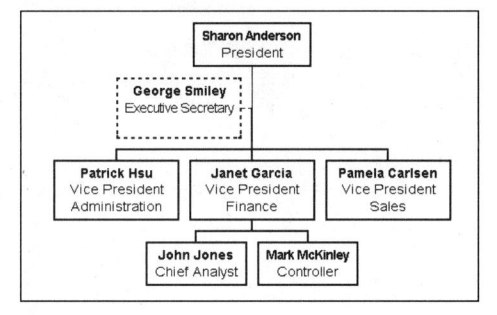

Figure 33. The Assistant box is formatted with a dotted line style.

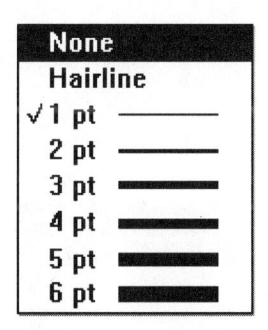

Figure 34. Line thicknesses

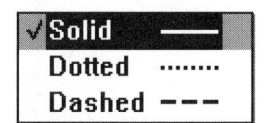

Figure 35. Line styles

Formatting the Lines

You can adjust the thickness (Figure 32), style (Figure 33), and color of the box borders and connecting lines.

1. To format connecting lines only, select Edit/Select/Connecting Lines.

   or

   To format box borders, select the appropriate boxes.

   See Selecting Boxes on page 90.

2. Use any of the following formatting commands on the Boxes menu:
   - Select Line Thickness to change the line thicknesses (Figure 34).
   - Select Line Style to select a different line style (Figure 35).
   - Select Line Color to change the color of the lines.

■ Tips

✓ Pressing Ctrl+A (or Edit/Select/All) selects all the boxes *and* the connecting lines.

✓ To select the boxes without selecting the connecting lines, Shift+click each box.

✓ When you are ready to return to PowerPoint, select File/Exit and Return to *xxx*.PPT, where *xxx*.PPT is the name of the presentation. Choose Yes to update the object.

95

CHAPTER 7

Zooming In and Out

The Chart menu (Figure 36) offers ways to change the display size of your organization chart. (It does not affect the printed size of the chart.) Figures 37 through 39 show examples of some of the zoom levels.

The Reduce/Enlarge tool is another way to zoom in/out (Figure 40).

Zooming In (Actual Size)

1. Click the Enlarge tool (Figure 40).
2. Click on the area of the chart you want to magnify.

Zooming Out (Size to Window)

1. Click the Reduce tool (Figure 40).
2. Click on the chart.

■ Tip

✓ Instead of using the Reduce/Enlarge tool in the toolbar, you can use a keyboard shortcut: Hold down Shift *and* Ctrl as you click on the chart.

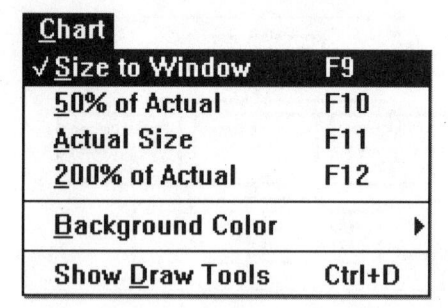

Figure 36. Use the Chart menu to zoom in (enlarge) or zoom out (reduce) the organization chart.

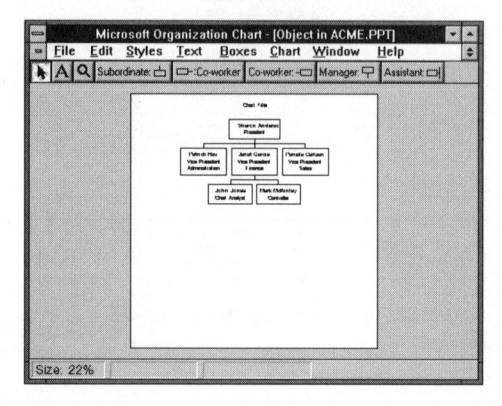

Figure 37. The Size to Window command gives you an overall feel for the chart (though you may not be able to actually read the text).

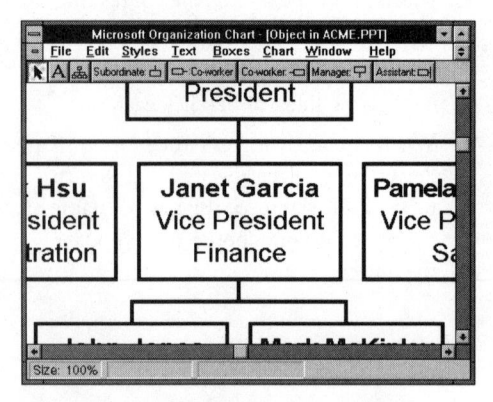

Figure 39. At Actual Size you can easily read box text and see more detail.

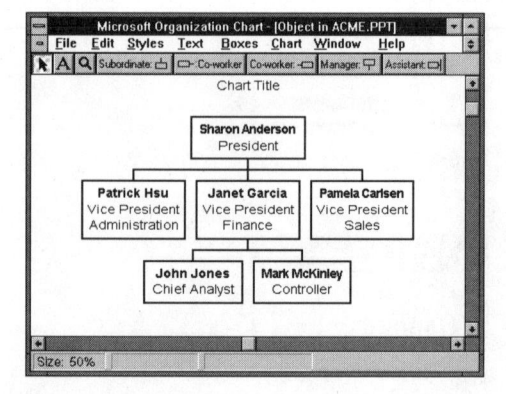

Figure 38. The 50% of Actual command shows the chart at 50% of printed size.

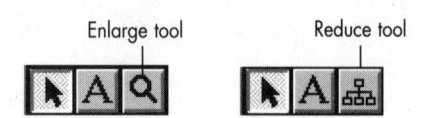

Figure 40. The button for the Reduce/Enlarge tool looks different depending on which view you are currently in.

BUILDING ORGANIZATION CHARTS

Double-click the embedded org chart.

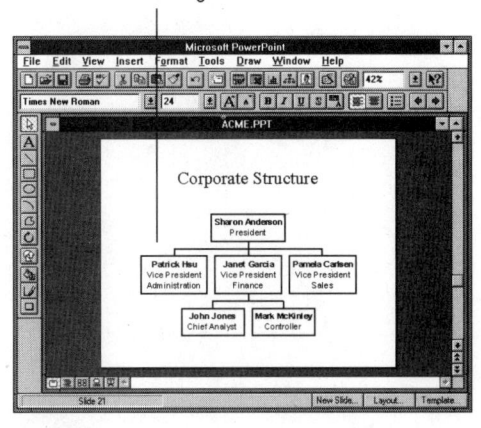

Figure 41. Opening the embedded org chart in Microsoft Organization Chart

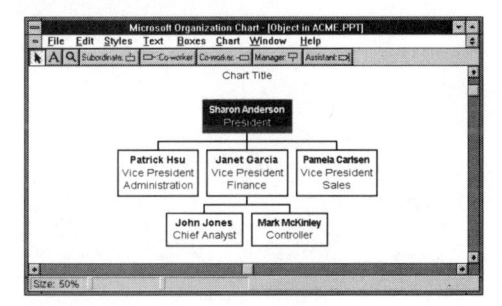

Figure 42. The chart after it is opened

Revising an Organization Chart

To revise an existing org chart you have previously created, you will need to reopen it in Microsoft Organization Chart.

1. Double-click the embedded org chart (Figures 41 and 42).
2. Make any desired changes to the chart (insert and/or rearrange the boxes, format the lines and boxes, and so forth).
3. Select File/Exit and Return to *xxx*.PPT, where *xxx*.PPT is the name of the PowerPoint presentation that contains the organization chart.
4. When asked if you want to update the object, select Yes (Figure 43).

   or

   If you want to abandon the changes you made to the chart, select No.

■ Tip

✓ To update the org chart object without exiting Microsoft Organization Chart, choose File/Update *xxx*.PPT, where *xxx*.PPT is the name of the presentation.

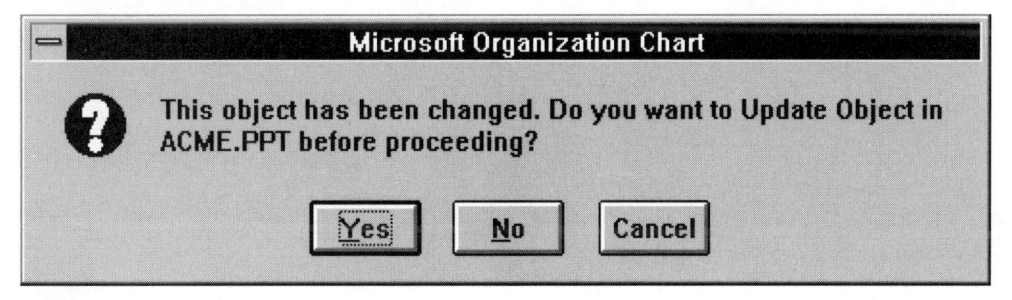

Figure 43. To save the changes you made in Microsoft Organization Chart, be sure to update the object.

CREATING TABLES 8

Figure 1. A four-column table

Figure 2. A three-column table

Figure 3. A table with side-by-side paragraphs

About Tables

The best way to present columns of data is in a Table slide. Figures 1 through 3 show examples of the kinds of tables you can create in PowerPoint.

Think of a table as a mini-spreadsheet, similar to the ones you may have created in Microsoft Excel or Lotus 1-2-3. You can even build formulas in PowerPoint tables.

When you create tables in PowerPoint, you actually use the *Microsoft Word 6* program (Figure 4). You will notice that the menu bar contains a Table item instead of a Draw item. The toolbars are different, too—that's how you know that another program is running.

Word 6 is not included with PowerPoint—it must be purchased separately. However, if you have Microsoft Office, Word and PowerPoint are included (along with several other programs). Note that you cannot create tables in PowerPoint unless you have Word 6.

To create or modify your table, double-click a table placeholder or an embedded table. This action launches Word. To return to PowerPoint, click anywhere on the slide outside of the table.

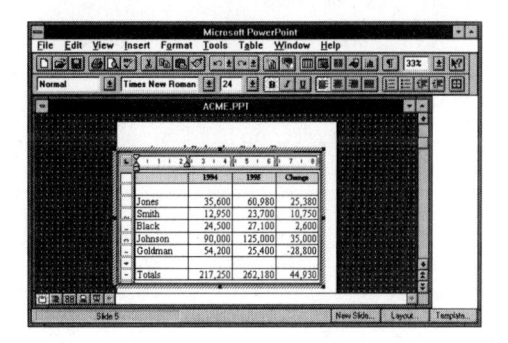

Figure 4. A table being edited in Word 6

Creating Tables

99

CHAPTER 8

Inserting a Table Slide

PowerPoint offers one AutoLayout for tables (Figure 5).

1. Click the New Slide button at the bottom of the PowerPoint window.
2. In the New Slide dialog box, choose the Table layout (Figure 5).
3. Click OK. The slide appears with title and table placeholders.
4. Click the title placeholder and type the title of your table.
5. Double-click the table placeholder to create your table. You are asked to specify the number of columns and rows (Figure 6).
6. Specify the Number of Columns and press Tab.
7. Specify the Number of Rows and click OK. A table appears in Word (Figure 7).

■ Tips

✓ The default size of a table is about 8 inches wide by 4.5 inches high. The columns and rows will be evenly spaced in this area. For instance, if you specify 2 columns by 3 rows, each column will be 4 inches wide and each row will be 1.5 inches high. However, the column widths and row heights can be adjusted at any time.

See Adjusting Column Widths on page 104 and Adjusting Row Heights on page 106.

✓ If you know that you want your table to be larger or smaller than the default size, you can adjust the table placeholder by dragging its selection handles.

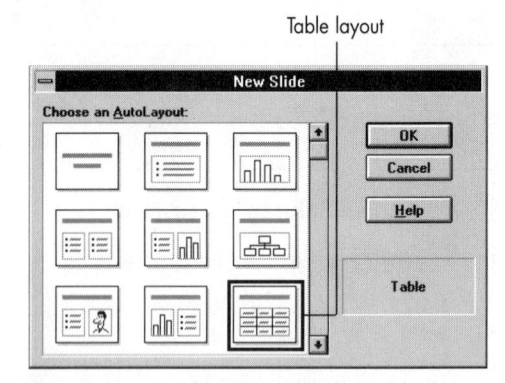

Figure 5. Choosing the Table layout

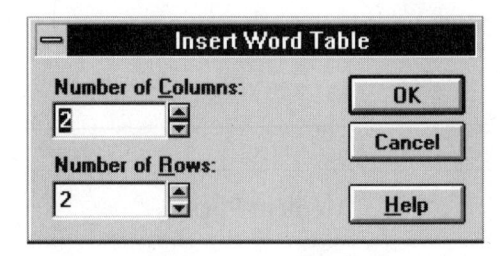

Figure 6. Specify the number of columns and rows in your table.

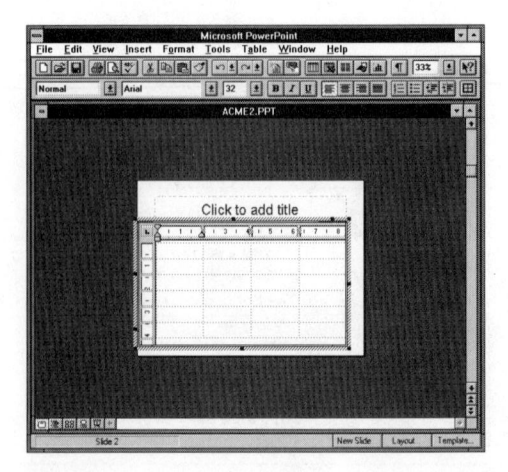

Figure 7. A table in Word 6

CREATING TABLES

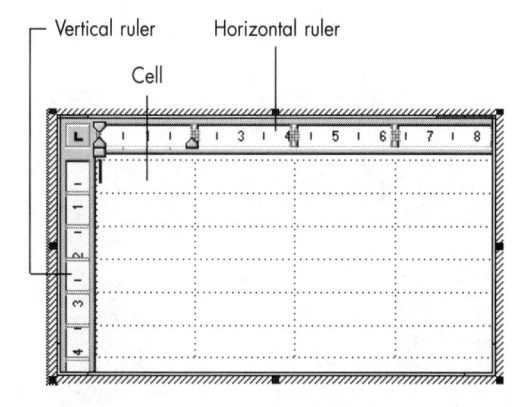

Figure 8. A table is a grid of cells.

Figure 9. Text automatically wraps within each cell, and the row heights automatically adjust.

Entering Text into a Table

A table is made up of rows and columns; the intersection of a row and column is called a *cell* (Figure 8).

Follow these steps to type text in a table:

1. Click a cell and start typing. Text that is wider than the column width will wrap automatically in the cell (Figure 9).
2. Press Tab to move the cursor to the next cell to the right. Press Shift+Tab to move to the previous cell.
3. After entering text in the last cell in the row, press Tab; this moves the cursor to the first cell in the next row.

■ Tips

- ✓ If you don't see gridlines between cells in your table, select Table/Gridlines.
- ✓ Pressing Enter in a cell drops the cursor down to the next line in the same cell. It does *not* move the cursor to a different cell.
- ✓ You can also position the cursor in a cell by clicking it or by using the arrow keys on the keyboard.
- ✓ To edit the contents of a cell, just click the cell to place the text cursor there, and then make the desired change.
- ✓ Pressing Tab from the last cell in a table inserts a new row and places the cursor in the first cell.
- ✓ If text wraps in a cell but you want it to fit on a single line, there are two solutions: You can either decrease the type size or adjust the column width.

  See Formatting Text on page 109, and Adjusting Column Widths on page 104.

- ✓ The table itself does not have a scroll bar. To move to a cell that has scrolled off the screen, use the arrow keys or press Tab.
- ✓ To return to PowerPoint, click the slide outside of the table, or press Esc.

101

CHAPTER 8

Revising a Table

To revise a table you have previously created, you need to reopen it in Microsoft Word.

1. Double-click the embedded table (Figures 10 and 11).
2. Make any desired changes to the table (add borders, change the font, adjust column widths, and so forth).
3. To return to PowerPoint, click the slide, outside of the table.

    or

    Press Esc.

■ Tip

✓ The rulers can be displayed or hidden (Figure 12) with the <u>V</u>iew/<u>R</u>uler command.

Double-click the embedded table.

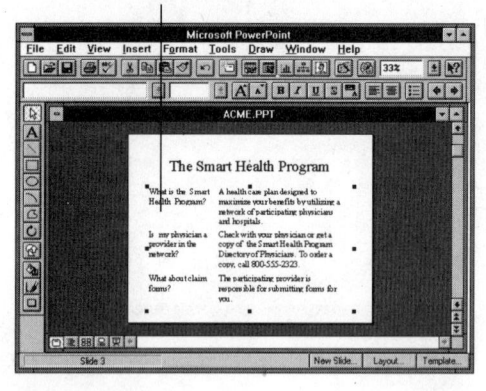

Figure 10. Opening the embedded table in Microsoft Word 6

Even though the title bar says PowerPoint, you are actually using Word 6 to edit the table.

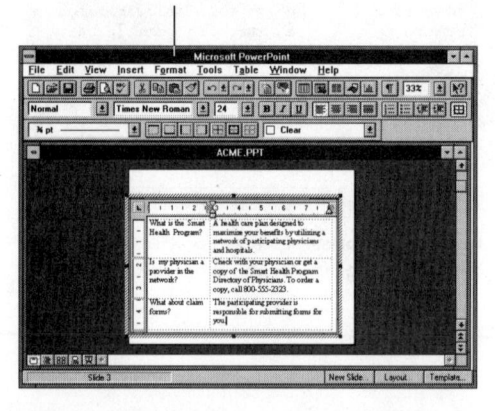

Figure 11. The table after it is opened in Word 6

Figure 12. A table without the ruler displayed

102

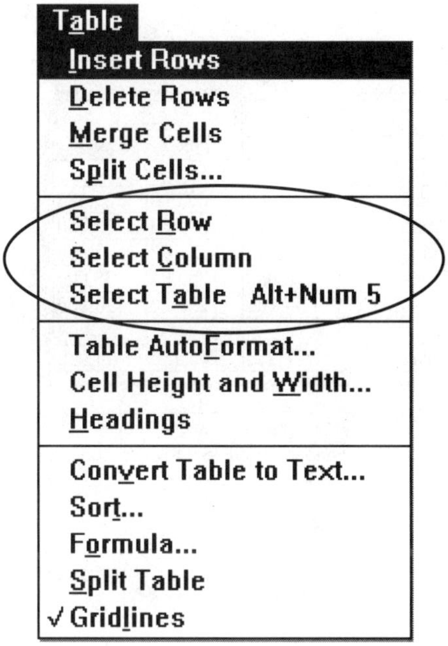

CREATING TABLES

Table
Insert Rows
Delete Rows
Merge Cells
Split Cells...

Select Row
Select Column
Select Table   Alt+Num 5

Table AutoFormat...
Cell Height and Width...
Headings

Convert Table to Text...
Sort...
Formula...
Split Table
✓ Gridlines

Figure 13. The Table menu contains three commands for selecting all or part of the table.

Selecting Cells

You will need to select cells in your table before formatting them. The Table menu (Figure 13) offers ways to select the current row or column, or the entire table.

With the mouse, you can select a range of cells by dragging across them (Figure 14).

You can select an entire column by clicking the gridline above the column (Figure 15). The mouse pointer displays as a down arrow when it is positioned properly for selecting the column.

To select an entire row (Figure 16), double-click the beginning of the row—to the left of the cell contents. The mouse pointer points up and to the right when it is positioned properly for selecting the row.

■ Tips

✓ The keyboard shortcut for selecting the entire table is Alt+5 (on the numeric keypad). For this shortcut to work, Num Lock *cannot* be turned on.

✓ A shortcut for selecting a column is to hold down Alt as you click a cell.

Click and drag across cells to select a range.

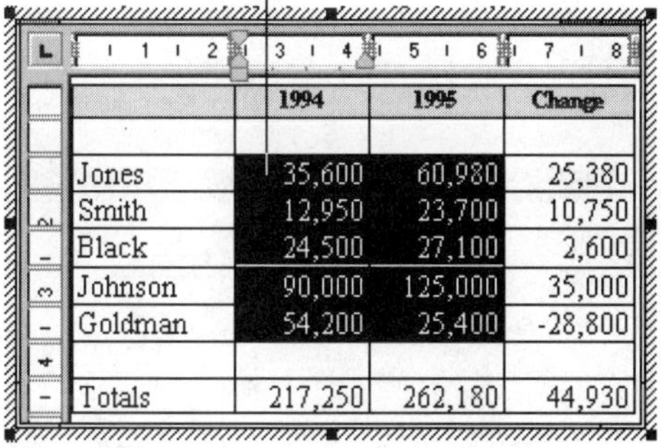

Figure 14. A selected range

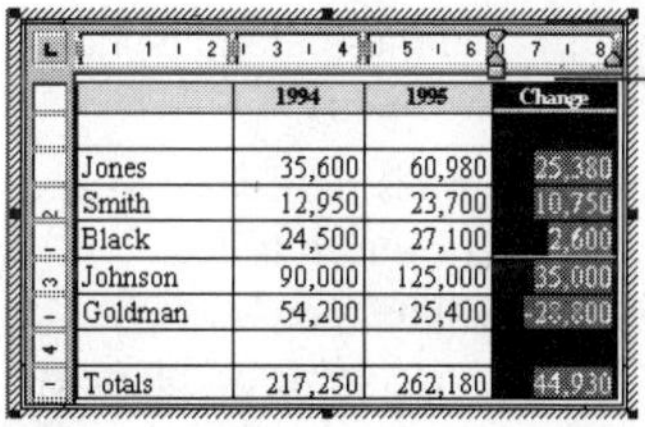

When you see the arrow (↓), click to select a column.

Figure 15. Selecting an entire column

When you see the arrow (↗), double-click to select a row.

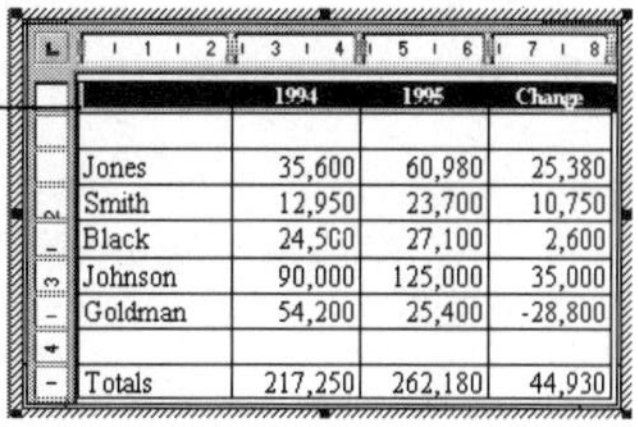

Figure 16. Selecting an entire row

103

CHAPTER 8

Adjusting Column Widths

By default, all the columns have equal widths in the table. There are three ways to adjust column widths: dragging markers in the ruler (Figure 17), dragging column boundaries (Figure 18), and in the Cell Height and Width dialog box (Figure 19).

When you adjust the width of a column, all columns to the right are resized proportionately. For some alternatives, see Figure 20 on the next page.

■ Tips

- ✓ If the rulers are hidden, select View/Ruler.
- ✓ Make sure no cells are selected when you drag the column markers or boundaries. (Otherwise, the width will change for only the selected cells.)
- ✓ Double-click a column marker in the ruler to quickly bring up the Cell Height and Width dialog box.
- ✓ The AutoFit button in the Cell Height and Width dialog box (Figure 19) automatically sets an appropriate width for the column, based on the longest entry in the column.
- ✓ To autofit with the mouse, double-click the right column boundary.
- ✓ If text in one column is right-aligned and the text in the next column is left-aligned, the text will be too close together. One way to fix this problem is to add extra space between columns.

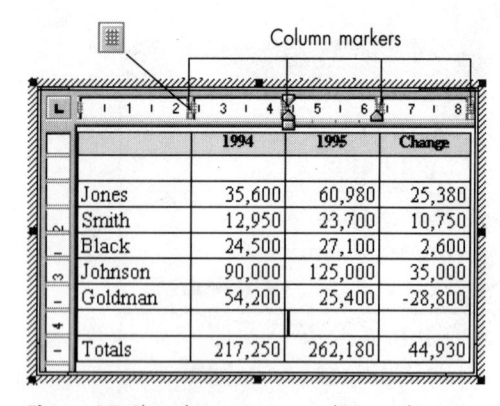

Figure 17. Place the pointer on a column marker. When the pointer changes to double arrows, drag to the right or left.

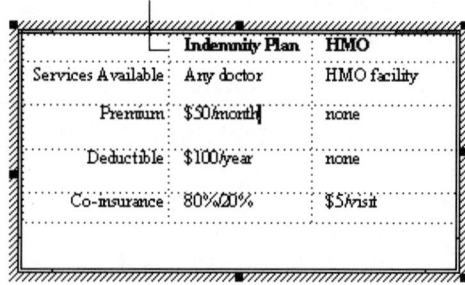

Figure 18. Dragging the column boundary is another way to adjust the column width.

Click the Column tab... ...then enter a value (in inches) for the column width.

Adds extra padding between all columns

These buttons let you set widths for other columns.

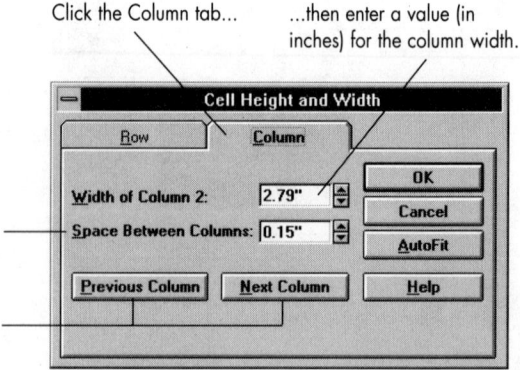

Figure 19. With the Table/Cell Height and Width command, you can enter exact values for your table's column widths.

Adjusting Column Widths (cont'd)

Figure 20. Compare each table with the first one.

At first, all columns have the same width.

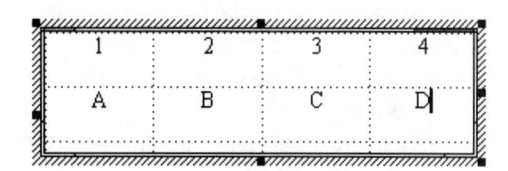

1	2	3	4
A	B	C	D

When you drag a column boundary, the columns to the right are resized proportionately. The overall table width is unchanged.

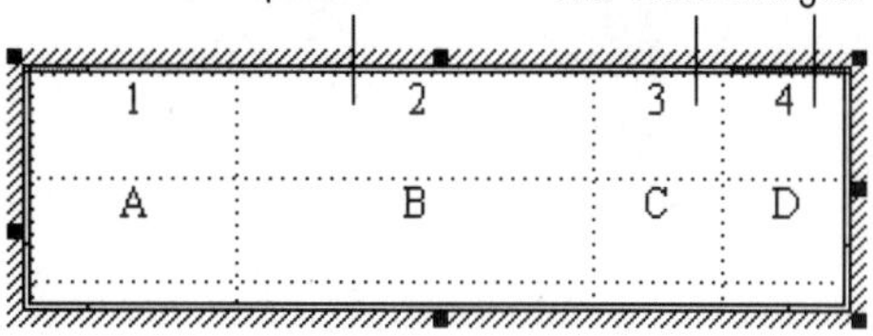

The width of column 2 was adjusted.

Notice that columns 3 and 4 also changed.

1	2	3	4
A	B	C	D

When you hold down Shift when dragging a column boundary, only the columns on either side of the boundary are resized. Other columns and the overall table width are unchanged.

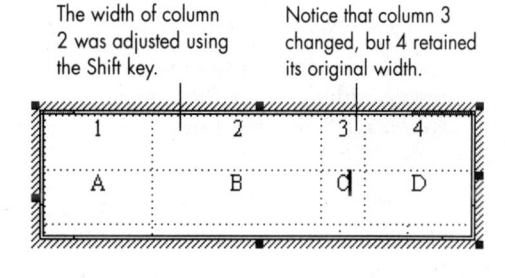

The width of column 2 was adjusted using the Shift key.

Notice that column 3 changed, but 4 retained its original width.

1	2	3	4
A	B	C	D

When you hold down Shift and Ctrl when dragging a column boundary, columns to the right do not change size but the overall width of the table changes.

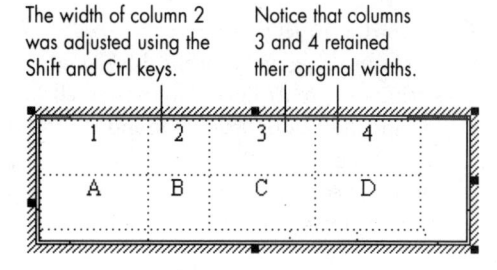

The width of column 2 was adjusted using the Shift and Ctrl keys.

Notice that columns 3 and 4 retained their original widths.

1	2	3	4
A	B	C	D

Adjusting Row Heights

By default, all rows are spaced evenly in the table. There are two ways to adjust the row height: You can drag the row's bottom divider line in the vertical ruler (Figure 21) to visually adjust the height, or use the Cell Height and Width dialog box (Figure 22) to enter a precise value. The following steps describe the latter technique.

1. Drag across at least one cell in the row whose height you want to adjust.
2. Select T*a*ble/Cell Height and *W*idth.
3. Click the Row tab (Figure 22).
4. For the H*e*ight, choose Exactly.
5. In the *A*t box, specify the number of points for the row height.
6. Click OK.

■ **Tips**

✓ The row height should be at least the point size of the text; otherwise, the characters will be cut off.

✓ Another way to add extra space between rows is with the F*o*rmat/*P*aragraph command. You can add space above or below the cell.

See Aligning Text Within a Cell on page 112.

✓ To set all rows to the same height, just click the text cursor (no cell should be selected) anywhere in the table before displaying the Cell Height and Width dialog box.

✓ If Word won't let you adjust the row height by dragging, it means the H*e*ight setting is set to At Least. Go to the Cell Height and Width dialog box and change this setting to Exactly, and specify a value for the *A*t setting. Then you will be able to adjust the row height with the mouse.

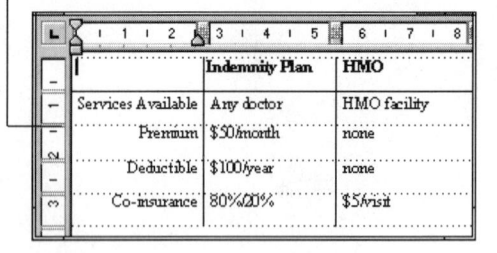

Figure 21. Adjusting the row height visually

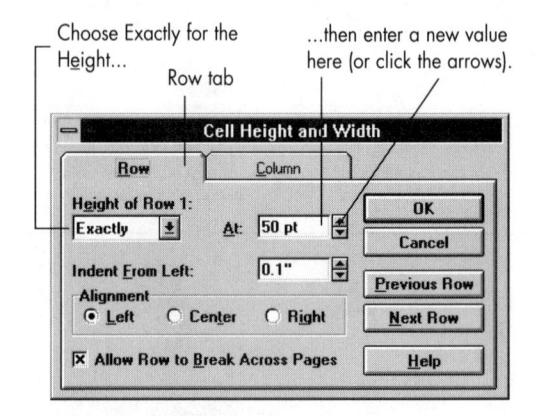

Figure 22. Adjusting the row height precisely

CREATING TABLES

The new row will be inserted above the selected row.

Figure 23. Before inserting a row

Inserted row

Figure 24. After inserting a row

Insert Rows (or Insert Columns if a column is selected)

Figure 25. The Standard toolbar in Word 6

Inserting Rows and Columns

If you underestimated the number of rows or columns in your table when ininitally creating it, you can insert them later. Figures 23 and 24 show a table before and after inserting a row.

Inserting a Row

1. Position the cursor, keeping in mind that rows are inserted *above* the cursor. Click the text cursor anywhere in the row, or select the entire row.

   See Selecting Cells on page 103.

2. Click the Insert Rows button (Figure 25).

Inserting a Column

1. Select an entire column. (The new column will insert to the *left* of the selected column).

   See Selecting Cells on page 103.

2. Click the Insert Columns button (Figure 25).

■ Tips

✓ To insert multiple rows (or columns) in the same location, select the number of rows (columns) you wish to insert. For instance, to insert two rows, select two rows; to insert three columns, select three columns.

✓ To insert a new row after the last row, position the cursor in the last cell in the table, and press Tab. A new row will appear.

✓ Inserted cells automatically adopt the formatting of neighboring cells.

107

CHAPTER 8

Deleting Rows and Columns

When you delete rows and columns, you not only remove the contents of the cells, you remove the cells as well (Figures 26 and 27).

1. Select the rows or columns to be deleted (Figure 26).

   See Selecting Cells on page 103.

2. Select Table/Delete Rows or Table/Delete Columns.

   or

   Press the right mouse button to display the shortcut menu. Then, select Delete Rows or Delete Columns.

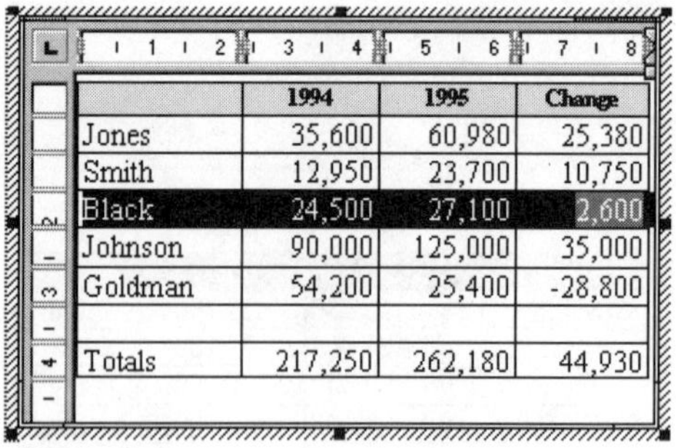

■ Tips

✓ If you accidentally delete rows or columns, immediately choose the Edit/Undo command.

✓ To erase the contents of selected cells, just press Delete. (The empty cells will remain, as shown in Figure 28.)

✓ If you select a cell or part of a row or column, the Table menu and shortcut menu include the command Delete Cells. Choosing this command displays the dialog box shown in Figure 29.

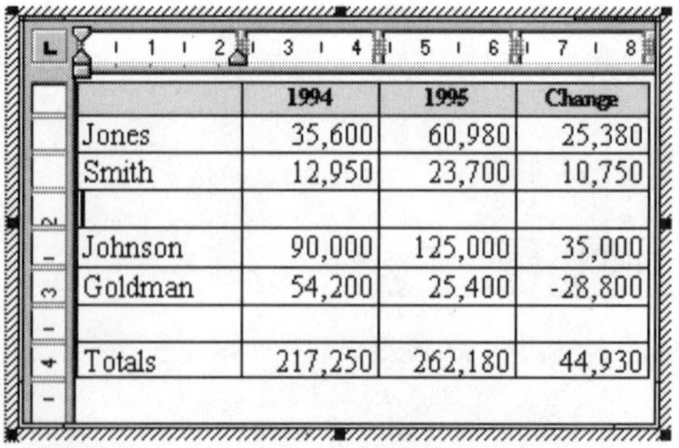

	1994	1995	Change
Jones	35,600	60,980	25,380
Smith	12,950	23,700	10,750
Black	24,500	27,100	2,600
Johnson	90,000	125,000	35,000
Goldman	54,200	25,400	-28,800
Totals	217,250	262,180	44,930

Figure 26. A row is selected for deleting.

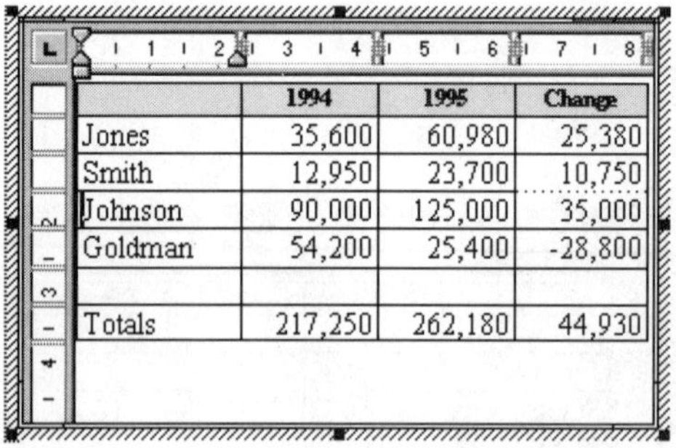

	1994	1995	Change
Jones	35,600	60,980	25,380
Smith	12,950	23,700	10,750
Johnson	90,000	125,000	35,000
Goldman	54,200	25,400	-28,800
Totals	217,250	262,180	44,930

Figure 27. The row that had contained Black's data has been deleted; that row no longer exists.

	1994	1995	Change
Jones	35,600	60,980	25,380
Smith	12,950	23,700	10,750
Johnson	90,000	125,000	35,000
Goldman	54,200	25,400	-28,800
Totals	217,250	262,180	44,930

Delete Cells
- ● Shift Cells Left
- ○ Shift Cells Up
- ○ Delete Entire Row
- ○ Delete Entire Column

[OK] [Cancel] [Help]

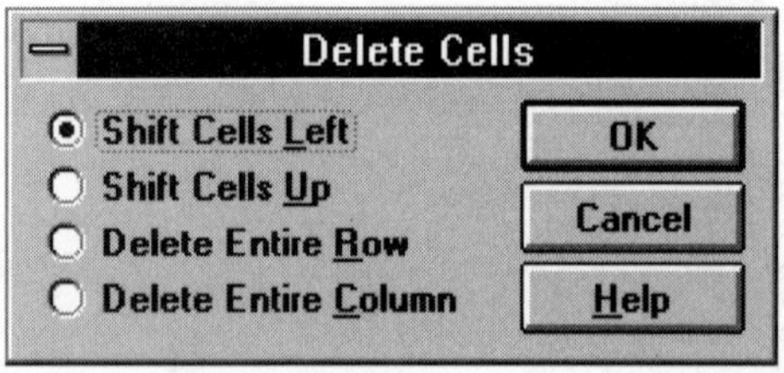

Figure 29. Select either Delete Entire Row or Delete Entire Column.

Figure 28. The row that had contained Black's data has been erased by pressing Delete; the row is now empty.

108

CREATING TABLES

	Indemnity Plan	HMO
Services Available	Any doctor	HMO facility
Premium	$50 / month	none
Deductible	$100 / year	none
Co-insurance	80% / 20%	$5 / visit

Figure 30. The text is 24-point Times New Roman.

	Indemnity Plan	**HMO**
Services Available	Any doctor	HMO facility
Premium	$50 / month	none
Deductible	$100 / year	none
Co-insurance	80% / 20%	$5 / visit

Figure 31. The text is 22-point Arial; the column headings are 24-point Arial Bold.

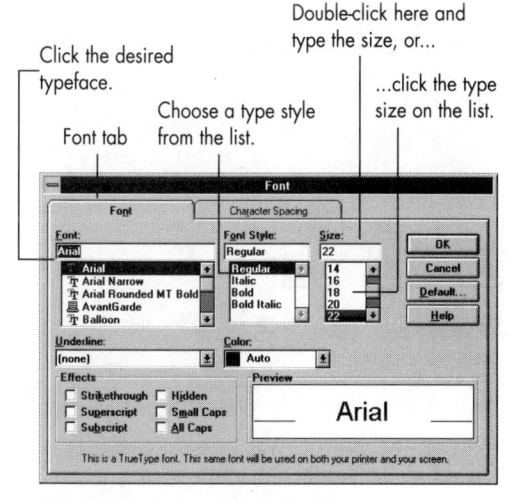

Figure 32. Choosing a font for table text

Formatting Text

You can format the text in the table with a particular typeface, size, and style, among other things (Figures 30 and 31).

1. Select the cells whose text you want to format; or within a cell, drag across the individual characters you want to format.

   See Selecting Cells on page 103.

2. Select Format/Font.

   or

   Press the right mouse button to display the shortcut menu, and choose Font.

3. Click the Font tab (Figure 32).

4. In the Font list, choose the desired typeface (use the scroll bar if necessary).

5. Select the desired Font Style (Regular, Italic, Bold, or Bold Italic).

6. In the Size list, choose the desired point size (use the scroll bar if necessary).

7. If you like, you can add an underline, or other effect, to the selection.

8. Click OK.

■ Tips

✓ Instead of displaying the Font dialog box, you can use the Font, Font Size, Bold, Italic, and Underline buttons (Figure 33).

✓ To avoid the "ransom note" look, use only one typeface in a table.

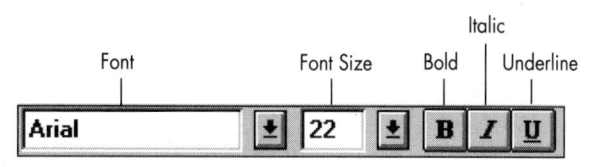

Figure 33. The Formatting toolbar in Word 6

109

CHAPTER 8

Adding Borders and Shading

The gridlines (Figure 34) between cells in a table do not print—they are there to help you distinguish cells on the screen. To print dividing lines between cells, you can add borders (Figure 35). You can also add shading to a range of cells (also Figure 35).

1. Select the cells to which you want to add borders or shading.

   See Selecting Cells on page 103.

2. Click the Borders button (Figure 36).

3. In the Line Style field in the Borders toolbar (Figure 37), choose a line thickness and style (Figure 38).

4. Choose one or more border types (Figure 37):
   Top Border   Horizontal line on the top of the selected range
   Bottom Border   Horizontal line on the bottom edge of the selected range
   Left Border   Vertical line on the left side of the selected range
   Right Border   Vertical line on the right side of the selected range
   Inside Border   Horizontal and vertical lines inside the selected range
   Outside Border   Outline around the selected range
   No Border   Removes lines from the selected range

5. Choose a shade in the Shading field, if desired (Figure 39).

6. To hide the Borders toolbar again, click the Borders button.

	1994	1995	Change
Jones	35,600	60,980	25,380
Smith	12,950	23,700	10,750
Black	24,500	27,100	2,600
Johnson	90,000	125,000	35,000
Goldman	54,200	25,400	-28,800
Totals	217,250	262,180	44,930

Figure 34. Non-printing gridlines

	1994	1995	Change
Jones	35,600	60,980	25,380
Smith	12,950	23,700	10,750
Black	24,500	27,100	2,600
Johnson	90,000	125,000	35,000
Goldman	54,200	25,400	-28,800
Totals	217,250	262,180	44,930

Figure 35. This table has inside and outside borders; the top row has a 20% shade.

Figure 36. The Formatting toolbar in Word 6

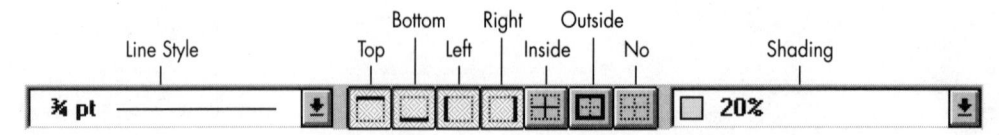

Figure 37. The Borders toolbar

CREATING TABLES

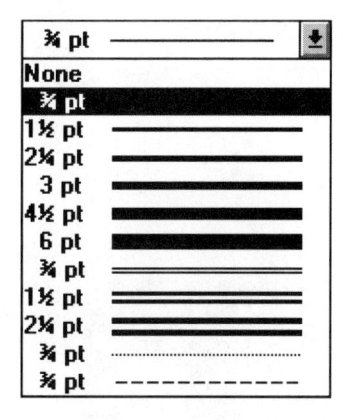

Figure 38. The list of line styles

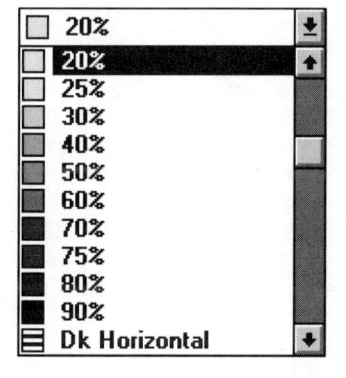

Figure 39. The list of shading percentages and patterns

Adding Borders and Shading (cont'd)

■ **Tip**

✓ Another way to specify borders is with the Format/Borders and Shading command (Figure 40). However, the Borders toolbar is more intuitive than this dialog box.

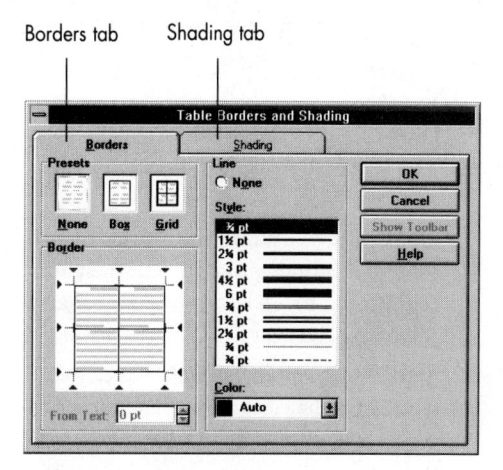

Figure 40. Use the Format/Borders and Shading command to display this dialog box.

CHAPTER 8

Aligning Text Within a Cell

By default, table text is aligned at the top-left edge of each cell (Figure 41). Using Word's paragraph formatting commands, you can adjust the horizontal and vertical alignment of text within a cell (Figure 42).

To control the horizontal alignment, use the alignment buttons (Figure 43). To add padding to the left or right of the text, drag the indent markers in the ruler (Figure 44). Finally, to control the vertical alignment, use the Format/Paragraph command to add space before or after the paragraph (Figure 45).

You must select cells before formatting them.

See Selecting Cells on page 103.

■ Tips

✓ The rulers can be turned on and off with the View/Ruler command.

✓ In the ruler, you adjust the indents one column at a time; just click anywhere in a column and the indent markers for that column will appear in the ruler.

✓ In the Paragraph dialog box, you can set indents for the entire table (assuming you've selected the entire table).

	Indemnity Plan	HMO
Services Available	Any doctor	HMO facility
Premium	$50 / month	none
Deductible	$100 / year	none
Co-insurance	80% / 20%	$5 / visit

Figure 41. Notice how close the text is to the cell borders.

	Indemnity Plan	HMO
Services Available	Any doctor	HMO facility
Premium	$50 / month	none
Deductible	$100 / year	none
Co-insurance	80% / 20%	$5 / visit

Figure 42. By adding indents and paragraph spacing, you can improve the appearance of this table.

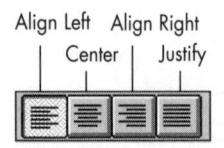

Figure 43. The Formatting toolbar in Word 6

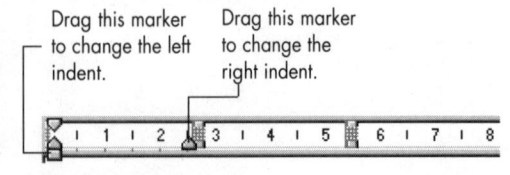

Figure 44. Drag the indent markers to position text horizontally in a cell.

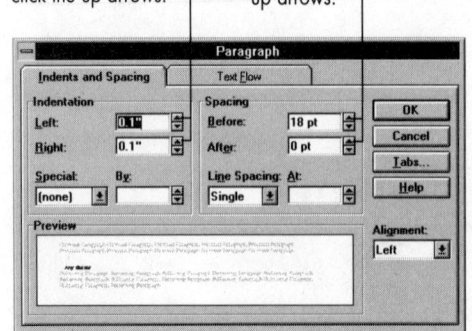

Figure 45. Use Format/Paragraph to position text horizontally and vertically in a cell. These are the settings used to format the table in Figure 42.

CREATING TABLES

	1994	1995	Change
Jones	35,600	60,980	25,380
Smith	12,950	23,700	10,750
Black	24,500	27,100	2,600
Johnson	90,000	125,000	35,000
Goldman	54,200	25,400	-28,800
Totals	217,250	262,180	44,930

Figure 46. An unformatted table

	1994	**1995**	**Change**
Jones	35,600	60,980	25,380
Smith	12,950	23,700	10,750
Black	24,500	27,100	2,600
Johnson	90,000	125,000	35,000
Goldman	54,200	25,400	-28,800
Totals	217,250	262,180	44,930

Figure 47. The List 4 AutoFormat

AutoFormatting a Table

With Word's AutoFormat feature, you can add borders, shading, and other formatting attributes by choosing one of several dozen predesigned formats. Figures 46 and 47 show a table before and after choosing an AutoFormat. This feature not only is a big time-saver, but you can also be assured of a well-designed format.

1. Select Table/Table AutoFormat.
2. Click different formats in the Formats list, and look at the Preview box to see what each looks like (Figure 48).
3. Choose the aspects of the format you want to apply: Borders, Shading, Font, Color, and/or AutoFit.
4. Select whether you want to apply special formatting to the Heading Rows, First Column, Last Row, and/or Last Column.
5. Click OK.

■ Tips

✓ You may want to turn off the AutoFit checkbox in the Table AutoFormat dialog box, especially if you have already manually adjusted the column widths. The AutoFit option will sometimes make the columns too narrow and will reduce the table width.

✓ Many formats offer unique formatting for the first and last rows and columns. As you preview a format, enable and disable the various options under Apply Special Formats To while looking at the Preview box. This box lets you see how the table will look with these options.

Click a format...   ...and see an example of it in the Preview box.

Select which aspects of the format to apply.

Select areas to apply special formats to.

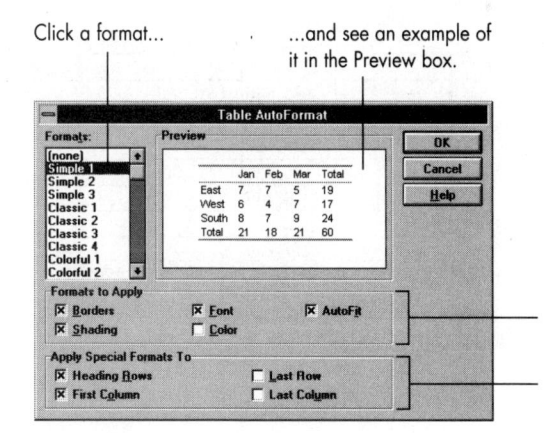

Figure 48. Selecting an AutoFormat

113

CHAPTER 8

Summing Columns

Just as with spreadsheet applications, Word tables can contain formulas to calculate totals. The main difference is that formulas are not typed directly into a cell—they are entered in the Formula dialog box (Figure 49).

1. Click the cell at the bottom of the column where you want the total to appear (Figure 50).
2. Select Table/Formula.
3. If necessary, edit the Formula box so that it reads =SUM(ABOVE).
4. Click OK.

The result is shown in Figure 51.

■ Tips

✓ To sum a row, the formula is =SUM(LEFT).

✓ In addition to the SUM function, there are 21 other functions available, such as AVERAGE, MAX, and MIN. The Paste Function field lists these functions. Choosing a function from the list displays it in the Formula box.

✓ You can also enter formulas that perform calculations on individual cells, such as =B3-C3.

To sum a column, make sure the Formula box has this function.

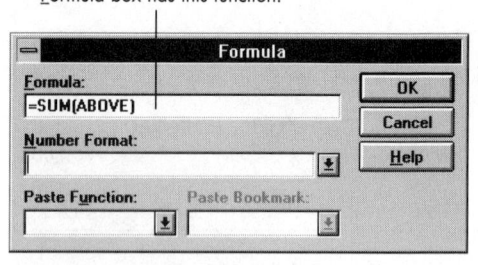

Figure 49. Entering a formula to sum a column

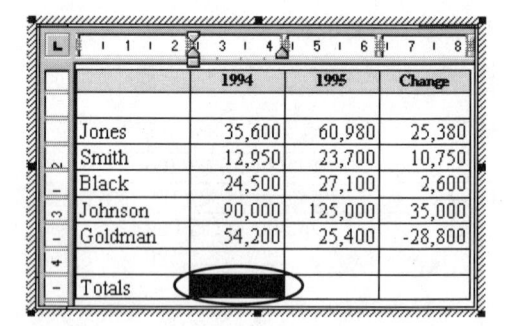

Figure 50. Click where you want the formula to appear.

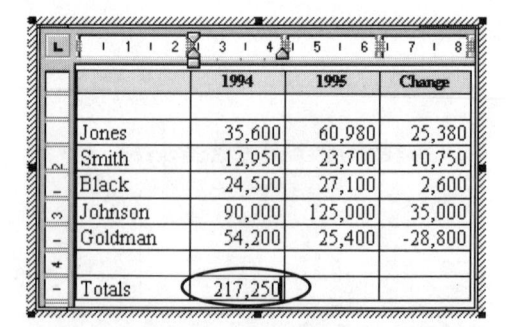

Figure 51. The result of the calculation

ADDING GRAPHIC OBJECTS 9

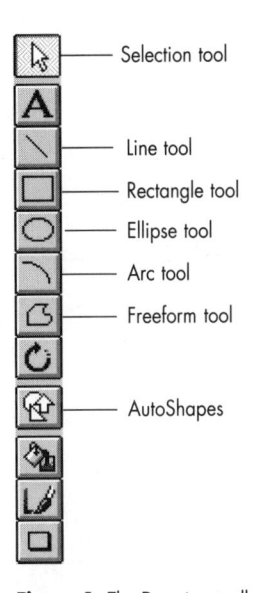

- Selection tool
- Line tool
- Rectangle tool
- Ellipse tool
- Arc tool
- Freeform tool
- AutoShapes

Figure 1. The Drawing toolbar

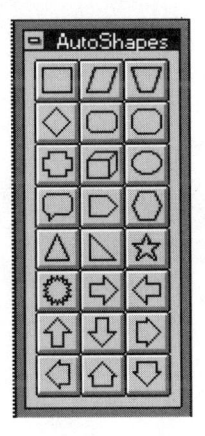

Figure 2. You can add any of these autoshapes to your slides.

Types of Graphic Objects

Graphic elements will contribute variety and interest to your slides. There are several ways to add graphic objects. First, you can draw them using the Drawing toolbar (Figure 1) which offers tools for drawing lines, boxes, circles, arcs, and so forth. With the AutoShapes toolbar (Figure 2), you can easily create predefined objects such as arrows, stars, diamonds, and triangles.

The second way to add graphic objects is by inserting *clip art* images that come with PowerPoint (Figure 3). You have hundreds to choose from.

See Inserting Clip Art on page 125.

Finally, you can import other graphic files—for example, an image you created in CorelDRAW.

See Inserting Graphic Files on page 127 and Pasting Graphics on page 128.

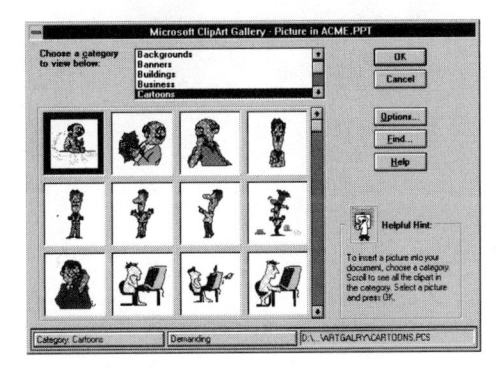

Figure 3. Use ClipArt Gallery to insert images on your slides.

Adding Graphic Objects

115

CHAPTER 9

Drawing Lines

Figure 4 illustrates how lines can become a graphic element on a slide.

1. In the Drawing toolbar, click the Line tool (Figure 5).
2. Place the mouse pointer (a crosshair) where you want to begin the line.
3. Hold down the mouse button as you drag in the direction you want the line to follow.
4. Release the mouse button when the line is the desired length.

■ Tips

✓ To make sure the line is perfectly straight (horizontally or vertically), hold down the Shift key as you draw the line.

✓ To change the length or angle of the line, click on the line to select it (Figure 6), and then drag a selection handle. To change the length without changing the angle, hold down Shift as you drag a handle.

✓ To reposition the line, select it and then drag it into position. Make sure you don't drag a selection handle or you will change the length of the line.

To change the line thickness, see Formatting Lines on the opposite page.

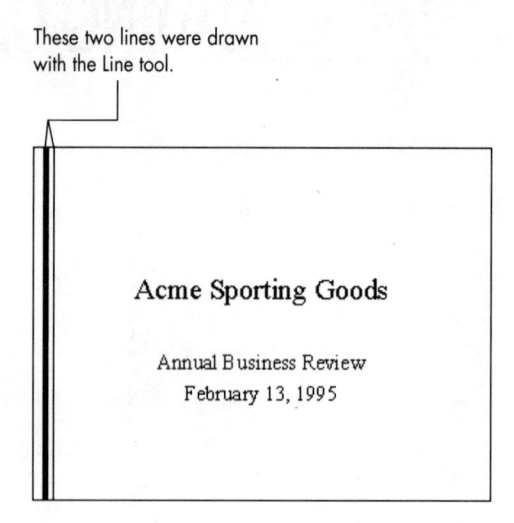

Figure 4. Lines created with the Line tool

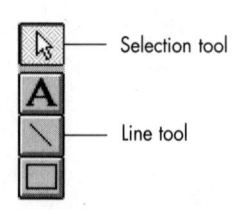

Figure 5. The Drawing toolbar

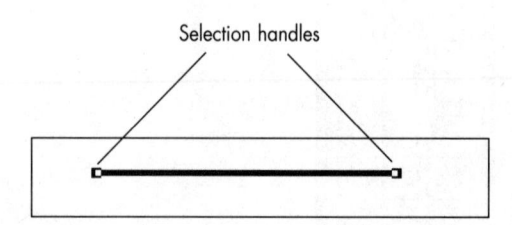

Figure 6. When a line is selected, selection handles appear.

Adding Graphic Objects

ADDING GRAPHIC OBJECTS

Formatting Lines

There are a variety of ways to format lines and borders. For instance, you can change the line thickness (Figure 7), choose a double-line style, create dashed lines, and add arrowheads (Figure 8).

1. Select the line or shape to be formatted.
2. Select Format/Colors and Lines. The Colors and Lines dialog box appears (Figure 9).

   or

   With the pointer on the line, press the right mouse button to display the shortcut menu. Then choose Colors and Lines.
3. In the Line field, choose a color.
4. In the Line Styles list, click the sample line with the thickness or style you prefer.
5. If desired, click one of the sample lines in the Dashed Lines list.
6. To create an arrow, choose one of the styles in the Arrowheads list.
7. Click OK.

■ Tips

✓ To select more than one line, hold down Shift as you click each one.

✓ You can also format lines with the Line Color, Line Style, Dashed Lines, and Arrowheads tools in the Drawing+ toolbar (Figure 10). Use View/Toolbars to display this toolbar.

Figure 7. The lines drawn on this slide have different line thicknesses.

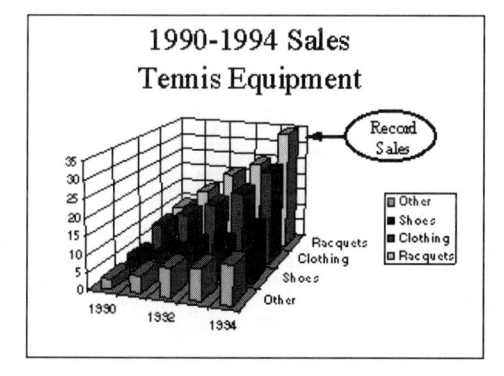

Figure 8. A line was turned into an arrow by formatting it with an arrowhead style.

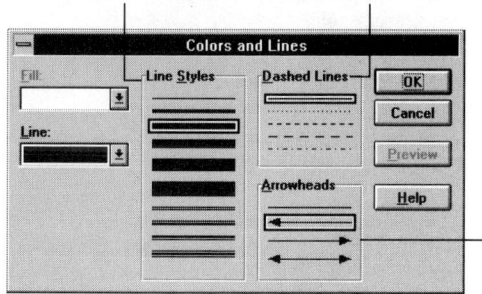

Figure 9. In this dialog box, you can choose line styles and colors, create dashed lines, and add arrowheads.

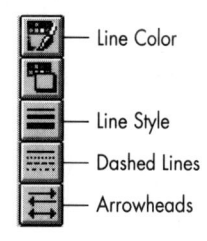

Figure 10. The Drawing+ toolbar

117

CHAPTER 9

Drawing Rectangles

Using the Rectangle tool (Figure 11), you can create rectangles and squares. Figure 12 shows an example of how a rectangle can be used on a slide.

1. In the Drawing toolbar, click the Rectangle tool (Figure 11).
2. Place the mouse pointer (a crosshair) where you want to begin the rectangle.
3. Hold down the mouse button as you drag towards the opposite corner of the box (Figure 13).
4. Release the mouse button when the box is the desired size.

■ Tips

- ✓ To create a perfect square, hold down Shift as you drag to draw the rectangle.
- ✓ To change the size of an object, click on it and drag a selection handle (Figure 14).
- ✓ To reposition the object, select it and then drag it into position. Make sure you don't drag a selection handle or you will change the size of the object.
- ✓ To type centered text inside a selected rectangle, just start typing. The text is actually part of the rectangle.
- ✓ To change the line weight of the object's border, use the Format/Color and Lines command.

See Formatting Lines on page 117.

See also Filling an Object on page 120.

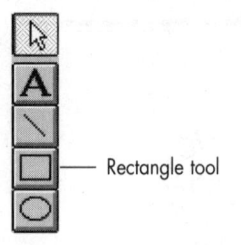

Figure 11. The Drawing toolbar — Rectangle tool

The gray rectangle was drawn on top of the black rectangle.

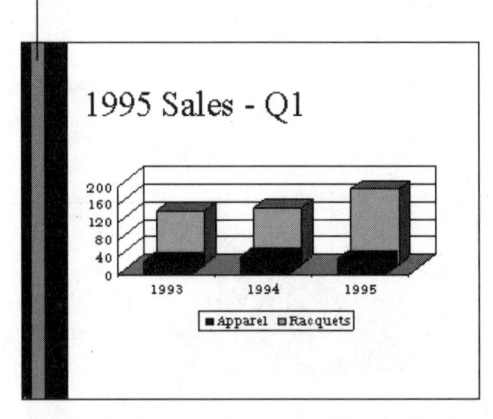

Figure 12. The Rectangle tool created the black and gray boxes on this slide.

Begin dragging at the upper-left corner of the box...

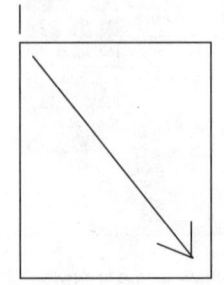

...then drag down and to the right until the box is the desired size.

Figure 13. Drawing a box

Selection handles

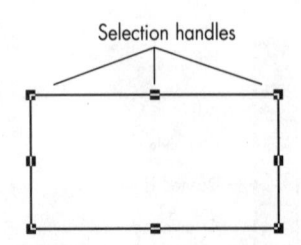

Figure 14. A selected rectangle

Adding Graphic Objects

ADDING GRAPHIC OBJECTS

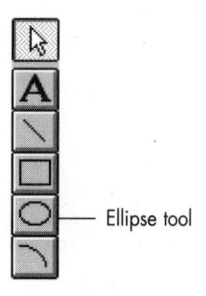

Figure 15. The Drawing toolbar

— Ellipse tool

Drawing Ellipses

Using the Ellipse tool (Figure 15), you can create ellipses and circles. Figure 16 shows an example of how an ellipse can be used to annotate a slide.

1. In the Drawing toolbar, click the Ellipse tool (Figure 15).
2. Place the mouse pointer (a crosshair) where you want to begin the ellipse.
3. Hold down the mouse button as you drag in a diagonal direction (Figure 17).
4. Release the mouse button when the ellipse is the desired size.

■ Tips

✓ To create a perfect circle, hold down Shift as you drag to draw the ellipse.

✓ To change the size and position of an ellipse, see the tips for Drawing Rectangles on the opposite page.

✓ To change the line weight of the ellipse's border, use the F̲ormat/C̲olor and Lines command.

✓ To type centered text inside a selected ellipse, just start typing. The text is actually part of the ellipse. This technique was used in Figure 16. (The text does not wrap, however—you must press Enter after each line.)

See Formatting Lines on page 117.

See also Filling an Object on the next page.

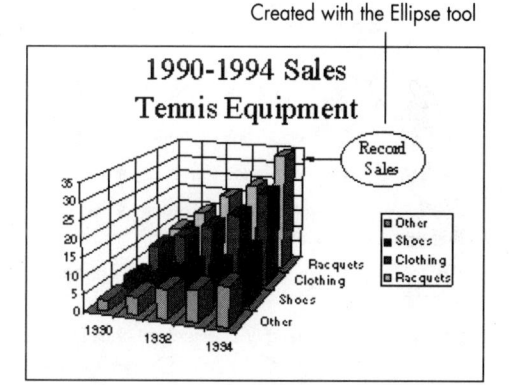

Figure 16. An ellipse encloses a graph annotation (*Record Sales*).

Begin dragging at the upper-left edge of the ellipse...

...then drag down and to the right until the ellipse is the desired size.

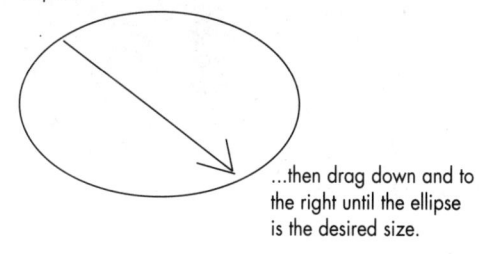

Figure 17. Drawing an ellipse

Adding Graphic Objects

119

CHAPTER 9

Filling an Object

You can choose a fill color or pattern for the rectangles, circles, arcs, freeform objects, and autoshapes you create in PowerPoint.

1. Select the object you want to fill.
2. Select Format/Colors and Lines. The Colors and Lines dialog box appears (Figure 18).

    or

    With the pointer on the object, press the right mouse button and choose Colors and Lines.

3. Display the Fill list (Figure 19) by clicking this field.
4. Choose a color, or click Other Color to display the large color palette (Figure 20).

    or

    Click Pattern on the Fill list, and then choose a pattern in the Pattern Fill dialog box (Figure 21).

    or

    To remove the fill, choose either No Fill for a transparent object or Background for an opaque object (Figure 22).

5. Click OK.

    For information on creating shades, refer to Creating a Gradient Background on page 146.

■ Tips

✓ Use the Fill On/Off button (Figure 23) to remove the fill from a selected object, and use the Fill Color button (Figure 24) to change the color.

✓ To remove the outline around an object, use the Line On/Off button (Figure 23).

✓ To add a drop shadow to a selected object (Figure 25), use the Shadow On/Off button (Figure 23). To adjust the color and offset of the shadow, use the Format/Shadow command (Figure 26) or the Shadow Color button (Figure 24).

Click here to display the Fill list.

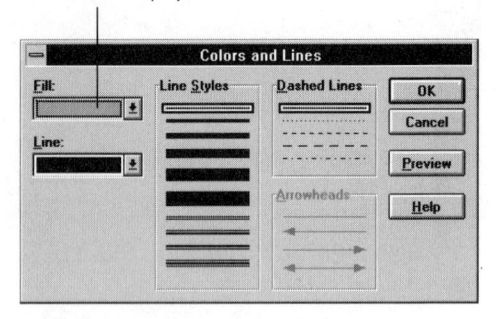

Figure 18. The Colors and Lines dialog box

- No Fill — Creates a transparent object
- Background — Creates an opaque object
- Shaded... — Creates a gradient fill
- Pattern... — Adds a pattern
- Other Color... — Displays large color palette

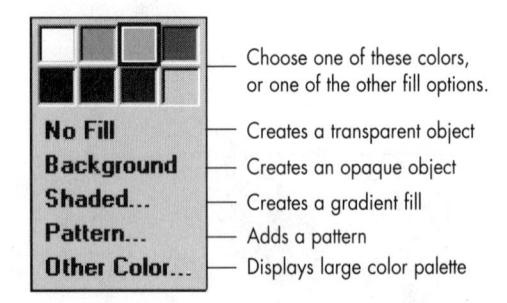

Choose one of these colors, or one of the other fill options.

Figure 19. Choosing a color or other type of fill for an object

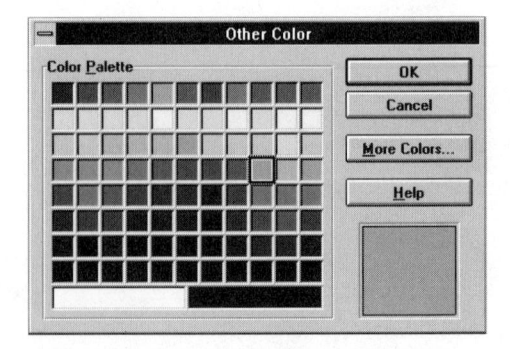

Figure 20. The large color palette

Adding Graphic Objects

120

ADDING GRAPHIC OBJECTS

Filling an Object (cont'd)

Choose a pattern style.

Choose a color for the pattern itself.

Choose a color for behind the pattern.

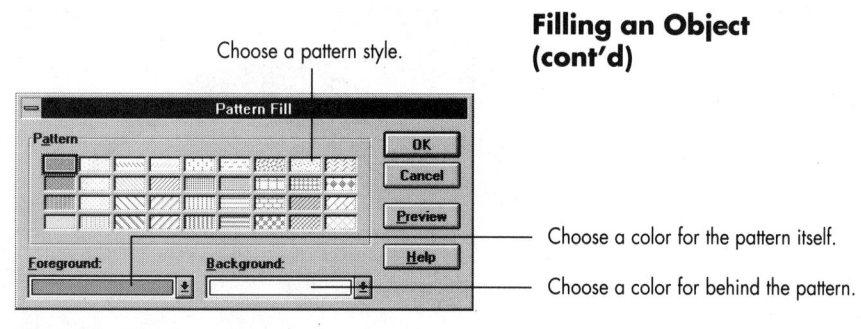

Figure 21. Choosing a pattern

This ellipse has no fill.

This ellipse has a Background fill.

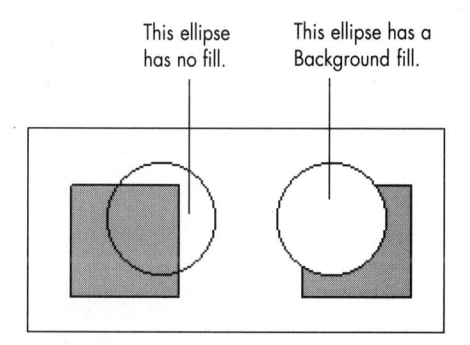

Figure 22. Choose No Fill for a transparent object and choose Background fill for an opaque object.

Figure 25. This rectangle has a drop shadow.

Fill On/Off
Line On/Off
Shadow On/Off

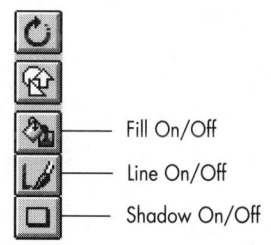

Figure 23. The Drawing toolbar

Fill Color
Line Color
Shadow Color

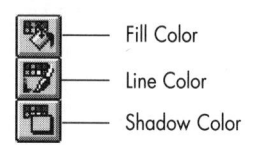

Figure 24. The Drawing+ toolbar

Click here to choose a color for the shadow.

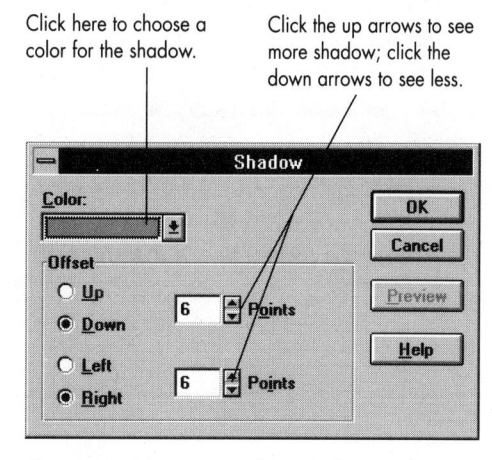

Click the up arrows to see more shadow; click the down arrows to see less.

Figure 26. Adjusting the color and offset of a drop shadow

121

CHAPTER 9

Drawing an Arc

Figure 27 shows a series of arcs you can create in PowerPoint. Here's how to create arcs:

1. Click the Arc tool (Figure 28).
2. Click at the beginning of the arc and drag to the end.

   or

   Hold down one of the following *constraint keys* as you drag:

   - Shift (to draw a quarter of a circle)
   - Ctrl (to center the arc on the starting point)
   - Shift+Ctrl (to draw a quarter of a circle and center the arc on the starting point)

3. Resize, reshape, and rotate the arc as necessary.

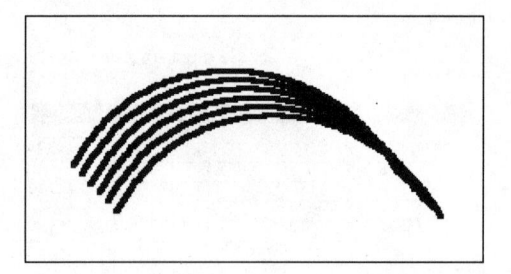

Figure 27. These arcs were created with the Arc tool.

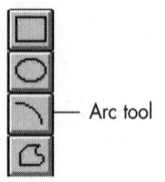

Figure 28. The Drawing toolbar

■ Tips

✓ To extend or contract the arc, double-click it to place control handles at the beginning and end of the arc. Drag a handle to resize the arc. Figure 29 shows an arc before and after resizing.

✓ To reshape the arc, click it to place a set of eight selection handles around the object. Drag these handles to reshape. Figure 30 shows an arc before and after reshaping.

To rotate the arc, see Rotating Objects on page 140.

To fill the arc (as in Figures 29 and 30), see Filling an Object on page 120.

To change the line thickness or style of the arc, see Formatting Lines on page 117.

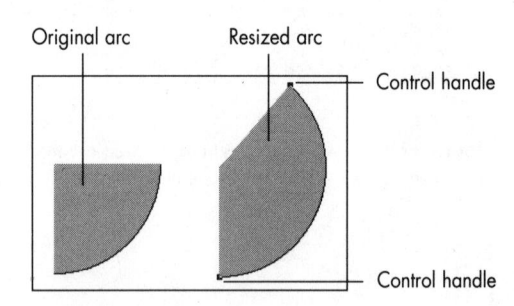

Figure 29. Filled arcs, before and after resizing

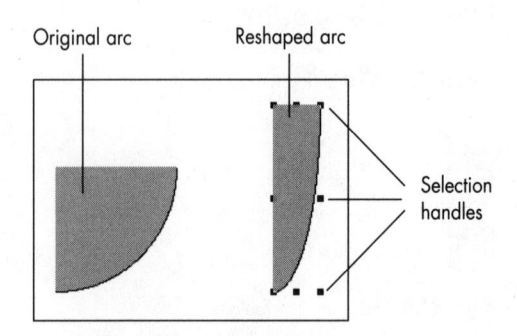

Figure 30. Filled arcs, before and after reshaping

Adding Graphic Objects

122

ADDING GRAPHIC OBJECTS

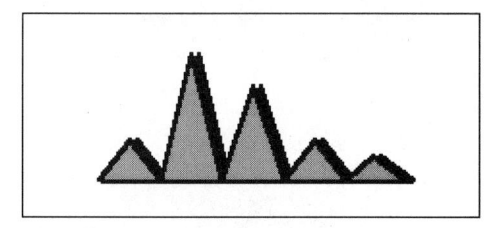

Figure 31. This geometric mountain range was created with the Freeform tool.

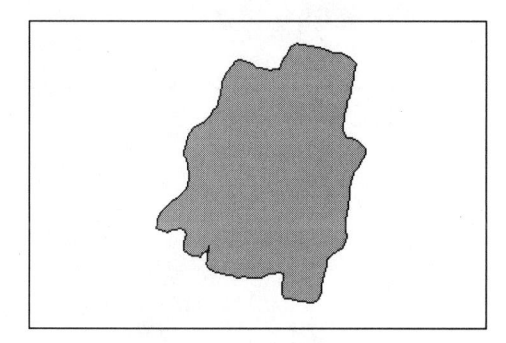

Figure 32. Hmmm...your author is obviously not artistically inclined and should stay clear of freehand drawing!

Click near starting point to create a closed shape.

Double-click at ending point to create an open shape.

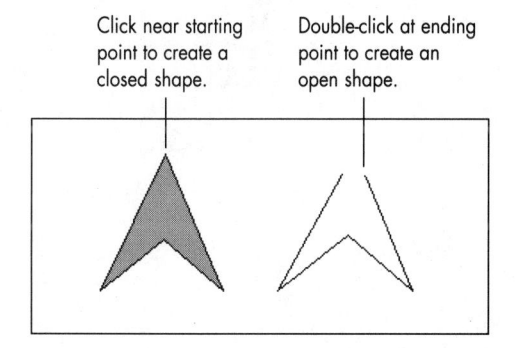

Figure 33. You can create closed or open shapes.

— Freeform tool

— Fill On/Off tool

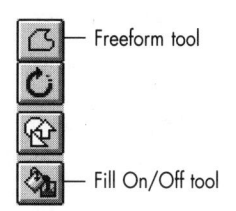

Figure 34. The Drawing toolbar

Creating Polygons and Freehand Drawings

The Freeform tool lets you create your own shapes, such as the one in Figure 31. In addition to creating a series of connected line segments, this tool also can be used to create freehand drawings, if you are artistically inclined (Figure 32).

Your shapes and drawings can be open or closed (Figure 33).

Creating Connected Line Segments

1. Click the Freeform tool (Figure 34).
2. Click at each point of the shape you want to draw—PowerPoint draws a line segment between each point.
3. To finish the drawing, click on or near the first point (to create a closed shape) or double-click (to create an open shape).

Creating a Freehand Drawing

1. Click the Freeform tool (Figure 34).
2. Place the crosshair pointer at the starting point of the drawing.
3. Hold down the mouse button—you'll see a drawing pencil appear.
4. Drag the mouse to draw with the pencil.
5. To finish the drawing, put the pencil on or near the starting point (to create a closed drawing) or double-click (to create an open drawing).

■ Tips

✓ Closed shapes are automatically filled; open shapes are not. Use the Fill On/Off tool (Figure 34) to remove or add a fill to a selected object.

✓ Shapes and drawings can have drop shadows (Figure 31).

See Filling an Object on page 120 for information on changing the fill color and adding drop shadows.

Adding Graphic Objects

123

CHAPTER 9

Creating Other Shapes

Autoshapes are a set of tools for creating more complex objects. The graph in Figure 35 has been enhanced with a couple of these tools. Figure 36 shows the complete set of autoshapes.

1. Click the AutoShapes button (Figure 37).
2. In the AutoShapes toolbar (Figure 36), click the desired tool.
3. Place the mouse pointer where you want to begin the object. (The pointer changes to a crosshair.)
4. Hold down the mouse button as you drag in the direction you want to create the object.
5. Release the mouse button when the object is the desired size.

■ Tips

✓ To type centered text inside a selected autoshape, just start typing. The text is actually part of the autoshape object. This technique was used in Figure 35. (The text does not wrap, however—you must press Enter after each line.)

✓ To replace an existing autoshape with another, select it and choose the Draw/Change AutoShape command; then choose the desired shape. The new shape will have the same size, text (if any), and line and fill attributes as the autoshape it replaces.

✓ To create a shape whose height is equal to its width, hold down Shift as you draw the object.

✓ The AutoShapes toolbar is like a window—it can be moved, sized, and closed.

See Filling an Object on page 120 for information on changing the fill color and adding drop shadows.

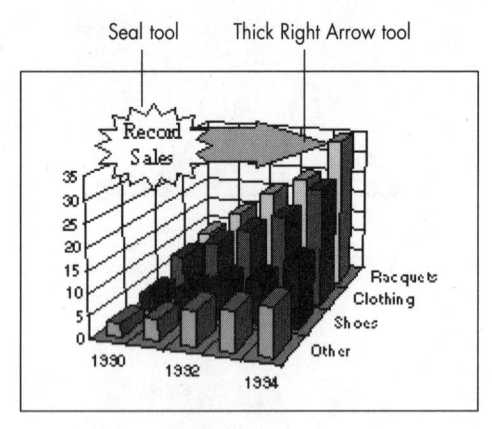

Figure 35. This graph was annotated with two autoshapes.

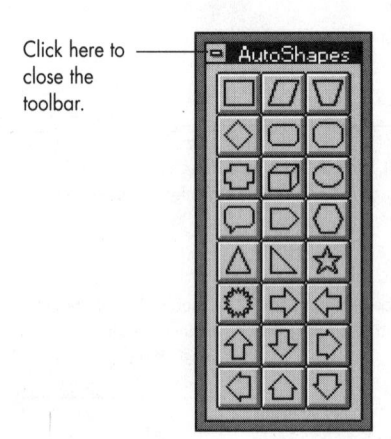

Figure 36. The AutoShapes toolbar

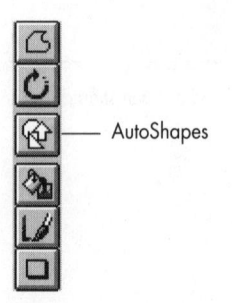

Figure 37. The Drawing toolbar

ADDING GRAPHIC OBJECTS

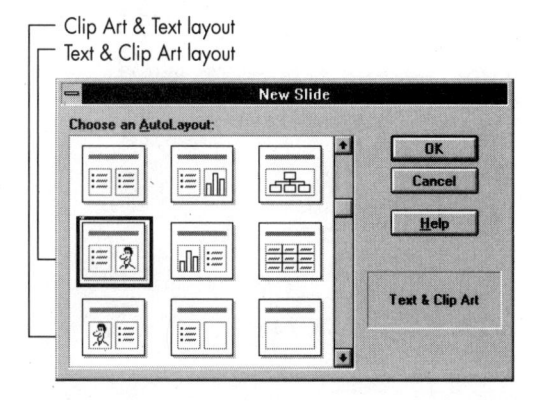

Clip Art & Text layout
Text & Clip Art layout

Figure 38. Choosing a layout with a clip art placeholder

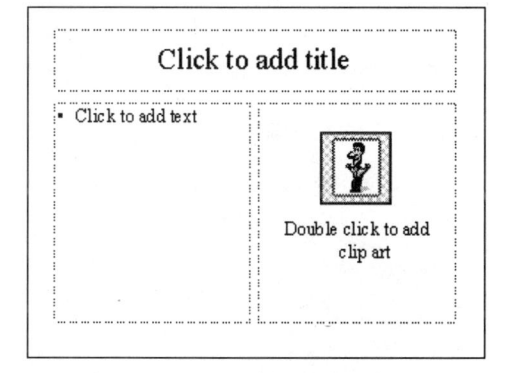

Figure 39. A slide with a clip art placeholder

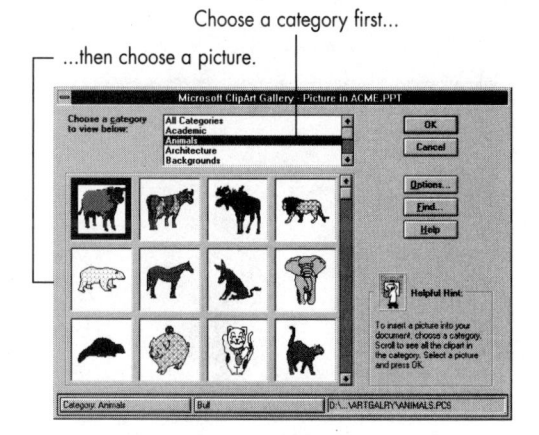

Choose a category first...
...then choose a picture.

Figure 40. Choosing a picture in ClipArt Gallery

Inserting Clip Art

PowerPoint comes with hundreds of *clip art* images that you can add to your slides. There are two ways to insert clip art.

When adding a new slide, you can choose one of the two clip art AutoLayouts (Figure 38). These layouts will insert a clip art placeholder (Figure 39); double-clicking this placeholder will bring up *Microsoft ClipArt Gallery* (Figure 40) from which you can select a clip art image.

Or, if you want to add clip art to an existing slide, use the Insert Clip Art button (Figure 41). This button inserts a placeholder and immediately launches ClipArt Gallery.

Once you are in ClipArt Gallery, follow these steps to choose an image:

1. Click a category (such as Animals or Backgrounds). Use the scroll bar to see additional categories.
2. Select a picture and click OK.

   or

   Double-click a picture.

■ Tips

✓ To resize a clip art image, select it and drag a *corner* selection handle. If you drag a *middle* handle the image will not maintain its original proportions.

✓ To move the image, select it and drag it into position. Make sure that you don't drag a selection handle, or you will resize the image.

Insert Clip Art

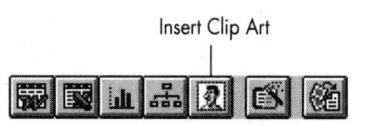

Figure 41. The Standard toolbar

Adding Graphic Objects

125

CHAPTER 9

Searching for Clip Art

An easy way to locate a particular clip art image is to have ClipArt Gallery search for it.

See previous page for information on inserting a clip art placeholder.

1. In ClipArt Gallery, click Find (Figure 42).
2. In the Find Picture dialog box (Figure 43), enter a word or part of a word in the box under With a Description Containing.

   or

   Enter a file name or part of a file name in the box under With a Filename Containing.
3. Click OK. ClipArt Gallery now displays all pictures that match your specifications (Figure 44).
4. Click the picture you want and choose OK.

■ Tip

✓ ClipArt Gallery displays only the pictures that match the conditions you entered in the Find Picture dialog box. To go back to viewing all the clip art again, click All Categories in the Choose a category list box.

Find button

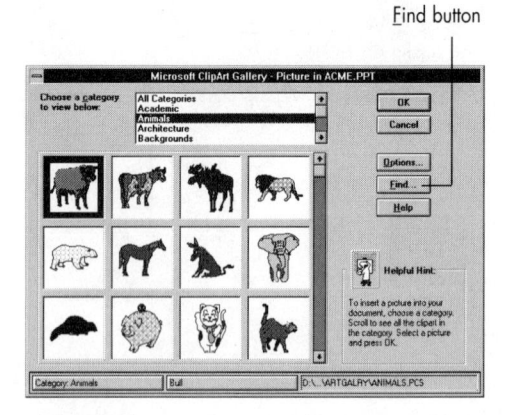

Figure 42. To search for clip art, click the Find button.

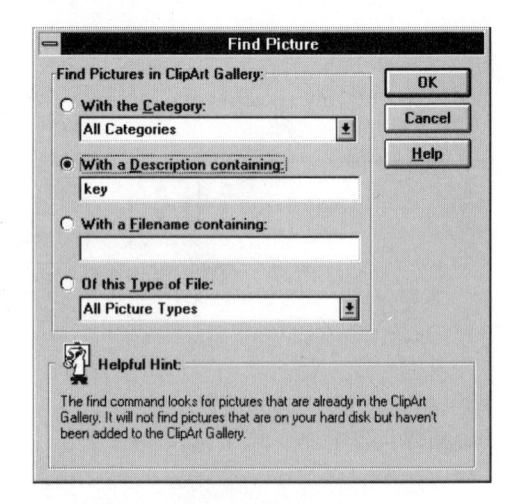

Figure 43. In this example, we are searching for pictures with the description *key*.

ClipArt Gallery found every image that had *key* in its description, such as...

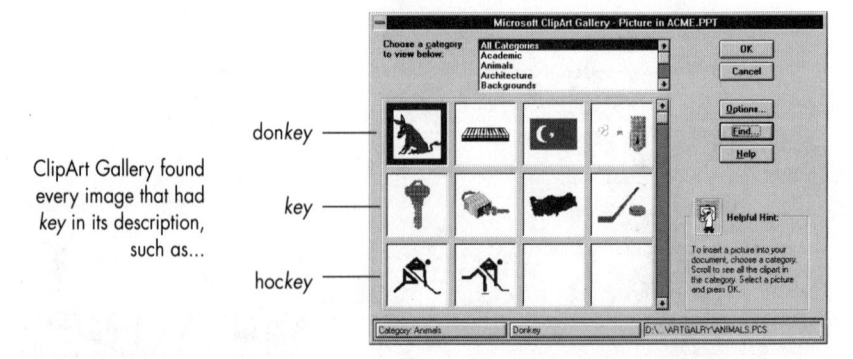

donkey

key

hockey

Figure 44. The results of the search

ADDING GRAPHIC OBJECTS

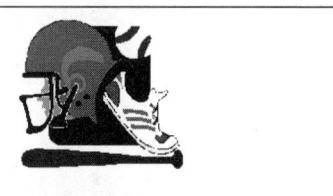

Figure 45. The sport graphic is an imported Windows Metafile.

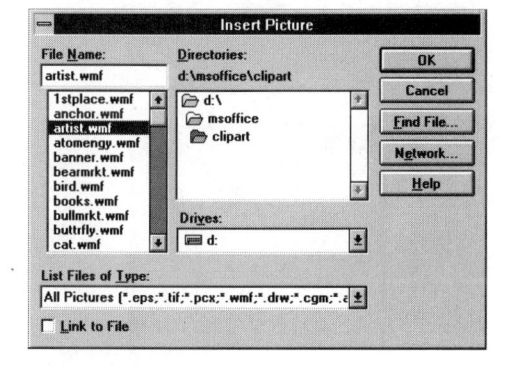

Figure 46. Inserting a graphic file

Inserting Graphic Files

You may want your slides to include graphic files that you have created or purchased. Figure 45 shows a graphic that has been imported to a PowerPoint slide.

1. Display the slide on which you want to insert the graphic file.
2. Select Insert/Picture. The Insert Picture dialog box appears (Figure 46).
3. In the List Files of Type field, choose a specific type of graphic format, such as Windows Metafile. (This step is optional because, by default, all pictures are displayed.)
4. To insert a file from another drive, click the Drives field and choose the desired drive letter.
5. To insert a file from another directory, navigate the Directories list.
6. Click the name of the graphic file in the File Name list.
7. Click OK.

■ Tips

✓ If the imported image may be edited in the future, enable the Link to File check box in the Insert Picture dialog box. That way, if the graphic file is modified, PowerPoint will automatically update the image in your presentation.

✓ To resize a graphic image, select it and drag a *corner* selection handle. If you drag a *middle* handle the image will not maintain its original proportions.

✓ To move the image, select it and then drag it into position. Make sure that you don't drag a selection handle, or you will resize the image.

See Pasting Graphics on the next page for another way to insert graphics.

127

Pasting Graphics

If you have created a graphic image in another program (such as CorelDRAW), you may want to use the copy-and-paste routine to bring it into PowerPoint (Figure 47). One advantage to using this method is that the image becomes an *embedded object* (like org charts, graphs, and tables) that can be easily modified.

1. Select the graphic in the source application, and use Edit/Copy to copy it to the Windows Clipboard.
2. Switch into PowerPoint and display the slide on which you want to insert the graphic.
3. Select Edit/Paste.

■ **Tip**

✓ As with any embedded object, you can modify it by double-clicking the object. PowerPoint will then launch the application that created the image and display the graphic, ready for editing. When you exit the source application, the graphic will be updated automatically in PowerPoint.

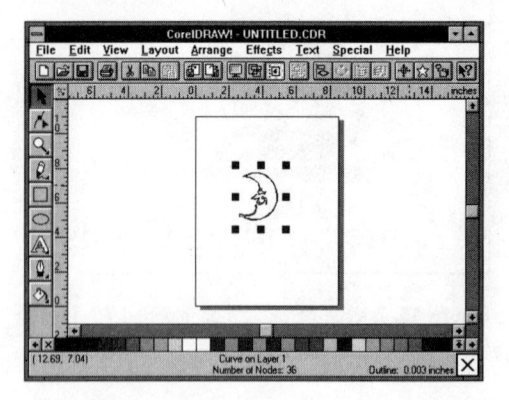

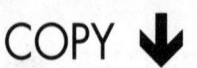

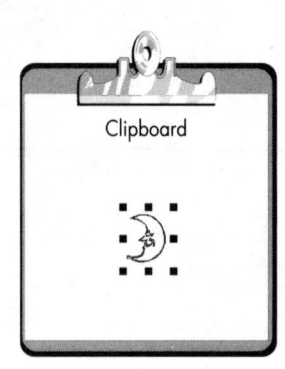

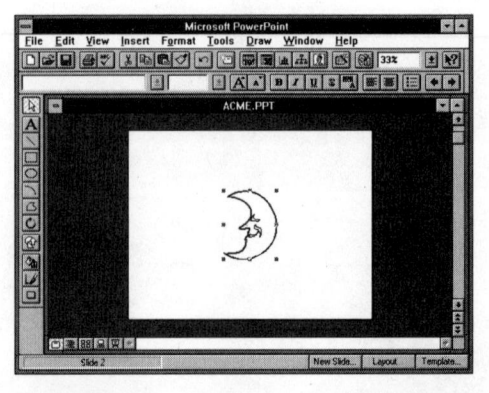

Figure 47. Pasting a graphic from CorelDRAW into PowerPoint

MANIPULATING GRAPHIC OBJECTS 10

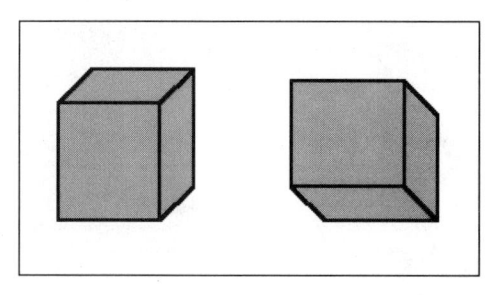

Figure 1. The cube on the right has been rotated.

Figure 2. The star on the right has been scaled to 50% of its original size.

Figure 3. The clip-art image of a woman has been cropped to show just her head and shoulders.

About Graphic Manipulation

PowerPoint offers a number of ways to manipulate the graphic objects you created with the drawing tools, as well as the images you imported from ClipArt Gallery and other programs.

The figures on this page demonstrate some of the techniques you can use to manipulate graphic objects. Objects can be flipped, rotated (Figure 1), scaled (Figure 2), cropped (Figure 3), aligned (Figure 4), and recolored.

In this chapter, you will also learn how to use PowerPoint's rulers, guides, and grid snap feature to place objects; copy graphic attributes; group a set of objects; and change the stacking order of objects.

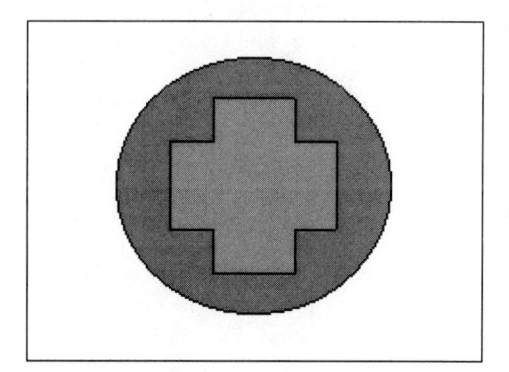

Figure 4. Alignment commands were used to center the cross exactly in the center of the circle.

Manipulating Graphic Objects

129

CHAPTER 10

Using Rulers and Guides

To help you precisely position graphic objects, you can use *rulers* and *guides* (Figure 5). For example, in Figure 6, the ruler helped position the squares exactly 1 inch apart, and a guide was used to align the boxes on a single baseline.

The View menu (Figure 7) allows you to turn rulers and guides on and off.

To display the rulers, select View/Ruler. The horizontal ruler appears above the slide; the vertical ruler appears to the left. Notice that the zero point is at the center of each ruler. This enables you to measure distances from the center of the slide.

To display the guides, select View/Guides. When you first display them, the horizontal and vertical guides intersect in the center of the slide. You can drag the individual guides to intersect at any position on the slide.

■ Tips

✓ You can turn the guides on and off with Ctrl+G.

✓ As you drag the guides, a number appears in the guide; this number represents the distance from the zero point. Thus, if you want to place objects 1.25 inches down from the center of the slide, you can easily drag the horizontal guide to this position (with or without the ruler displayed).

✓ A broken line appears in the rulers to represent the position of the mouse pointer on the slide. Use this line to help you measure the size of objects as you draw them, or to position objects as you drag them.

✓ When positioning an object horizontally, be sure to drag the *left* border, so that the broken line in the ruler reflects the left edge of the object.

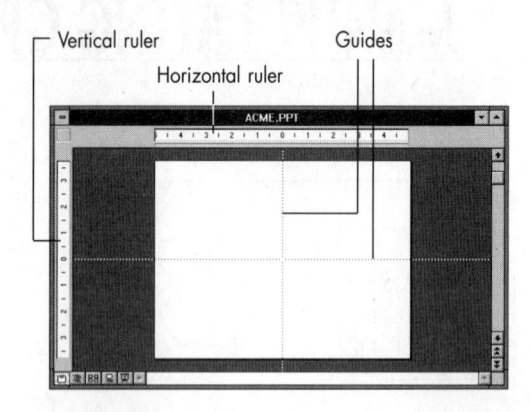

Figure 5. The rulers and guides

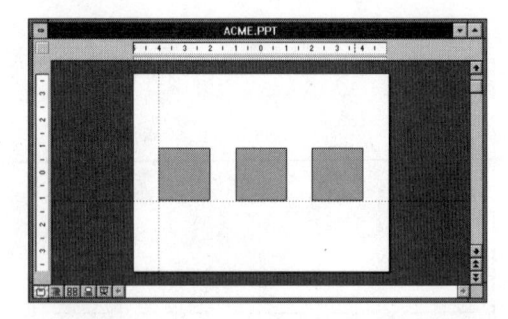

Figure 6. The horizontal ruler made it easy to space the boxes 1 inch apart; the horizontal guide helped align the boxes along the bottom.

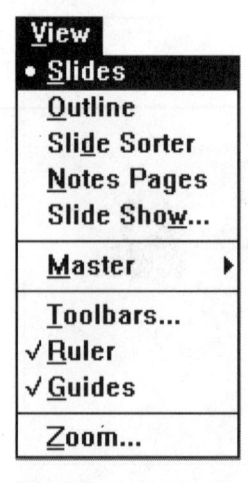

Figure 7. The check marks next to Ruler and Guides indicate these screen elements are currently displayed.

Using Grid Snap

Another tool that helps position objects is the *grid*, a series of invisible, horizontal and vertical lines, about 1/12 inch apart. Whenever you draw, size, or move an object, the object borders jump to the grid, as though it were a magnet.

The grid is always there, although you can never actually see it. To activate the magnetic effect of the grid, use the Draw/Snap to Grid command. To see if grid snap is enabled, pull down the Draw menu; if there is a check mark next to Snap to Grid, the feature is already enabled (Figure 8).

■ Tips

✓ If PowerPoint is not letting you position an object exactly where you want it, grid snap may be interfering and you may want to disable it.

✓ The effect of jumping from one gridline to the next is more apparent in zoomed-in views.

See Zooming In and Out on the next page.

✓ Because you don't actually see the gridlines, grid snap is not as useful as it could be.

✓ To temporarily disable grid snap when positioning an object, hold down Alt as you drag.

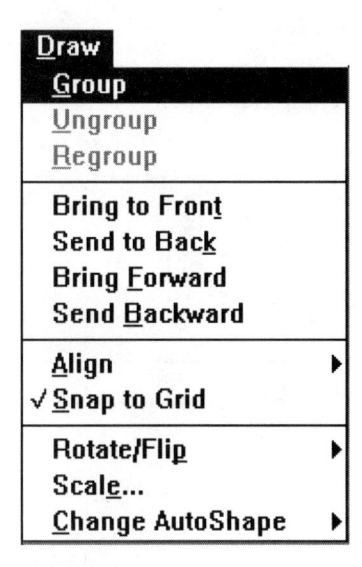

Figure 8. Snap to Grid is enabled, as indicated by the check mark.

CHAPTER 10

Zooming In and Out

As you are drawing, sizing, and moving objects, you may want to zoom in to make sure they are positioned properly. Though objects may look fine when zoomed out (Figure 9), zooming in may help you discover small inaccuracies (Figure 10).

There are three ways to zoom in and out:

- Click the arrow in the Zoom Control field (Figure 11) to display a list of zoom percentages. Then click the desired number.

  or

- Click the box in the Zoom Control field, type a number between 10 and 400, and press Enter.

  or

- Select View/Zoom and choose the desired zoom percentage in the Zoom dialog box (Figure 12).

■ Tip

✓ To zoom in on a particular area of the slide, click an object in this area before choosing a zoom percentage; the selected object will then be centered in the window.

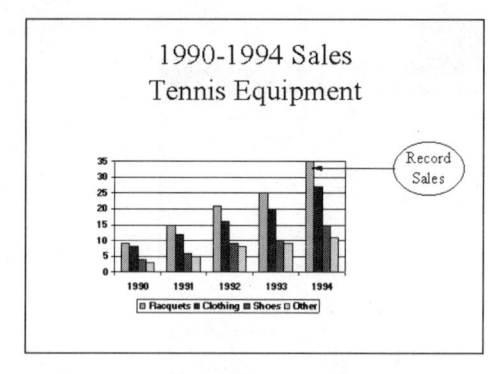

Figure 9. At a 50% zoom, the arrow looks perfectly straight.

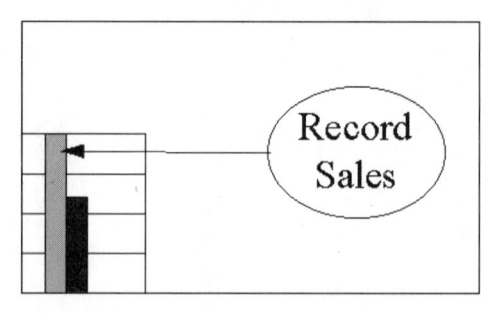

Figure 10. When you zoom in to 100%, you can see that the arrow is crooked.

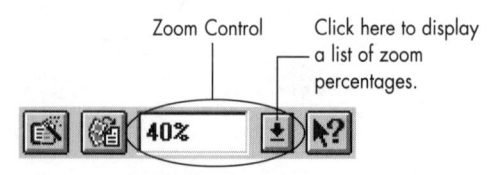

Figure 11. The Standard toolbar

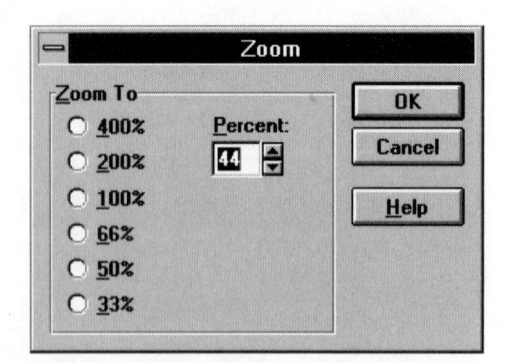

Figure 12. Choose a zoom percentage, or enter any value between 10 and 400 in the Percent field.

132

MANIPULATING GRAPHIC OBJECTS

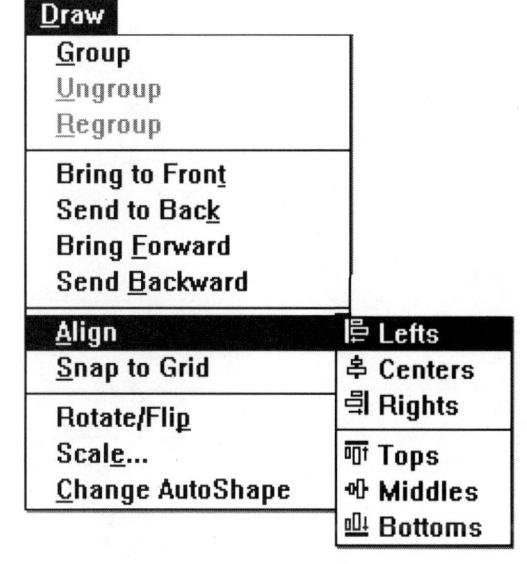

Figure 13. Options for aligning objects

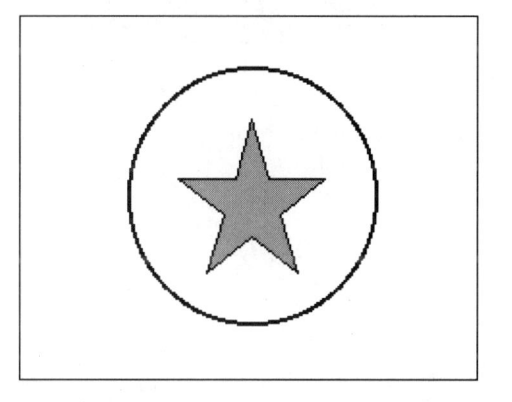

Figure 14. The star is centered—horizontally and vertically—inside the circle.

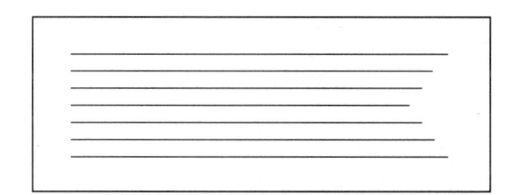

Figure 15. The seven lines are aligned on the left.

Aligning Objects

As explained on the preceding pages, you can use guides and rulers to help line up several objects. However, perhaps the easiest way to align objects is automatically with the Draw/Align command (Figure 13). For example, you can center one object inside another (Figure 14) or align a group of objects on the left (Figure 15).

1. Click to select the first object you want to align.
2. Hold down Shift as you click additional objects to be aligned.
3. Select Draw/Align.
4. Choose one of the alignment options.

■ Tips

✓ The first set of Align options (Lefts, Centers, and Rights) aligns the objects horizontally; the second set (Tops, Middles, and Bottoms) aligns vertically.

✓ To center one object inside another, you need to issue two alignment commands: one to align the objects horizontally (Centers) and the other to align vertically (Middles).

✓ Another way to select multiple objects is to drag a selection rectangle around them.

133

Grouping Objects

When you have a set of objects that you want to manipulate as a whole, it's easier to *group* them. Once the objects are grouped, you can move, resize, scale, flip, and rotate the group as if it were a single object.

1. Click to select the first object you want in the group. Then hold down Shift as you click additional objects to be grouped (Figure 16).

    or

    Drag a selection rectangle around the objects.

2. Select <u>D</u>raw/<u>G</u>roup.

The group is now treated as a single object (Figure 17).

■ Tips

- ✓ Another way to group objects is with the Group button on the Drawing+ toolbar (Figure 18) or by pressing Ctrl+Shift+G.
- ✓ To select all objects on a slide, press Ctrl+A.
- ✓ You cannot modify any objects inside the group until you deactivate the group, using <u>D</u>raw/<u>U</u>ngroup, the Ungroup button, or Ctrl+Shift+H.
- ✓ For more complex drawings, you can create groups within groups.

Figure 16. All the objects in this design are selected.

Figure 17. After grouping, one set of selection handles surround the design.

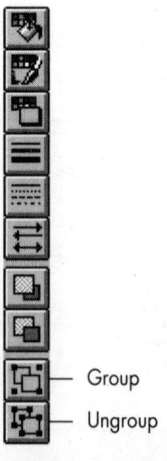

Figure 18. The Drawing+ toolbar

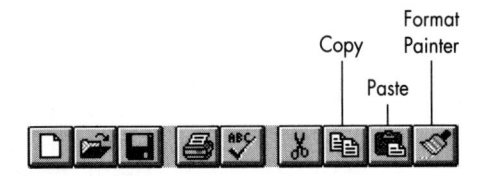

Figure 19. The Standard toolbar

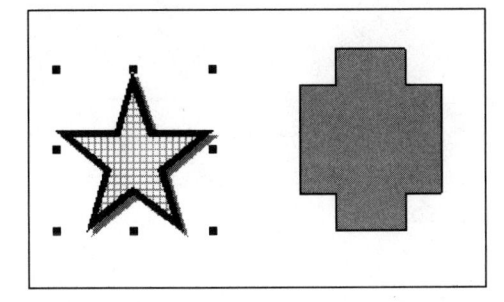

(labels: Copy, Format Painter, Paste)

Figure 20. The star has the attributes you want to copy to the cross.

The cross now has a thick border, a shadow, and a pattern fill.

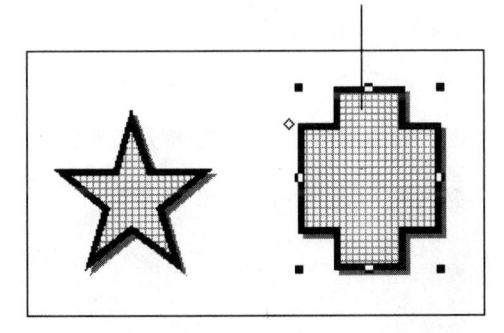

Figure 21. After applying the format with the Format Painter tool, the cross has the same attributes as the star.

Copying Graphic Attributes

Use the Format Painter tool (Figure 19) to copy attributes from one object to another. Some of the attributes you can copy are color, pattern, shadow, and line thickness.

1. Select the object whose attributes you want to copy (Figure 20).
2. Click the Format Painter button (Figure 19). The pointer changes to a paintbrush.
3. Click the object to which you want to apply the attributes (Figure 21).

■ Tips

✓ You can also use the Format Painter tool to copy text attributes (such as font, size, and style) between text boxes.

✓ Format Painter cannot copy attributes of images imported or pasted from other applications.

✓ To copy the object as well as its attributes, use the Copy and Paste buttons (Figure 19).

✓ To copy attributes to more than one object, use either of the following methods:

- After clicking the Format Painter button, draw a selection rectangle around the objects to be formatted.

  or

- Select the object with the desired format to be copied, and double-click the Format Painter button. Then click as many objects as you want to format, and when done, press Esc.

MANIPULATING GRAPHIC OBJECTS

Manipulating Graphic Objects

135

CHAPTER 10

Recoloring a Picture

If, after inserting a clip art image or other graphic, you decide to change the colors in the image, you can do so right in PowerPoint, using the Tools/Recolor command. What this command does, essentially, is replace one color with another.

1. Select the picture to be recolored.
2. Select Tools/Recolor. The Recolor Picture dialog box appears (Figure 22).
3. Choose whether you want to change all Colors (fills and lines) or just the Fills.
4. In the Original column, locate the color you want to replace. This column lists all the colors used in the picture. (There are just three colors listed in Figure 22.)
5. Click the arrow in the adjacent New field to display the small palette.
6. Choose a new color (Figure 23).

   or

   Click Other Color to display additional color choices (Figure 24). Choose the new color from this palette and then click OK.
7. Repeat steps 4 through 6 for any other colors you want to change.
8. Click OK.

■ **Tips**

✓ To see how the picture looks with the new colors, click the Preview button (Figure 22).

✓ You must ungroup a group before you can recolor it.

   See Grouping Objects on page 134.

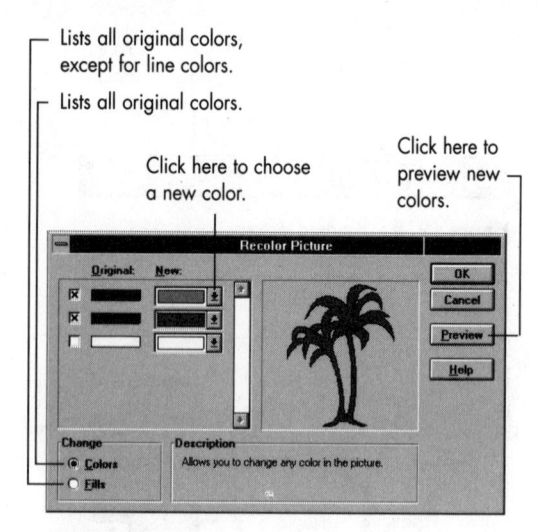

Figure 22. Recoloring a picture

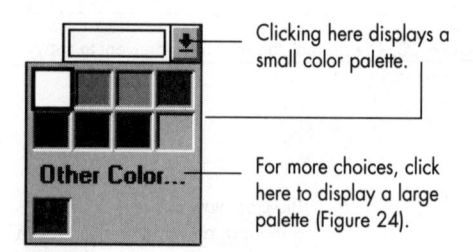

Figure 23. Choosing a new color

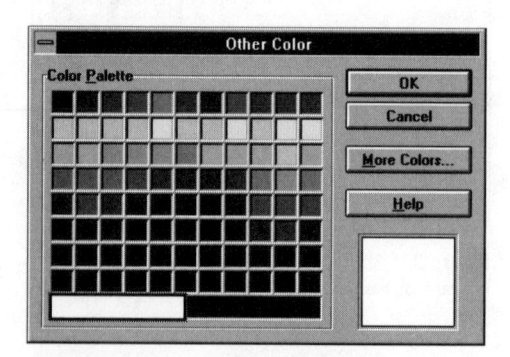

Figure 24. The Other Color dialog box displays a palette with a wide variety of colors.

MANIPULATING GRAPHIC OBJECTS

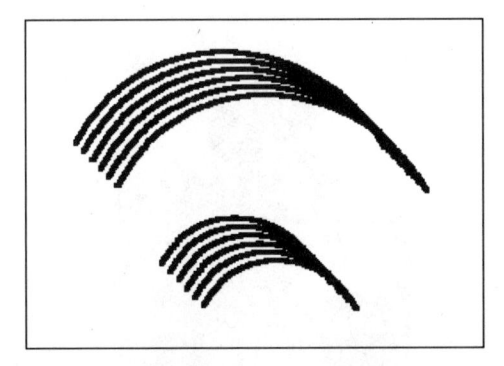

Figure 25. The design at the top is the original size; the copy at the bottom has been scaled 50%.

Enter a scale percentage here...   ...or click the arrows to increase or decrease 1% at a time.

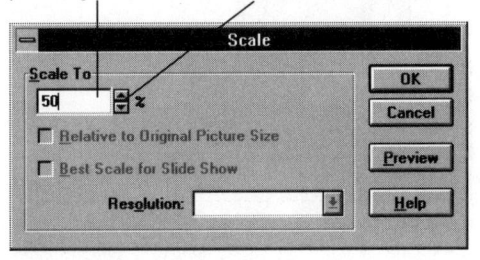

Figure 26. Scaling an object

The original set of objects

These two objects were selected and then scaled.

These two objects were grouped and then scaled.

Figure 27. For best results, group multiple objects before scaling.

Scaling an Object

Scaling resizes an object by a designated percentage and ensures that the object maintains its original proportions. This feature is similar to the enlarge and reduce buttons on your copy machine.

Figure 25 shows a group of objects before and after scaling. You can scale objects drawn in PowerPoint, as well as pictures you have inserted.

1. Select the object or group to be scaled.
2. Select Draw/Scale. The Scale dialog box appears (Figure 26).
3. In the Scale To field, specify a percentage. A number greater than 100 enlarges the object; a number less than 100 reduces.
4. Click OK.

■ Tips

✓ To resize an object or group manually, hold down Shift as you drag a corner selection handle. The Shift key ensures that the object's original proportions are maintained. (This isn't necessary for inserted pictures.)

✓ To see how the object looks with the new scale factor, click the Preview button in the Scale dialog box.

✓ Because you can scale your designs at any time, you don't have to worry about the final size of your artwork as you are creating it.

✓ To scale more than one object at a time, group them first. If you select multiple objects without grouping them, they may lose their relative arrangement (Figure 27).

See Grouping Objects on page 134.

✓ To restore a picture to its original size, hold down Ctrl and double-click a handle. To restore its original proportions, use the Shift key.

137

CHAPTER 10

Cropping a Picture

Cropping is a term that refers to trimming away an unwanted section of a picture. For example, if a graphic displays a person's full body, you can crop it so that only the person's face appears. Figures 28 and 29 show another example of cropping.

1. Select the picture to be cropped.
2. Select Tools/Crop Picture. The pointer changes to the shape shown in Figure 30.
3. Place the cropping pointer on a selection handle (Figure 31), and click and drag toward the middle of the picture until you have trimmed away the unwanted portion.
4. If necessary, drag other selection handles to crop other portions.
5. When you are finished cropping, click an empty area of the slide, or press Esc.

■ Tips

✓ When you crop, you are temporarily hiding part of the picture. If you want to redisplay any part of the hidden section, you can crop again.

✓ You may want to zoom in for more accuracy in cropping.

See Zooming In and Out on page 132.

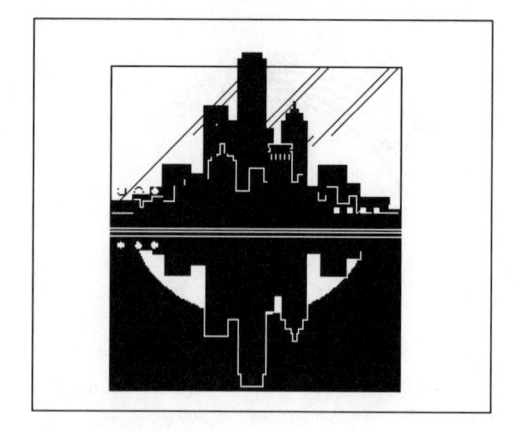

Figure 28. The original picture

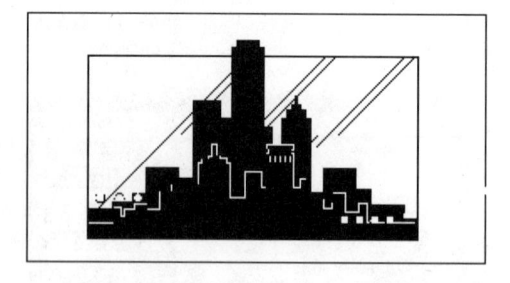

Figure 29. The bottom half of the picture was cropped out.

Figure 30. The cropping pointer

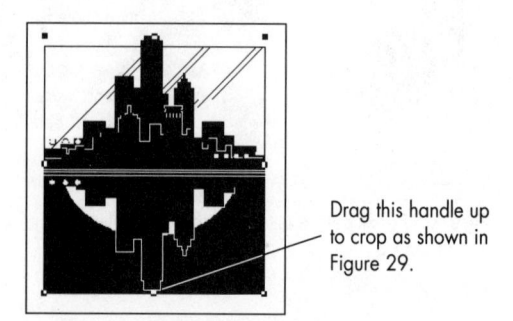

Drag this handle up to crop as shown in Figure 29.

Figure 31. Drag the selection handles to crop the picture.

MANIPULATING GRAPHIC OBJECTS

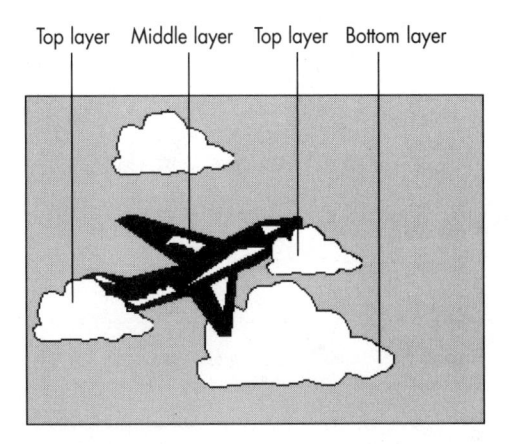

Top layer   Middle layer   Top layer   Bottom layer

Figure 32. Overlapping objects are layered.

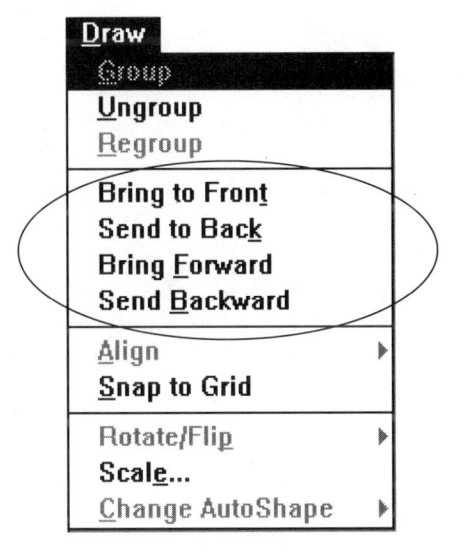

Figure 33. The circled commands let you change the stack order of the selected object.

— Bring Forward
— Send Backward

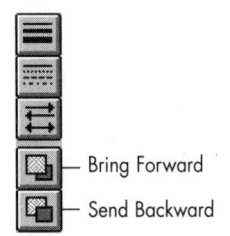

Figure 34. The Drawing+ toolbar

Changing the Stack Order

As you draw objects or place pictures on a slide, PowerPoint layers them one on top of the other. In Figure 32, you can see how the clouds and airplane are on different layers.

To control the order in which the objects are stacked, use commands on the Draw menu (Figure 33). The Bring Forward and Send Backward commands are also available as buttons on the Drawing+ toolbar (Figure 34).

■ **Tips**

✓ Send Backward moves the selected object down to the next layer in the stack. Send to Back places the object on the bottom of the stack (Figure 35).

✓ Bring Forward moves the selected object up to the next layer in the stack. Bring to Front places the object on the top of the stack.

✓ Choosing the Send Backward command several times will ultimately produce the same results as choosing Send to Back once. Likewise, selecting Bring Forward several times is the equivalent of choosing Bring to Front.

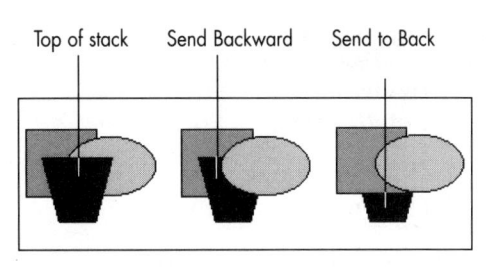

Top of stack   Send Backward   Send to Back

Figure 35. The difference between the effects of Send Backward and Send to Back

Manipulating Graphic Objects

139

CHAPTER 10

Rotating Objects

Figure 36 shows an example of rotated objects.

1. Select the object to be rotated.
2. Select the Free Rotate tool (Figure 37). You will see the Free Rotate pointer.
3. Place the Free Rotate pointer (Figure 38) on a selection handle. You will then see the four-arrow pointer. Drag in a clockwise or counterclockwise direction.
4. Release the mouse button when you are finished rotating.
5. If you want to rotate the object further, repeat steps 3 and 4.
6. Click off the object to deactivate the Free Rotate tool.

■ Tips

✓ The Drawing+ toolbar contains two additional tools for rotating objects (Figure 39). Rotate Left rotates the object 90 degrees counterclockwise, and Rotate Right rotates 90 degrees clockwise.

✓ Anther way to rotate is with the Rotate/Flip command on the Draw menu. This command displays the options shown in Figure 40.

✓ You cannot rotate clip art or other pictures unless you first convert them to PowerPoint objects. To convert an image, ungroup it; then, to rotate the entire image, you must group it again.

See Grouping Objects on page 134.

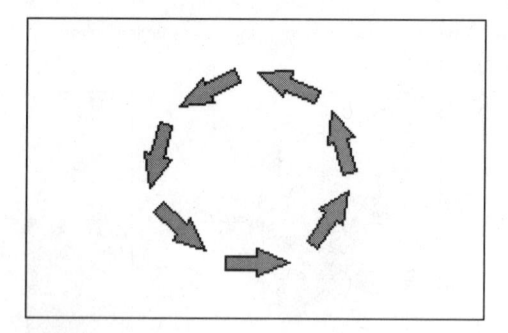

Figure 36. To create this circle of arrows, each arrow was rotated.

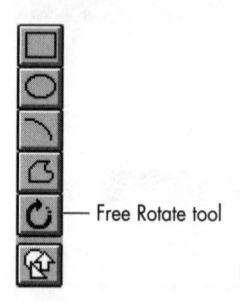

Figure 37. The Drawing toolbar

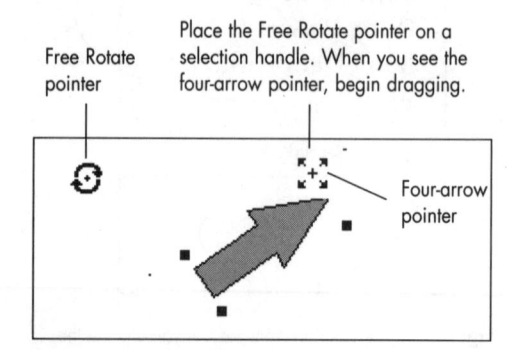

Figure 38. Rotating an object

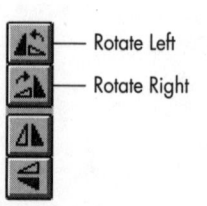

Figure 39. The Drawing+ toolbar

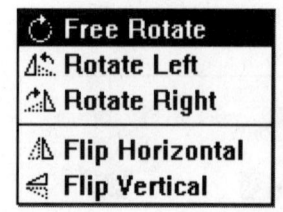

Figure 40. Choose the Rotate/Flip command on the Draw menu to display these choices.

MANIPULATING GRAPHIC OBJECTS

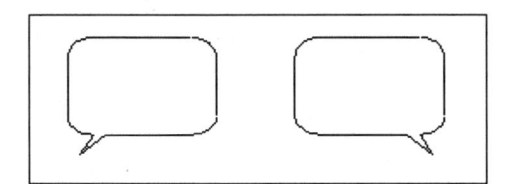

Figure 41. The balloon on the left is the original object; the balloon on the right has been flipped horizontally.

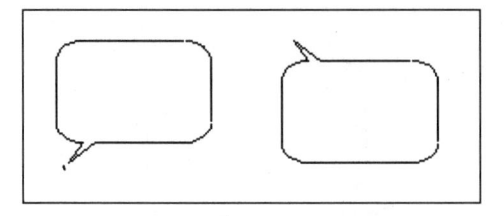

Figure 42. The balloon on the left is the original object; the balloon on the right has been flipped vertically.

— Flip Horizontal
— Flip Vertical

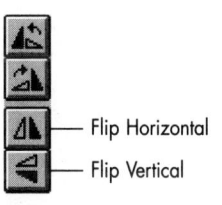

Figure 43. The Drawing+ toolbar

Figure 44. The original clip-art image is on the left; the image on the right was flipped horizontally.

Flipping Objects

You can flip objects horizontally (Figure 41) and vertically (Figure 42).

1. Select the object to be flipped.
2. On the Draw menu, select Rotate/Flip.
3. Choose either Flip Horizontal or Flip Vertical.

■ Tips

✓ Another way to flip objects is with the Flip Horizontal and Flip Vertical buttons in the Drawing+ toolbar (Figure 43).

✓ You cannot flip clip art or other pictures unless you first convert them to PowerPoint objects. To convert an image, ungroup it; then, to flip the entire image, you must group it again. Figure 44 shows a clip art image that was flipped horizontally.

See Grouping Objects on page 134.

Manipulating Graphic Objects

141

MAKING GLOBAL CHANGES 11

```
           Agenda
1994 Annual Business Review

    • Introduction
    • Corporate Goals
    • 1994 Sales Performance
        – By Region
        – By Product Line
    • 1995 Budget
```

Figure 1. The original slide, before global formatting

Formatting a Presentation

This chapter shows you how to quickly format an entire presentation—without having to change each slide. Some global changes, such as replacing fonts and changing colors or backgrounds, are done with commands on the Tools or Format menu.

Other changes, such as formatting slide titles and adding logos or page numbers to every slide, are done by editing the *Slide Master*. The Slide Master contains default formatting, as well as any background items you want repeated on each slide. Figures 1 and 2 show a slide before and after modifying the Slide Master. While these figures show just one slide, bear in mind that *all* slides would be formatted similarly.

Perhaps the most dramatic global change you can make to your presentation is to apply a *template*. A template controls the color scheme, text formatting, and repeating graphic elements—and it's applied with a single command. Figure 3 shows the slide after applying a template.

```
**Agenda
1994 Annual Business Review**

■ Introduction
■ Corporate Goals
■ 1994 Sales Performance
    ▸ By Region
    ▸ By Product Line
■ 1995 Budget
```

Figure 2. After editing the Slide Master

```
       Agenda
1994 Annual Business Review

    ■ Introduction
    ■ Corporate Goals
    ■ 1994 Sales Performance
        – By Region
        – By Product Line
    ■ 1995 Budget
```

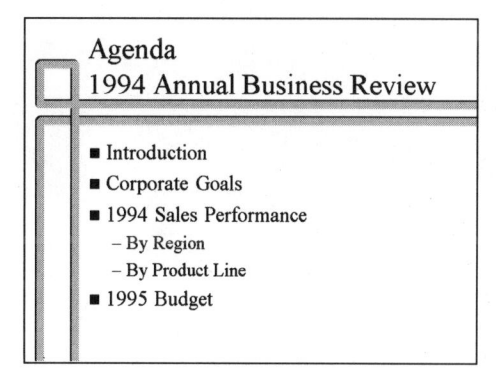

Figure 3. After applying a template

143

CHAPTER 11

Replacing a Font

Suppose you want all your slide text to be Arial instead of Times New Roman (Figures 4 and 5). You can accomplish this task easily with the Tools/Replace Fonts command.

1. Select Tools/Replace Fonts. The Replace Font dialog box appears (Figure 6).
2. In the Replace field, choose the font you want to replace in the presentation.
3. In the With field, choose the new font.
4. Click the Replace button.
5. Repeat steps 2 through 4 to replace other fonts.
6. Click Close.

■ Tips

✓ The Replace Fonts command does not substitute typefaces in graphs, tables, and org charts.

✓ To replace the font in only the slide titles or only the bullet text, you need to edit the Slide Master.

See Changing the Default Format for Text on page 149.

Retail Store Comparison
Acme Stores vs. XYZ Stores

Acme	XYZ
■ 1200 stores	■ 750 stores
■ Convenient locations in every major city	■ Few locations in East
■ Everyday low prices	■ Suggested retail prices
■ Monthly sales	■ Seasonal sales only

Figure 4. The current font for text on this slide (and all other slides) is Times New Roman.

Retail Store Comparison
Acme Stores vs. XYZ Stores

Acme	XYZ
■ 1200 stores	■ 750 stores
■ Convenient locations in every major city	■ Few locations in East
■ Everyday low prices	■ Suggested retail prices
■ Monthly sales	■ Seasonal sales only

Figure 5. After replacing fonts, the text on this slide (and on all other slides) is Arial.

Click here to list all fonts used in the presentation.

Click here to list all fonts available on your system.

Replace Font

Replace: Times New Roman
With: Arial

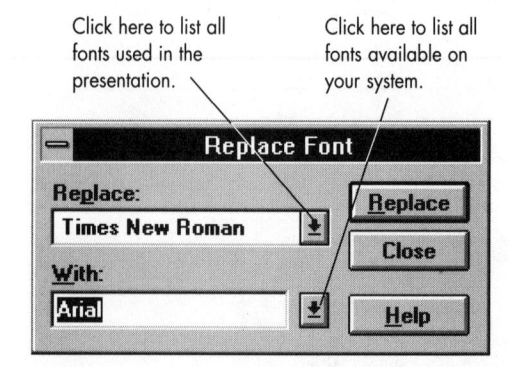

[Replace] [Close] [Help]

Figure 6. Replace one font with another using the Tools/Replace Fonts command.

MAKING GLOBAL CHANGES

First, choose a slide element.

Then, click here to choose a color.

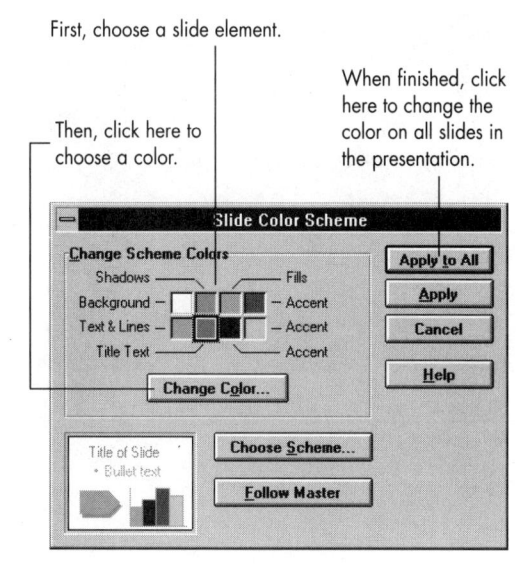

When finished, click here to change the color on all slides in the presentation.

Figure 7. Changing color globally

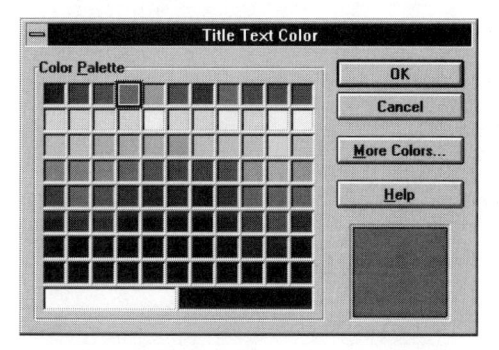

Figure 8. Choosing a color

Changing Default Colors in a Presentation

There are several slide elements whose colors you can change globally: the slide background, slide titles, text and lines, drop shadows, and object fills. Any new slides you create will use the new color scheme.

1. Select Format/Slide Color Scheme. The Slide Color Scheme dialog box appears as shown in Figure 7.
2. In the Change Scheme Colors area, click the box associated with the element you want to change. For instance, click the Title Text box.
3. Click the Change Color button. A color palette appears, as shown in Figure 8.
4. Click a color box and then click OK.
5. Repeat steps 2 through 4 for each element you want to change.
6. Click Apply to All to apply the new colors to the entire presentation.

■ Tips

✓ Instead of clicking the Change Color button for an element, you can display the color palette by double-clicking the color box.

✓ When you change the Text & Lines color, it affects the color of bullet, graph, org chart, and table text. It also changes the color of lines and objects drawn in PowerPoint, lines inside graphs (such as gridlines and legend borders), and connecting lines in org charts. The color of table borders does not change, however.

✓ When you change the Fills color, only the objects using the default fill color will be affected. Objects for which you have assigned a specific new color will retain that color.

Making Global Changes

145

CHAPTER 11

Creating a Gradient Background

A *gradient* is a gradual progression from one color to another; PowerPoint calls this a *shade*. Figure 9 shows a slide with a shaded background. Shades have a primary color of your choosing and are blended with different amounts of black or white.

1. Select Format/Slide Background. The Slide Background dialog box appears (Figure 10).
2. To choose the shade's primary color, click the Change Color button. A color palette appears.
3. Click a color box and then click OK.
4. Choose one of the Shade Styles (Vertical, Horizontal, etc.).
5. Click one of the Variants (these are variations of the style you selected in step 4).
6. To lighten the blended color, click the right arrow on the Dark/Light slider (Figure 11).

   or

   To darken the blended color, click the left arrow on the Dark/Light slider.
7. Click Apply To All.

■ Tips

✓ As you darken the blended color, you are adding more black. As you lighten, you are adding more white.

✓ You may need to adjust your color scheme after creating a shaded background. For example, for a dark shade, you might want to choose white for slide titles, text, and lines.

See Changing Default Colors in a Presentation, on the previous page.

Figure 9. This slide has a shaded (gradient) background.

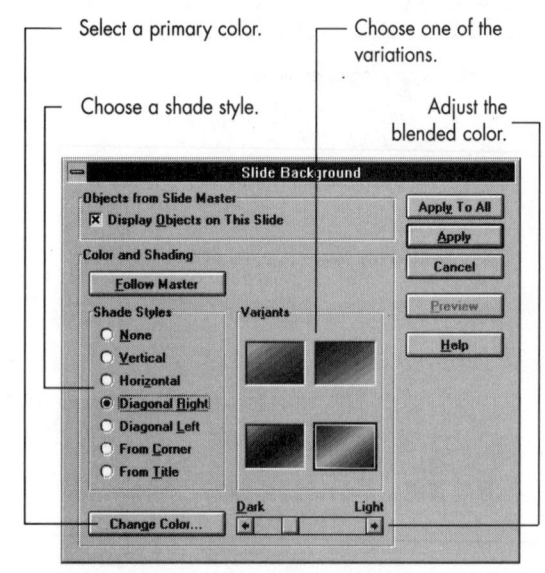

Figure 10. Creating a shaded background

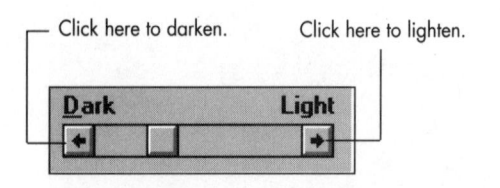

Figure 11. Use the Dark/Light slider to control the amount of black and white in the blended color.

146

MAKING GLOBAL CHANGES

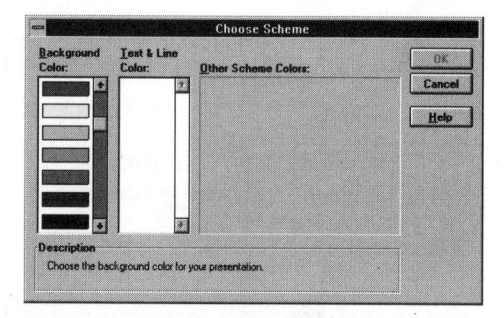

Figure 12. First choose a background color.

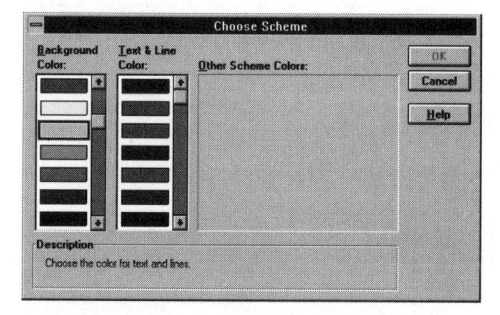

Figure 13. Then choose one of the compatible text and line colors.

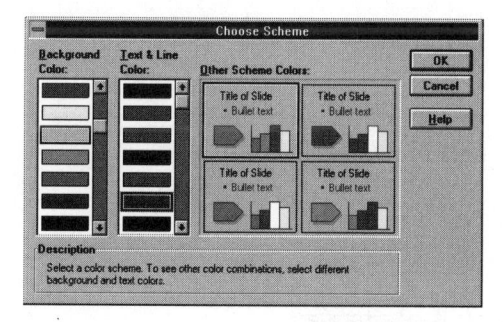

Figure 14. Finally, choose a preview that contains the desired combination of colors for slide titles, fills, shadows, and accents.

Choosing Compatible Colors

If you feel overwhelmed by all the possible choices when selecting colors for your presentation, PowerPoint can help you choose a set of compatible colors. After you select a background color, PowerPoint will then narrow down the possibilities for Text & Line colors to those that work well with your choice. Based on your selection, PowerPoint then presents complementary color choices for slide titles, fills, and other slide elements.

1. Select F*o*rmat/Slide *C*olor Scheme.
2. Click the Choose *S*cheme button. The Choose Scheme dialog box appears (Figure 12).
3. In the *B*ackground Color list, scroll until you find the desired background color. When you click it, the *T*ext & Line Color list displays colors compatible with your choice (Figure 13).
4. In the *T*ext & Line Color list, scroll until you find the desired color. When you click it, the *O*ther Scheme Colors section displays four previews, each with a different set of colors for slide titles, fills, shadows, and accents (Figure 14).
5. In the *O*ther Scheme Colors section, click one of the previews.
6. Try different background and text color choices until you find a scheme you like.
7. Click OK to close the Choose Scheme dialog box.
8. Click Apply *t*o All.

■ Tip

✓ If you're not happy with the colors after you apply a new color scheme, you can immediately select *E*dit/*U*ndo to restore your previous color scheme.

See also Changing Default Colors in a Presentation on page 145.

147

Editing the Slide Master

The Slide Master (Figure 15) contains the default formatting for your presentation, as well as any background items you want to appear on each slide. Any changes you make to the Slide Master automatically affect all slides in your presentation. When you format the Master title and Master text, you are actually formatting all the titles and text in your presentation.

Figure 16 is an example of a formatted Slide Master. To edit the Slide Master, follow these steps.

1. Select <u>V</u>iew/<u>M</u>aster.
2. Choose <u>S</u>lide Master. The Slide Master appears (Figure 15).
3. Make desired changes to the Master.
   See Changing the Default Format for Text, Adding Background Items, and Inserting Page Numbers on the following pages.
4. When you're finished, click the Slide View button (Figure 17). All slides will now have the formatting and background items you added to the Master.

The following pages show some common ways to edit the Slide Master.

■ Tips

✓ A quick way to display the Slide Master is to hold Shift as you click the Slide View button.

✓ Another change you can make to the Slide Master is to adjust the size and position of the title area and object area placeholders. (These placeholders are pointed out in Figure 15).

See Manipulating Text Placeholders on page 33.

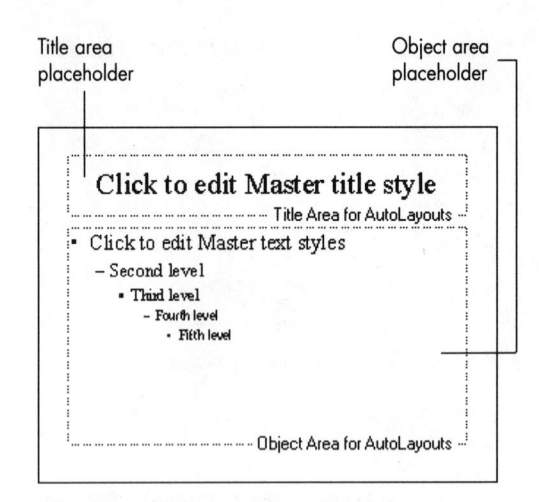

Figure 15. The Slide Master

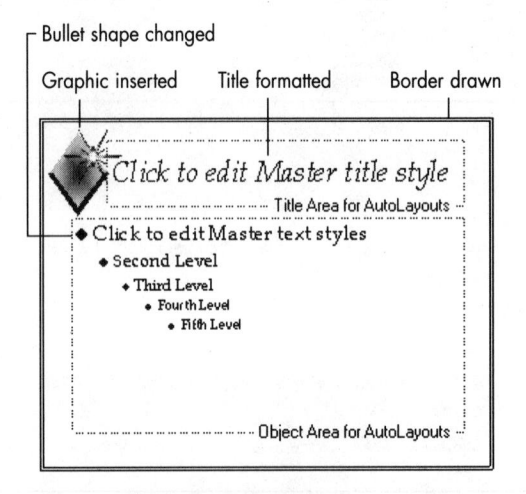

Figure 16. A formatted Slide Master

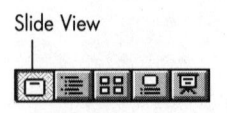

Figure 17. The View buttons

MAKING GLOBAL CHANGES

```
        Agenda
1994 Annual Business Review

• Introduction
• Corporate Goals
• 1994 Sales Performance
   – By Region
   – By Product Line
• 1995 Budget
```

Figure 18. This Bulleted List slide uses the default Slide Master.

```
        Agenda
1994 Annual Business Review

■ Introduction
■ Corporate Goals
■ 1994 Sales Performance
   ‣ By Region
   ‣ By Product Line
■ 1995 Budget
```

Figure 19. The same slide after formatting the Slide Master—all Bulleted List slides are formatted identically.

Click this line to format first-level bullets.

Click this line to format slide titles.

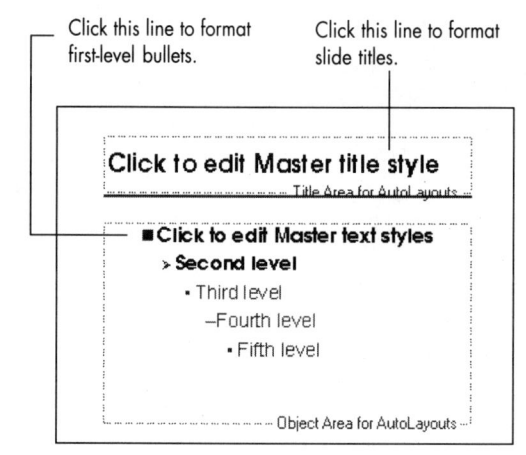

```
Click to edit Master title style
............ Title Area for AutoLayouts .............

■ Click to edit Master text styles
   ‣ Second level
       • Third level
         –Fourth level
            • Fifth level


............ Object Area for AutoLayouts .............
```

Figure 20. The formatted Slide Master

Changing the Default Format for Text

Suppose you want all your slide titles to be in a larger type size and aligned on the left, all first-level bullets to be squares, and all bullet text to be anchored in the middle. By making these changes on the Slide Master, you only need to format the text once—all new and existing slides will conform to the modified format.

Figures 18 and 19 show a Bulleted List slide before and after editing the Slide Master. Figure 20 shows the modified Slide Master.

1. Select <u>V</u>iew/<u>M</u>aster/<u>S</u>lide Master.

2. To format slide titles, click the Master title and make desired changes. (You do not need to select all the text.)

   See pages 39–43 for information on formatting text.

3. To format first-level bullets, click where it says "Click to edit Master text styles" and make desired changes.

   See Changing the Bullet Shape on page 37, Adjusting the Bullet Placement on page 38, and Setting Anchor Points in a Text Placeholder on page 42.

4. To format other bullet levels, click the line (such as "Second level") and make desired changes.

5. Click the Slide View button (Figure 17 on previous page) when you're finished.

■ Tips

✓ When you format text directly on a slide, your formatting overrides the Slide Master. Therefore, for consistent formatting throughout your presentation, try to use direct formatting as little as possible.

✓ If you format a slide before modifying the Slide Master, the slide will retain its direct formatting and not conform to the Master.

149

Adding Background Items

When background items are placed on the Slide Master, they are repeated on every slide in the presentation. Common background items are company names and logos, borders, rules, dates, and page numbers.

Figure 21 shows several examples of background items you may want repeated on each slide.

1. Select <u>V</u>iew/<u>M</u>aster/<u>S</u>lide Master. The Slide Master appears, as shown in Figure 22.
2. Do any of the following to add background items:
   - Use tools on the Drawing toolbar to create lines and boxes on the Master.
     See Drawing Lines on page 116 and Drawing Rectangles on page 118.
   - Use the Text tool to insert text placeholders on the Master.
     See Creating a Text Placeholder on page 32.
   - Use the <u>I</u>nsert/<u>C</u>lip Art or <u>I</u>nsert/Picture commands to add graphics to the Master.
     See Inserting Clip Art on page 125 and Inserting Graphic Files on page 127.
3. When you're finished, click the Slide View button (Figure 23).

■ Tips

✓ If you don't want any background items to appear on a particular slide, select F<u>o</u>rmat/Slide Background, and then turn off the Display <u>O</u>bjects on This Slide check box. Click <u>A</u>pply.

✓ To create the border shown in Figure 21, use the Rectangle tool to draw a box around the slide, and then turn off the fill. Use the F<u>o</u>rmat/Colors and <u>L</u>ines command to choose a line style (such as the double-line in the figure).

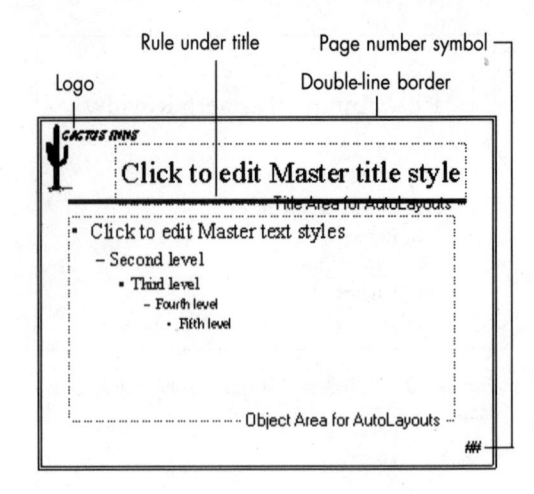

Figure 21. Background items added to a Slide Master

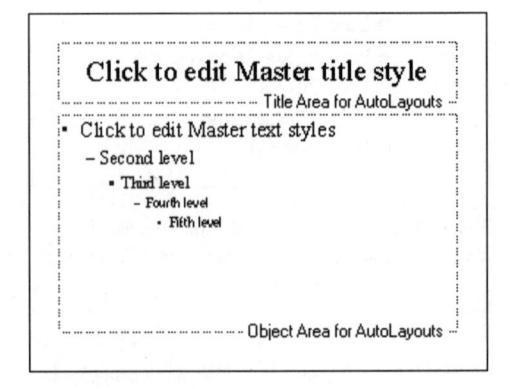

Figure 22. The Slide Master

Slide View

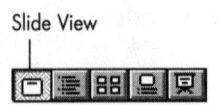

Figure 23. The View buttons

MAKING GLOBAL CHANGES

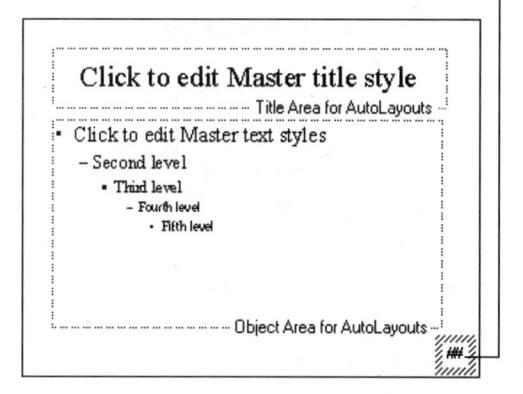

Figure 24. A text placeholder containing a page number

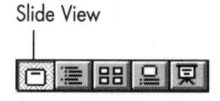

Figure 25. The View buttons

Figure 26. The actual page numbers appear during a slide show.

Inserting Page Numbers

To automatically number the slides in your presentation, insert a page number symbol on the Slide Master.

1. Select <u>V</u>iew/<u>M</u>aster/<u>S</u>lide Master. The Slide Master appears.
2. Make sure the cursor is not in an existing text placeholder, and then select <u>I</u>nsert/Page N<u>u</u>mber. A text placeholder containing ## appears in the center of the slide.
3. Move the placeholder into position (Figure 24).

   For information on moving placeholders, see Manipulating Text Placeholders on page 33.

4. Click the Slide View button (Figure 25).

When you insert a page number symbol on the Slide Master, ## appears on each slide. You will see the actual slide number during the slide show (Figure 26) and when you print.

■ Tips

✓ An alternate way of placing a page number is to insert a text placeholder where you want the page number to appear and then select <u>I</u>nsert/Page N<u>u</u>mber.

✓ The page number can be formatted just as any other text can, and you can insert text in front of the page number or around it. For instance, you can insert the word *Slide* before the page number.

✓ To allow ample space for the page number, you may want to make the object area a little smaller.

For information on resizing placeholders, see Manipulating Text Placeholders on page 33.

✓ To change the starting page number, select <u>F</u>ile/Slide Set<u>u</u>p, and specify a new number under <u>N</u>umber Slides From.

Making Global Changes

151

Applying a Template

A *template* is a presentation in which the Slide Master and color scheme have been specifically designed for a particular look so that it can be easily cloned in other presentations. By applying a template, you can instantly change the format of the text, add background items to each slide, and adjust the colors used in the presentation. PowerPoint comes with over 100 templates.

Figure 27 shows a slide before a template has been applied; Figures 28 and 29 show the same slide after applying two different templates.

1. Click the Template button at the bottom of the PowerPoint window.

   or

   Select Format/Presentation Template.

2. In the Directories list, choose the appropriate template subdirectory (Figure 30).

4. In the File Name list, click a .PPT file (Figure 31). A preview of this template is shown in the bottom right corner of the dialog box.

5. Preview other templates, and when you find one you like, click Apply.

■ Tips

✓ You can also choose a template as you are creating a new presentation.

   See Choosing a Template on page 18.

✓ A template can be any .PPT file. Thus, if you want the current presentation to look like another you've previously created, choose this file name for the presentation template.

✓ The name of the template applied to the current presentation is listed in the Summary Info dialog box. (Select File/Summary Info to display this box.)

Figure 27. Before applying a template

Figure 28. After applying the THEATREB.PPT template

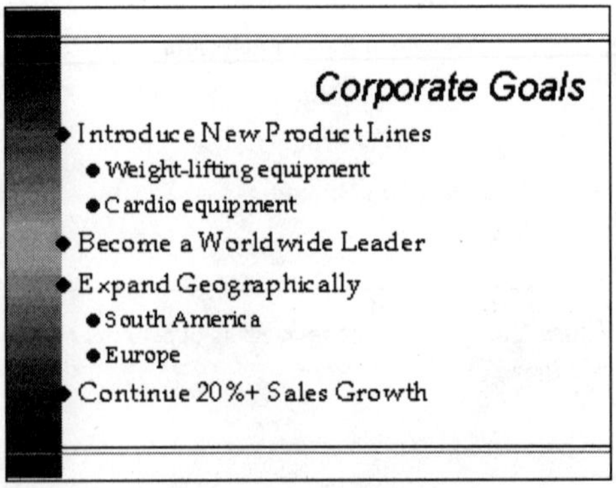

Figure 29. After applying the BLACKB.PPT template

MAKING GLOBAL CHANGES

Applying a Template (cont'd)

✓ After applying a template, you may want to make your own adjustments to the new Slide Master. You may also want to fine-tune the slide background or color scheme.

See Editing the Slide Master on page 148.

✓ Suppose, after applying a template, you change the slide background or color scheme, and then decide you want to revert back to the template's original settings. To do this, select Format/Slide Background or Format/Slide Color Scheme, and click Follow Master. Then click Apply to All.

Black-and-white overheads
Color overheads
Onscreen slide shows

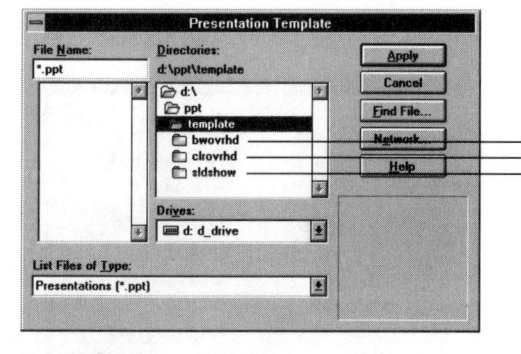

Figure 30. Choose the appropriate template subdirectory.

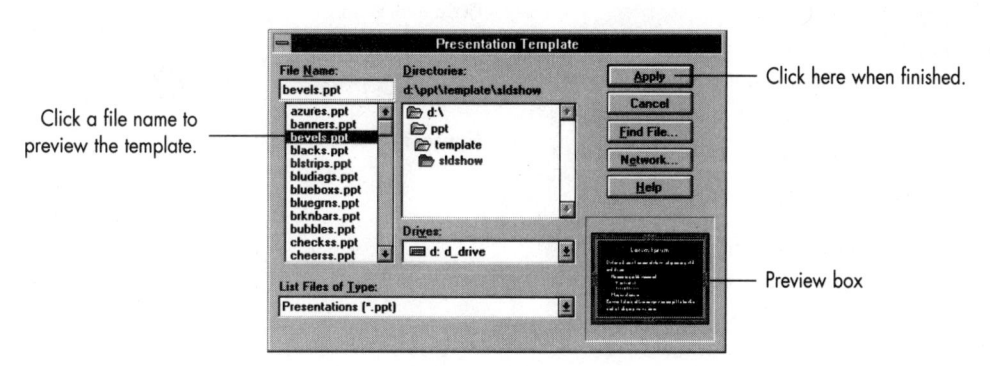

Click a file name to preview the template.

Click here when finished.

Preview box

Figure 31. Choose a template in this dialog box.

153

CHAPTER 11

Using the Pick a Look Wizard

The *Pick a Look Wizard* is a quick and friendly way to design a presentation; it steps you through the process of choosing a template and placing background text (such as a company name, date, and page number) on each slide.

You can activate this Wizard at any time—when creating a new presentation, or when working on an existing presentation.

1. Select File/New, choose Pick a Look Wizard (Figure 32), and click OK.

   or

   In an existing presentation, select Format/Pick a Look Wizard.

2. In each of the dialog boxes that appears, make your choices and click the Next button (Figure 33).

3. Click the Finish button when you reach the final dialog box (Step 9 of 9).

■ Tips

✓ Another way to activate this Wizard in an existing presentation is with the Pick a Look Wizard button (Figure 34).

✓ The Wizard asks you about output (Figure 33) so that you can choose an appropriate template.

✓ The Pick a Look Wizard also helps you design the Masters for outlines, handouts, and notes pages.

   See pages 188–194 for information on outlines, handouts, and notes pages.

✓ Another Wizard that PowerPoint offers is the *AutoContent Wizard*. To give you a headstart on the content of your presentation, you can choose AutoContent Wizard in the New Presentation dialog box (Figure 32).

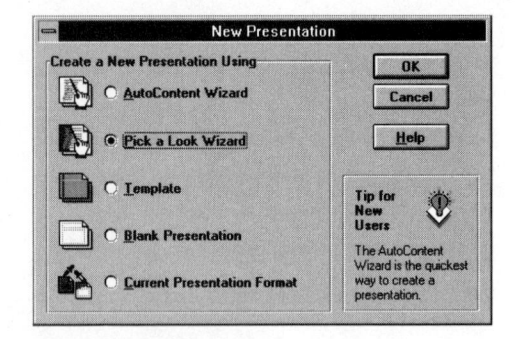

Figure 32. Choosing Pick a Look Wizard when creating a new presentation

Figure 33. Using Pick a Look Wizard

Pick a Look Wizard

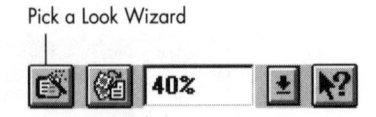

Figure 34. The Standard toolbar

154

WORKING IN OUTLINE VIEW 12

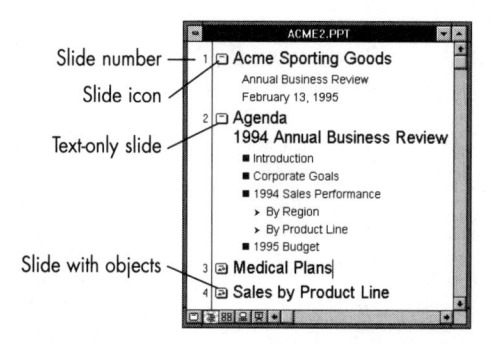

Figure 1. Outline view

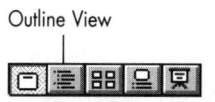

(Labels: Slide number, Slide icon, Text-only slide, Slide with objects)

ACME2.PPT
1. Acme Sporting Goods
   Annual Business Review
   February 13, 1995
2. Agenda
   1994 Annual Business Review
   ■ Introduction
   ■ Corporate Goals
   ■ 1994 Sales Performance
   ▸ By Region
   ▸ By Product Line
   ■ 1995 Budget
3. Medical Plans
4. Sales by Product Line

Figure 2. The View buttons

Figure 3. Outlining toolbar

Introducing Outline View

Outline view displays an outline of your presentation; you can see each slide's title and main text, such as bulleted items (Figure 1). Outline view is ideal for seeing the structure of your presentation and for reordering slides.

Another advantage to Outline view is that it offers a quick way to type a series of Bulleted List slides. Later in this chapter, you will see how easy it is to type one list after another, without having to give a special command to insert a new slide for each list.

Switch to Outline view by clicking the Outline View button (Figure 2) or by selecting the View/Outline command. Note that Outline view has its own toolbar (Figure 3).

The *slide icon* to the left of each slide's title (Figure 1) indicates whether the slide contains only text or contains an object such as a graph, table, org chart, or picture. Clicking the slide icon once selects the slide (so that you can move, copy, or delete it); clicking it twice displays that slide in Slide view.

See page 188 for information on printing outlines.

155

CHAPTER 12

Hiding Text Formatting

As you can see in Figure 4, Outline view shows text formatting and displays the actual bullet symbols for Bulleted List slides. Since you aren't as concerned with formatting when you are in Outline view, you may wish to hide the formatting (Figure 5).

Use the Show Formatting button (Figure 6) to toggle the formatting on and off.

■ Tips

✓ When formatting is hidden, you can see more slides in the outline.

✓ Another way to hide and display formatting is with the slash key (/) on the numeric keypad.

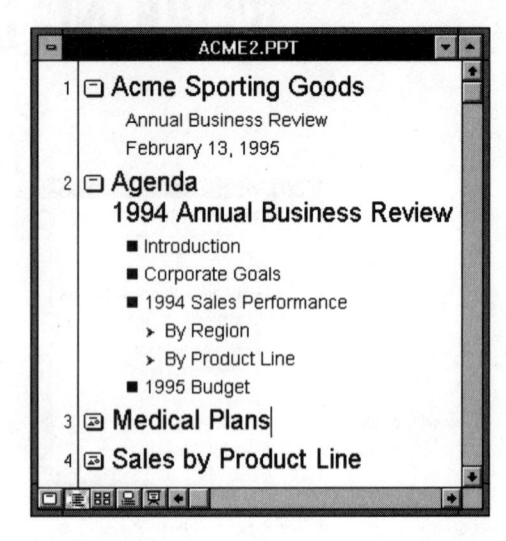

Figure 4. Text formatting is displayed in this outline.

— Show Formatting

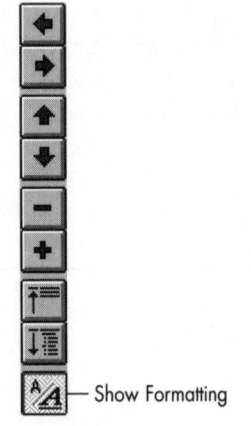

Figure 6. Outlining toolbar

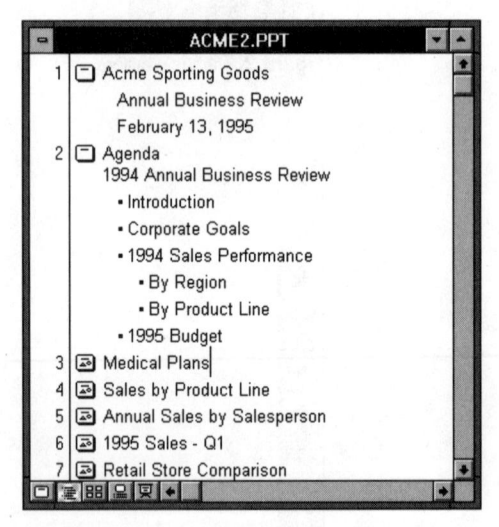

Figure 5. Formatting is hidden in this outline.

Working in Outline View

156

WORKING IN OUTLINE VIEW

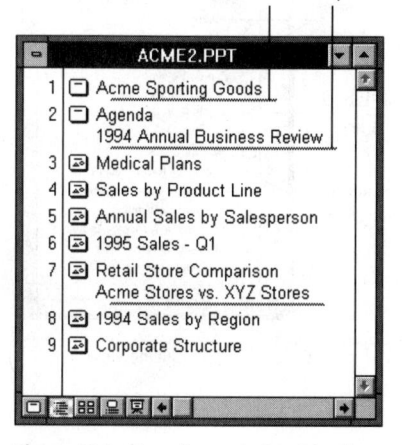

Figure 7. In this outline, only the slide titles are displayed.

These lines indicate the slides are collapsed.

- Collapse Selection
- Expand Selection
- Show Titles
- Show All

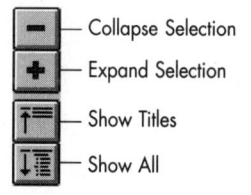

Figure 8. The Outlining toolbar

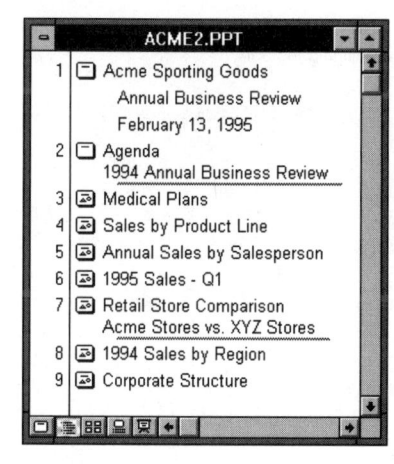

Figure 9. The text in Slide 1 is expanded; the text in Slides 2 and 7 is collapsed.

Displaying Slide Titles Only

When you display just the slide titles in Outline view, you can get a better picture of your presentation's structure (Figure 7). Furthermore, when text is hidden, you can see more slides in the window. When you hide text, you are *collapsing* the outline.

Use the Show Titles button to collapse the outline. Use the Show All button to display all *(expand)* the text again (Figure 8).

PowerPoint also allows you to selectively collapse and expand parts of the outline. This capability is useful if you want to see the text on some slides but not on others. Figure 9 shows an example of a partially collapsed outline.

1. Click anywhere in the slide whose text you want to hide.

   or

   To hide text in consecutive slides, drag across some of the text in each slide.

2. Click the Collapse Selection button (Figure 8).

■ Tips

✓ Use the Expand Selection button to redisplay collapsed text.

✓ Suppose you want to collapse all text in the outline except the text on one slide. First, use the Show Titles button to hide all the main text. Then click the slide whose text you want to show, and use the Expand Selection button.

✓ If you aren't sure whether a particular slide is collapsed or not, look for a gray line underneath its slide title (Figure 7). This line indicates text is hidden.

✓ Here are some keyboard shortcuts:

Alt+Shift+1	Show Titles
Alt+Shift+A	Show All
Alt+Shift+Plus	Expand Selection
Alt+Shift+Minus	Collapse Selection

157

CHAPTER 12

Creating Bulleted Lists

You can create one Bulleted List slide after another in Outline view, without having to issue a command to insert a slide for each one.

1. Click the slide before which you want to insert the new slide. (Slides are inserted after the current slide.)
2. Click the New Slide button at the bottom of the PowerPoint window.
3. Type the slide title and press Enter.
4. Press Tab to insert a bullet (Figure 10).
5. Type the bullet item and press Enter.
6. Continue typing bullet items, following the same rules you do in Slide view:
   - Press Enter to type another bullet.
   - Press Tab to indent the current line.
   - Press Shift+Tab to unindent the current line.
7. To create another slide, press Ctrl+Enter after the last bullet in the list.
8. Repeat steps 3 through 7 for each Bulleted List.

■ Tips

✓ Another way to create a new slide is to click at the beginning of an existing slide title and press Enter. A new slide appears just before the current one.

✓ To create a two-line title (like the one in Slide 2 in Figure 10), press Shift+Enter after the first line.

✓ If you inadvertently type an item at the wrong level, use the Promote or Demote buttons (Figure 11) to change the indent level of the current line.

✓ To move a bullet item up or down in a list, click the item and then click the Move Up or Move Down button (Figure 11) until the item is in position.

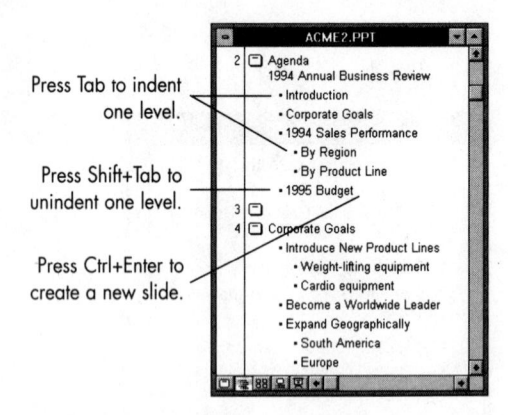

Figure 10. Typing Bulleted Lists in Outline view

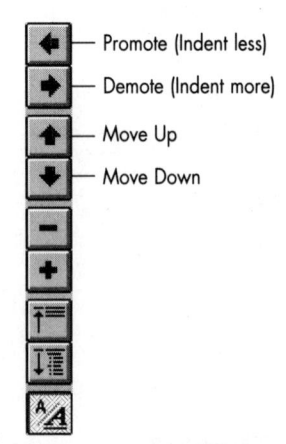

Figure 11. Outlining toolbar

WORKING IN OUTLINE VIEW

— Move Up
— Move Down

— Show Titles

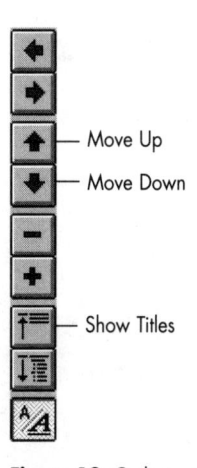

Figure 12. Outlining toolbar

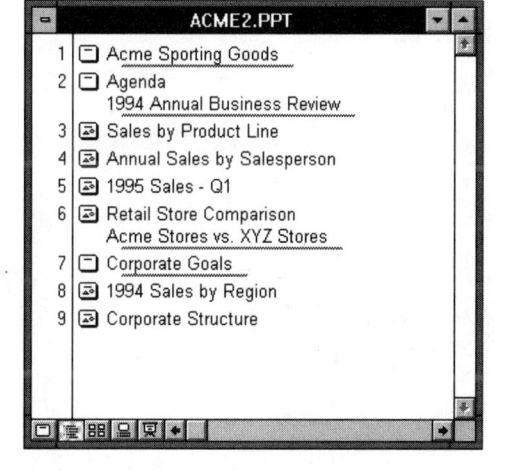

Figure 13. Reordering slides is easier if only the slide titles are displayed.

Drag the slide icon. —

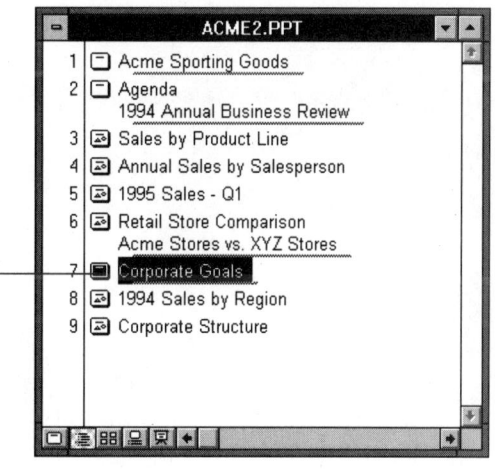

Figure 14. Using the drag-and-drop technique

Reordering the Slides

Because you can see many slides at once in Outline view, it is ideal for repositioning slides in a presentation. PowerPoint offers three ways to move slides: the Move buttons, the drag-and-drop technique, and the cut-and-paste technique.

The Move Buttons

1. Click the Show Titles button (Figure 12) so that only slide titles are displayed (Figure 13).
2. Click anywhere in the title of the slide you want to move.
3. Click either the Move Up or Move Down button (Figure 12) until the slide is in position.

The Drag-and-Drop Technique

1. Click the Show Titles button so that only slide titles are displayed.
2. Drag the slide icon for the slide you want to move (Figure 14). A horizontal line indicates where the slide will be inserted.
3. When the horizontal line is in position, release the mouse button.

CHAPTER 12

Reordering the Slides (cont'd)

The Cut-and-Paste Technique

1. Click the slide icon for the slide you want to move (Figure 15); this selects the entire slide.
2. Click the Cut button (Figure 16).
3. Position the cursor at the slide's new destination (Figure 17). Be sure to place the cursor at the beginning of a slide title.
4. Click the Paste button (Figure 16). The slide is inserted *above* the cursor. Figure 18 shows the results.

■ Tip

✓ The Move Up and Move Down buttons and the drag-and-drop technique are best for short distance moves. The cut-and-paste technique works well when the target location has scrolled off the screen.

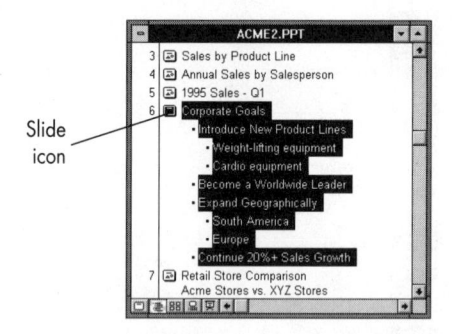

Figure 15. Select a slide before cutting it.

Figure 16. The Standard toolbar

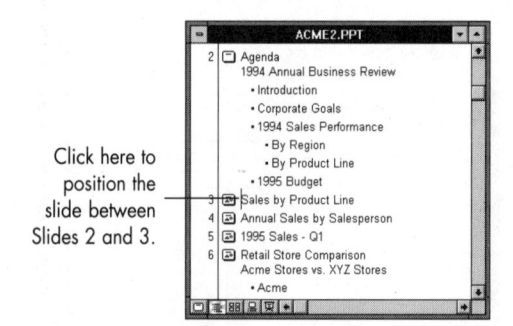

Figure 17. Position the cursor before pasting the slide.

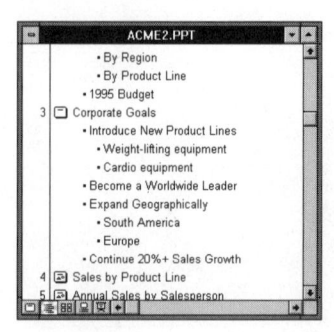

Figure 18. The pasted slide

Working in Outline View

160

WORKING IN OUTLINE VIEW

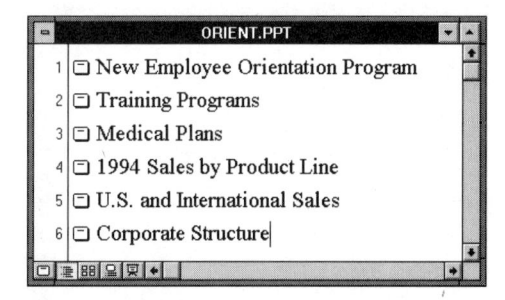

Figure 19. Typing an outline in Outline view

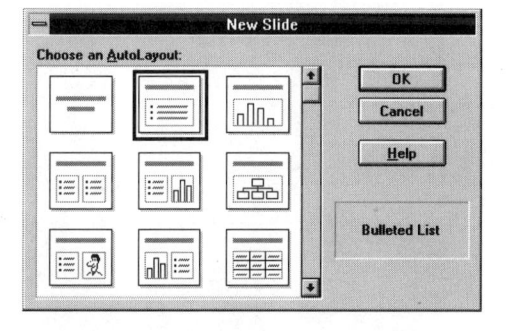

Figure 20. Choosing the Bulleted List layout gives you the flexibility of typing bullet items, if you choose to, while developing your outline.

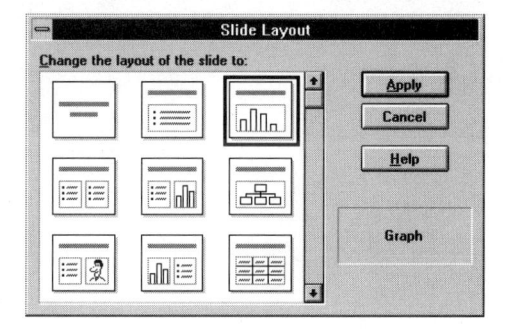

Figure 21. This dialog box lets you choose a different layout for an existing slide.

Outlining a Presentation

When initially creating a presentation, you may want to focus on developing the overall content and structure rather than on creating individual slides. You can do this by typing slide titles in Outline view (Figure 19); you do not choose a slide type at this time.

Once you have typed your outline, you can go back to Slide view and complete each slide.

Here are the specific steps for creating a new outline:

1. Select File/New to create a new presentation.
2. Choose Blank Presentation and click OK.
3. In the New Slide dialog box, choose the Bulleted List layout (Figure 20) and click OK.
4. Click the Outline View button.
5. For each slide, type the title and press Enter.
6. When finished, press Ctrl+Home to move the cursor to the first slide in the presentation.
7. Click the Slide View button.
8. To change the layout for a particular slide, go to that slide and click the Layout button at the bottom of the PowerPoint window. Choose the appropriate AutoLayout for the current slide (Figure 21) and click OK.
9. Complete the slide—for example, create a graph, table, or org chart.
10. Go to the next slide and repeat steps 8 and 9.

■ Tip

✓ As you are creating your outline, you may also want to type your bulleted lists.

See Creating Bulleted Lists on page 158.

161

CHAPTER 12

Importing an Outline

If you have created an outline in your word processor (Figure 23), you can import it into an existing PowerPoint presentation, or simply open it to create a new presentation.

If you intend to import an outline into PowerPoint, you need to follow a few simple rules when typing the outline in your word processor:

- Type each slide title in a separate paragraph (that is, press Enter after each title).
- For a two-line slide title, press Shift+Enter between lines.
- Press Tab to indent bullet items (but don't insert any bullet symbols).

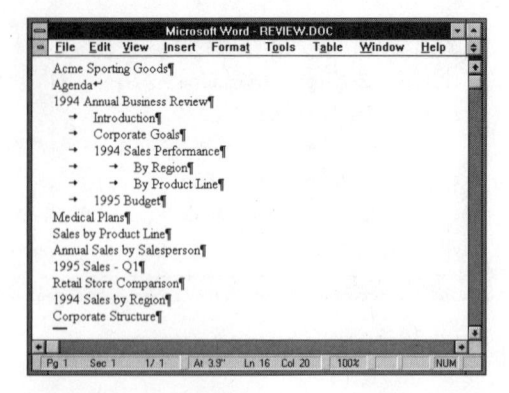

Figure 23. An outline created in Word for Windows

Inserting an Outline into an Existing Presentation

1. Select Insert/Slides from Outline. The Insert Outline dialog box appears (Figure 24).
2. Navigate to the drive and directory in which your outline is stored.
3. In the File Name list, click the name of the outline file to import.
4. Click OK.

Creating a Presentation by Opening an Outline

1. Select File/Open.
2. In the List Files of Type field, choose Outlines (Figure 25).
3. Navigate to the drive and directory in which your outline is stored.
4. In the File Name list, click the name of the outline file to import.
5. Click OK.

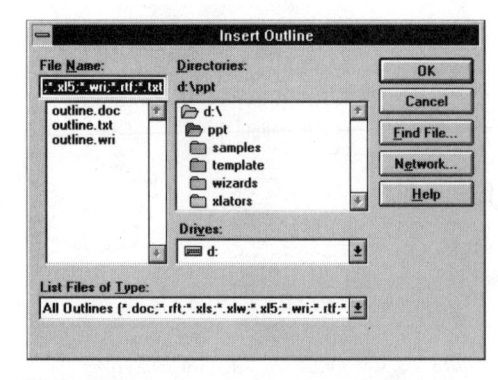

Figure 24. Inserting an outline into an existing presentation

■ Tip

✓ PowerPoint can import outlines from Word for Windows, Word for Macintosh, WordPerfect, Excel, and Windows Write. It can also import .TXT and .RFT files.

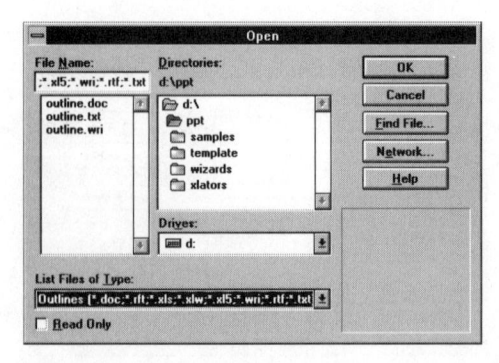

Figure 25. By opening an outline file, you can create a presentation from that outline.

WORKING IN OUTLINE VIEW

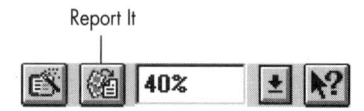

Figure 26. The Standard toolbar

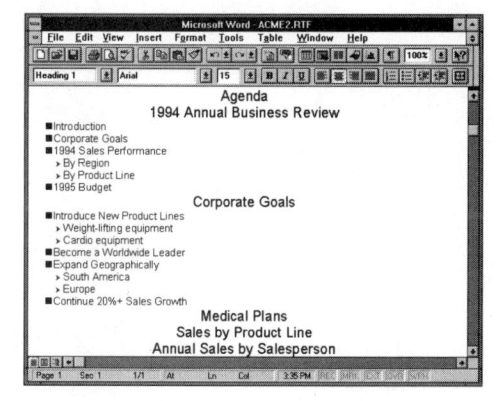

Figure 27. After you click the Report It button, the outline appears in Word 6.

Figure 28. The formatted outline in Word 6

Editing an Outline in Word 6

If you have Word 6, you can easily bring in a presentation's outline to edit, format, and print.

1. Click the Report It button (Figure 26). The outline appears in Word 6 (Figure 27).
2. Edit the outline as needed (Figure 28), and print it if you like.
3. Save your changes.
4. Select File/Exit to return to PowerPoint.

■ Tips

✓ When the outline is brought into Word, each paragraph is assigned an appropriate style: Heading 1 (for slide titles), Heading 2 (for first-level bullets), Heading 3 (for second-level bullets), and so forth. By editing the styles, you can quickly reformat the entire outline.

✓ You can use Outline view in Word 6 to reorganize, collapse, and expand the outline.

✓ Unless you specify otherwise, Word saves the outline as an .RTF (Rich Text Format) file. To save it as a Word .DOC file, use File/Save As.

✓ The changes you make to the outline in Word do not affect your PowerPoint presentation.

163

WORKING IN SLIDE SORTER VIEW 13

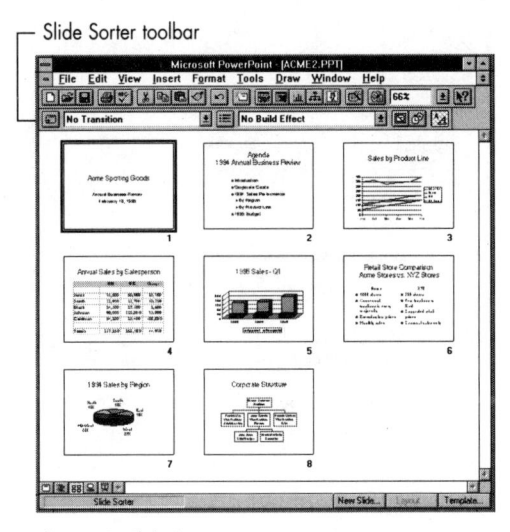

Figure 1. Slide Sorter view

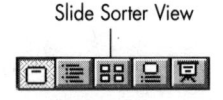

Figure 2. The View buttons

Figure 3. Slide formatting is turned off.

Introducing Slide Sorter View

Slide Sorter view shows miniatures of each slide in your presentation (Figure 1). It's similar to Outline view in that you see many slides at once, but in Slide Sorter view you have the advantage of displaying all objects on the slides (text, graphs, tables, and so forth).

Slide Sorter view lets you observe the flow of your presentation, and change the order of your slides if necessary. You can easily copy and delete slides as well. This view is useful for copying and moving slides to other presentations. And you will see in Chapter 14 how to use Slide Sorter view to add transitions to your slide shows.

See Adding a Transition Effect to a Slide on page 178.

Switch to Slide Sorter view by clicking the Slide Sorter View button (Figure 2) or by selecting the View/Slide Sorter command. Note that Slide Sorter view has its own toolbar (pointed out in Figure 1).

■ Tips

- ✓ Use Slide Sorter view when making global changes to your presentation (applying a template, changing the color scheme, etc.) so that you can instantly see the effect on all the slides.

  See Chapter 11, starting on page 143, for information on making global changes.

- ✓ Double-click a slide to display it in Slide view.

- ✓ Slide Sorter view runs a little faster when you don't display the slide formatting and objects (Figure 3). The Show Formatting button toggles formatting on and off.

Working in Slide Sorter View

165

CHAPTER 13

Zooming In and Out

You can control the number of slides you see in Slide Sorter view, as well as the level of detail you see on each slide, by zooming in and out. To see more slides, zoom out (Figure 4). To see more detail, zoom in (Figure 5).

There are three ways to zoom in and out:

- Click the arrow in the Zoom Control field (Figure 6) to display a list of zoom percentages. Then click the desired number.

    or

- Click the box in the Zoom Control field, type a number between 10 and 400, and press Enter.

    or

- Select View/Zoom and choose the desired zoom percentage in the Zoom dialog box (Figure 7).

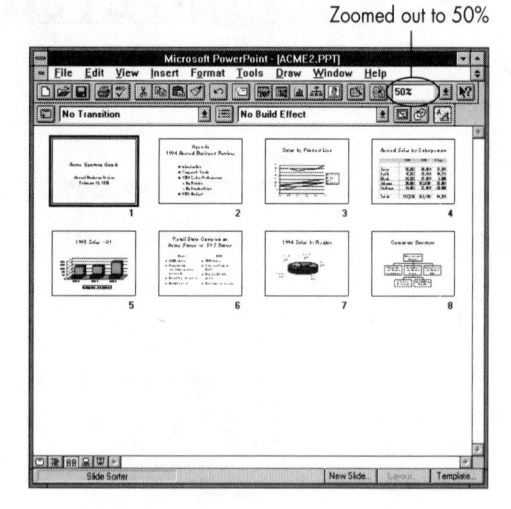

Figure 4. When you zoom out to 50%, you can see more slides at once.

Zoom Control
Click here to display a list of zoom percentages.

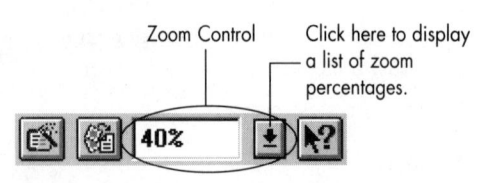

Figure 6. The Standard toolbar

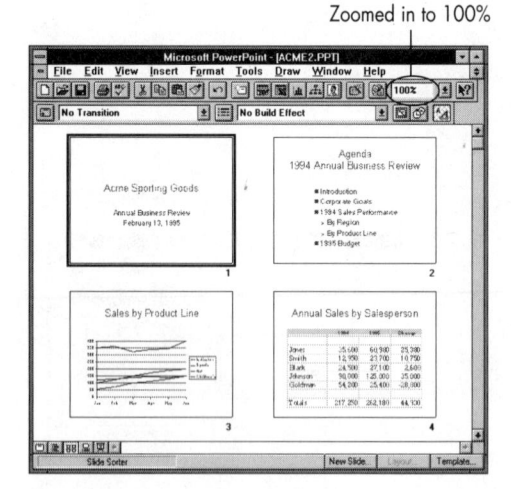

Figure 5. When you zoom in to 100%, you can see more detail on the slides.

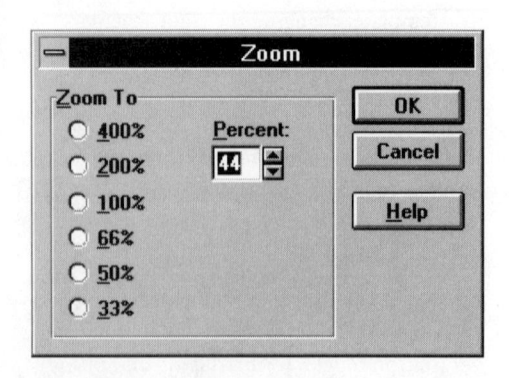

Figure 7. Choose a zoom percentage, or enter any value between 10 and 400 in the Percent field.

Working in Slide Sorter View

WORKING IN SLIDE SORTER VIEW

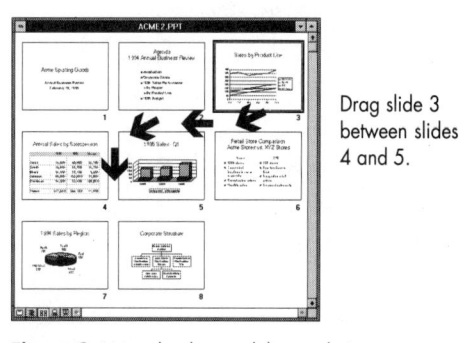

Figure 8. Using the drag-and-drop technique to move a slide

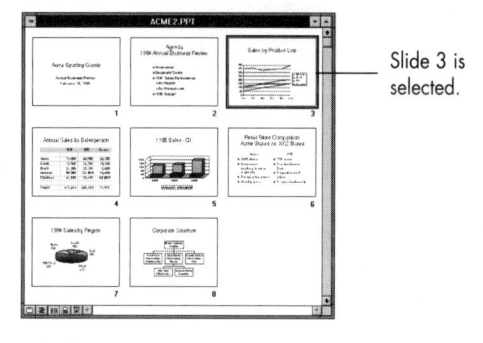

Drag slide 3 between slides 4 and 5.

Figure 9. Select a slide before cutting it.

Slide 3 is selected.

Figure 10. The Standard toolbar

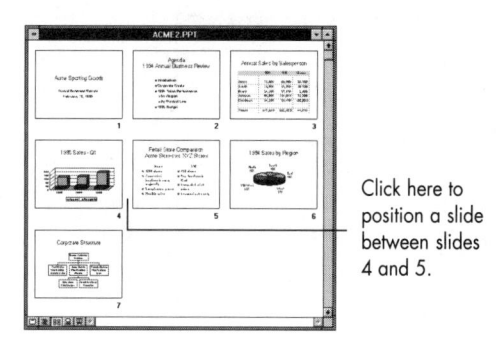

Cut   Paste

Figure 11. Position the cursor before pasting the slide.

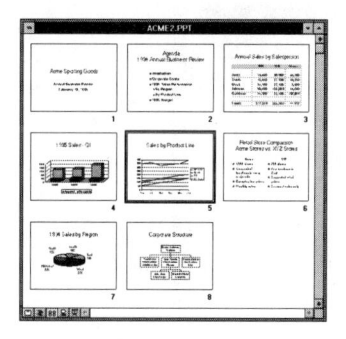

Click here to position a slide between slides 4 and 5.

Figure 12. The pasted slide

Reordering the Slides

Because you can see many slides at once in Slide Sorter view, it is ideal for reordering slides in the presentation. PowerPoint offers two ways to move slides in this view.

The Drag-and-Drop Technique

1. Zoom out until you can see the slide you want to move as well as the target location.
2. Drag the slide you want to move (Figure 8). When the pointer is between slides, a vertical line indicates where the slide will be inserted.
3. When the vertical line is in position, release the mouse button.

The Cut-and-Paste Technique

1. Click the slide you want to move (Figure 9). When a slide is selected, it is surrounded by a thick border.
2. Click the Cut button (Figure 10).
3. Click between two slides where you want to move the selected slide (Figure 11). A tall cursor (the height of a slide) indicates where the slide will be inserted.
4. Click the Paste button (Figure 10) to insert the slide (Figure 12).

■ **Tip**

✓ When you reorder, all the slides in the presentation are renumbered.

167

CHAPTER 13

Copying Slides

Sometimes you may want to create a slide that is similar to an existing one. Rather than creating the new slide from scratch, you can create a copy of the existing slide, and then make any necessary revisions.

There are three ways to copy slides.

The Drag-and-Drop Technique

1. Zoom out until you can see the slide you want to copy as well as the target location.
2. Hold down Ctrl and drag the slide you want to copy (Figure 13). When the pointer is between slides, a vertical line indicates where the copy will be inserted.
3. When the vertical line is in position, release the mouse button.

The Duplicate Technique

1. Select the slide to be copied.
2. Select Edit/Duplicate or press Ctrl+D. A copy appears to the right of the original.
3. Drag the copy into place, if necessary.

The Copy-and-Paste Technique

1. Click the slide to be copied (Figure 14).
2. Click the Copy button (Figure 15).
3. Click where you want to insert the copy (Figure 16). A tall cursor indicates where the slide will be inserted.
4. Click the Paste button (Figure 15) to insert a copy of the slide (Figure 17).

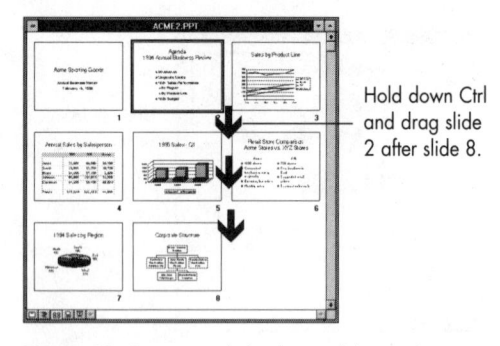

Figure 13. Copying with the drag-and-drop technique

Hold down Ctrl and drag slide 2 after slide 8.

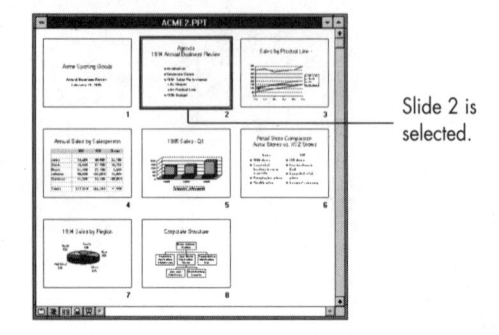

Figure 14. Select a slide before copying it.

Slide 2 is selected.

Figure 15. The Standard toolbar

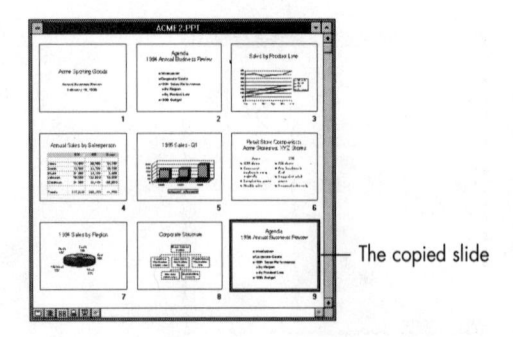

Copy
Paste

Figure 17. After pasting the copied slide

The copied slide

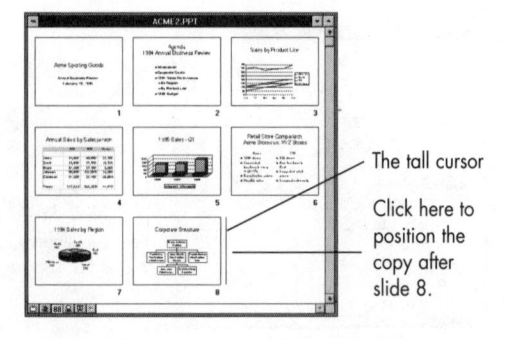

Figure 16. Position the cursor before pasting the slide.

The tall cursor

Click here to position the copy after slide 8.

Working in Slide Sorter View

WORKING IN SLIDE SORTER VIEW

This ensures that both presentations have the same color scheme and Slide Master.

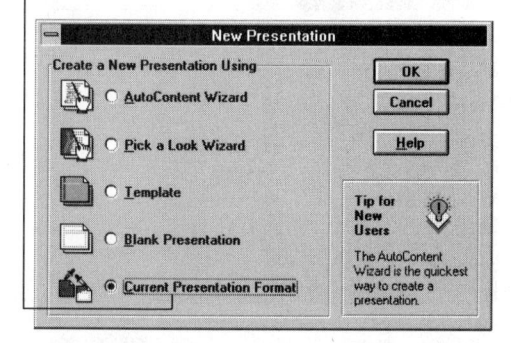

Figure 18. Creating a new presentation that has the same format as the current one

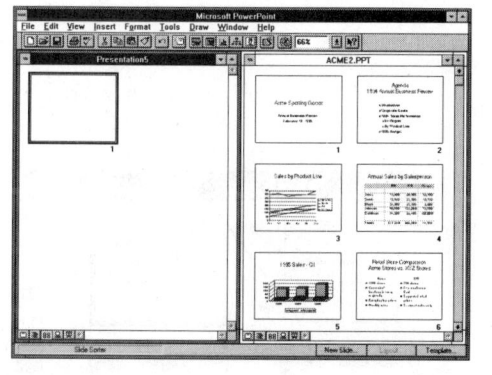

Figure 19. The new presentation is in the left window; the original presentation is in the right window

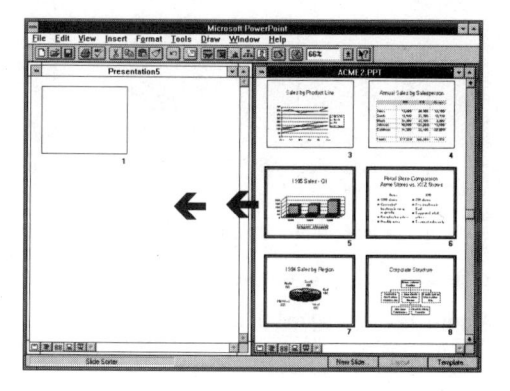

Figure 20. Select all the slides to be moved. Drag one selected slide to the other presentation, and all the others will follow.

Moving Slides Between Presentations

If a presentation gets so large that it becomes unwieldy, you may want to divide it into two or more different files. One way to do this is to move some of the slides into a new presentation. (If you want to move slides into an existing presentation, skip steps 2 through 4 below.)

1. Open the presentation that needs to be divided, and switch to Slide Sorter view.
2. Select File/New.
3. Choose Current Presentation Format (Figure 18) and click OK.
4. In the New Slide dialog box, click OK.
5. Select Window/Arrange All to display the two presentations side by side (Figure 19).
6. Hold down Shift as you click each slide to be moved. A thick border appears around each selected slide.
7. Drag one of the slides you want to move to the other presentation window (Figure 20).
8. Release the mouse button. All selected slides are moved.

■ **Tip**

✓ Another way to move slides between presentations is with the cut-and-paste technique.

See Reordering the Slides on page 167.

169

CHAPTER 13

Copying Slides Between Presentations

Sometimes while working on a presentation you'll realize there are slides in another presentation that you can use in your current project. By having both presentations open at the same time (Figure 21), you can copy slides from one to the other.

1. Open both presentations, and switch to Slide Sorter view in each one.
2. Select Window/Arrange All to display the two presentations side by side.
3. Click the slide to be copied.

   or

   To copy more than one slide, hold down Shift as you click each one. A thick border appears around each selected slide (Figure 22).
4. Hold down Ctrl and drag one of the slides to the other presentation window. When the pointer is between slides, a vertical line indicates where the copies will be inserted.
5. When the vertical line is in position, release the mouse button.

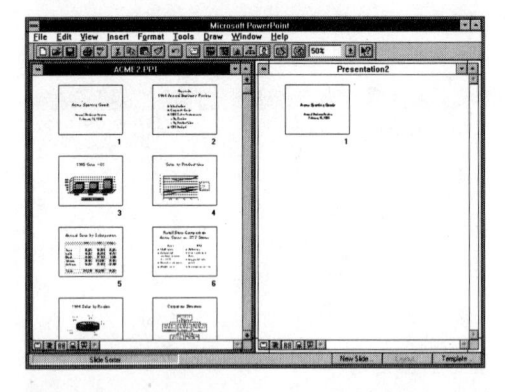

Figure 21. Side-by-side windows make it easy to copy slides between presentations.

Figure 22. Selecting multiple slides

WORKING IN SLIDE SORTER VIEW

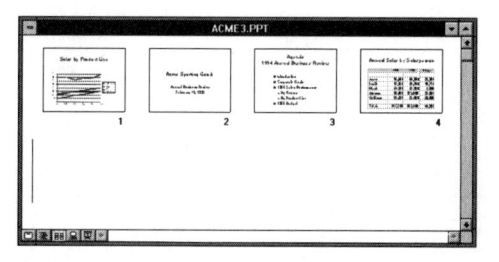

Figure 23. The target presentation currently contains four slides.

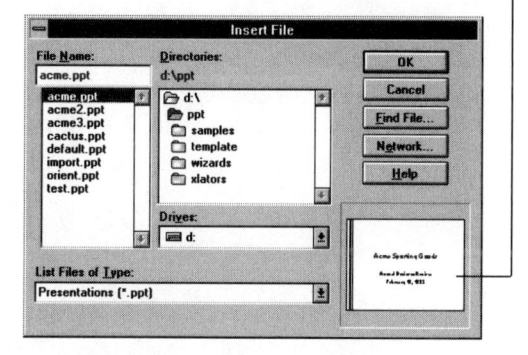

Figure 24. Selecting a presentation file to insert

A preview of the first slide in the selected presentation

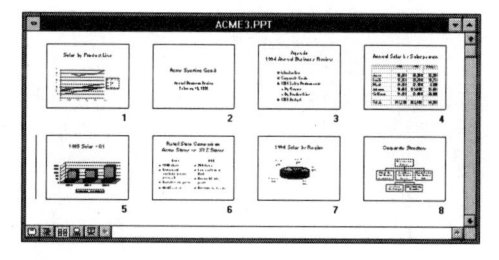

Figure 25. After inserting slides from another file, this presentation contains eight slides.

Copying Slides Between Presentations (cont'd)

PowerPoint offers an easy way to consolidate presentations when you want to copy all the slides from one presentation into another. This is useful when you need to combine the slides created by several individuals, into a single presentation.

1. Open the presentation into which you want to copy the slides (Figure 23).
2. In Slide Sorter view, click where you want the slides to be inserted. A vertical line appears.
2. Select Insert/Slides from File. The Insert File dialog box appears (Figure 24).
3. In the File Name list, select the presentation file containing the slides you want to insert.
4. Click OK.

All the slides from the selected presentation file are inserted into the target presentation (Figure 25).

■ Tips

✓ The copied slides adopt the Slide Master and color scheme of the target presentation.

✓ The Insert/Slides from File command lets you copy slides from other programs, such as Harvard Graphics and Freelance.

Working in Slide Sorter View

171

CHAPTER 13

Deleting Slides

You can delete slides in any view, but doing it in Slide Sorter offers several advantages. First, you see miniatures of the slides, so you can be sure you are selecting the right ones for deletion. Second, you can delete more than one slide at a time.

1. Click the slide you want to delete.

   or

   To select multiple slides, hold down Shift as you click each one (Figure 26).

2. Press Delete or select Edit/Delete Slide.

■ Tip

✓ If you accidentally delete slides, immediately select Edit/Undo or use the Undo button (Figure 27).

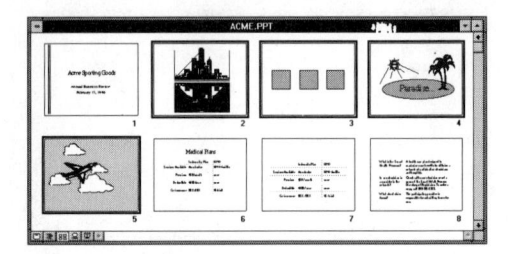

Figure 26. Four slides are selected for deletion.

Figure 27. The Standard toolbar

172

PRODUCING A SLIDE SHOW   14

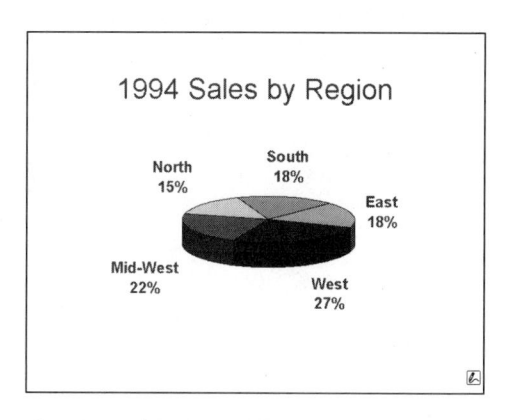

Figure 1. A slide presented full screen in a slide show

About Slide Shows

PowerPoint's *slide show* feature displays one slide at a time, full screen (Figure 1). Since your computer becomes the equivalent of a slide projector, you can see how your presentation will look to your audience. In this full-screen view, you can concentrate on individual slides, and perhaps spot mistakes you may have missed in the other views. However, you cannot edit slides during a slide show.

You can present your slide show directly on your monitor with one or two people looking over your shoulder; or, for a larger audience, you will want to project the show onto a big screen. Projection requires special equipment; you will need either an LCD panel and an overhead projector, or an RGB projector. Projecting a slide show in this manner saves you the time and expense of producing 35mm slides and allows you to make last-minute changes.

To spice up your slide show, you may want to add special *transition effects* for drawing slides on the screen. Blinds, checkerboards, fade, and dissolve are a few of these effects.

Because the Slide Sorter toolbar (Figure 2) contains options for slide shows, you will usually want to be in Slide Sorter view when working on your slide show.

See Chapter 13, starting on page 165, for more information on Slide Sorter view.

Figure 2. The Slide Sorter toolbar

CHAPTER 14

Organizing a Slide Show

During a slide show, slides are displayed in the order they appear in your presentation. Therefore, before presenting your slide show, you should give some thought to the order of your slides, and rearrange them if necessary.

To change the slide order, move the slides in Outline view (Figure 3) or Slide Sorter view (Figure 4).

See Reordering the Slides on pages 159 and 167.

To move a slide in the outline, drag the slide icon.

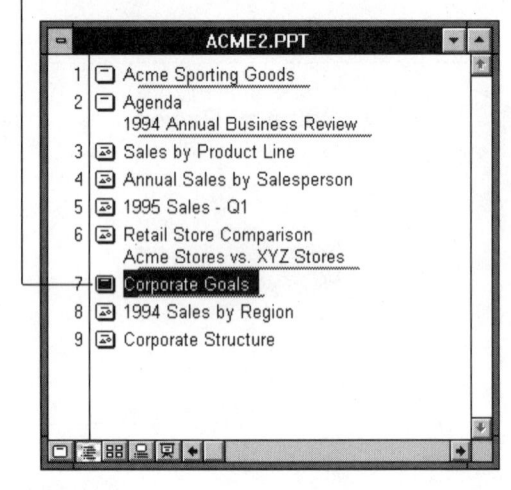

Figure 3. Using the drag-and-drop technique to move a slide in Outline view

Drag the slide to a new location.

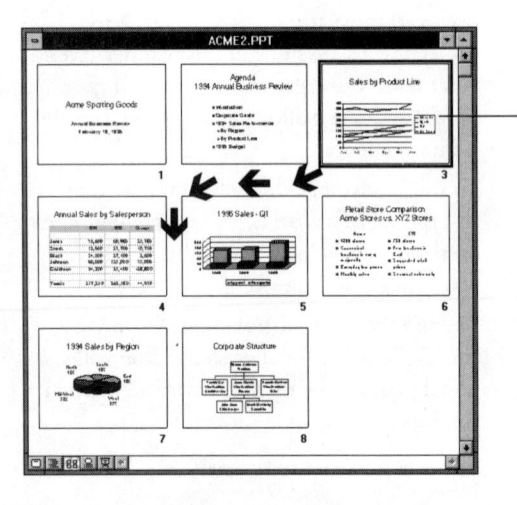

Figure 4. Using the drag-and-drop technique to move a slide in Slide Sorter view

PRODUCING A SLIDE SHOW

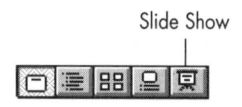

Figure 5. The view buttons

(Slide Show label points to the view buttons)

The first slide number to display goes here.

The last slide number goes here.

Figure 6. Entering a range of slides to display in a slide show

Navigating a Slide Show	
Next Slide	Left mouse button
	Right Arrow
	Down Arrow
	Page Down
	Spacebar
	Enter
Previous Slide	Right mouse button
	Left Arrow
	Up Arrow
	Page Up
	Backspace
First Slide	Home
Last Slide	End

Displaying a Slide Show

To view the current presentation in a slide show, do the following:

1. In any view, press Ctrl+Home to go to the first slide in the presentation.
2. Click the Slide Show button (Figure 5).
3. Press the left mouse button to view the next slide.
4. Keep pressing the left mouse button until you have viewed all the slides.

To view a range of slides, follow these steps:

1. Select View/Slide Show.
2. In the Slide Show dialog box (Figure 6), click in the From field, enter the first slide number you want to view, press Tab, and then enter the last number in the To field.
3. Click Show.
4. Press the left mouse button to view the next slide.
5. Keep pressing the left mouse button until you have viewed all the slides.

■ Tips

✓ To cancel the slide show while you're viewing it, press Esc.

✓ For a list of ways to navigate a slide show, see the boxed table to the left.

✓ To preview the current slide, just click the Slide Show button. When you're ready, press Esc to cancel the show.

175

CHAPTER 14

Annotating a Slide

During a slide show, you may want to mark up a slide to emphasize an important point. Using your mouse like a pencil, you can draw circles, lines, arrows, and so forth (Figure 7). These annotations are temporary, and as soon as you move on to the next slide in the show, your freehand drawings disappear.

1. Click the Freehand Annotation icon in the lower-right corner of the screen (Figure 8). Note that you don't see this icon until you start moving the mouse.
2. Position the pencil pointer where you want to begin drawing.
3. To draw, hold down the left or right mouse button and drag.
4. To turn off Annotation mode, click the Pointer icon (Figure 9) or press Esc.

■ Tips

✓ To erase the annotations on the slide, press E.

✓ To draw straight lines, hold down Shift as you drag.

✓ If you forget to turn off Annotation mode (step 4 above), you won't be able to use the mouse buttons to continue the slide show. Keyboard navigation keys such as the arrow keys, however, will operate with Annotation mode on or off.

Figure 7. The arrow and circle are annotations that were drawn during a slide show.

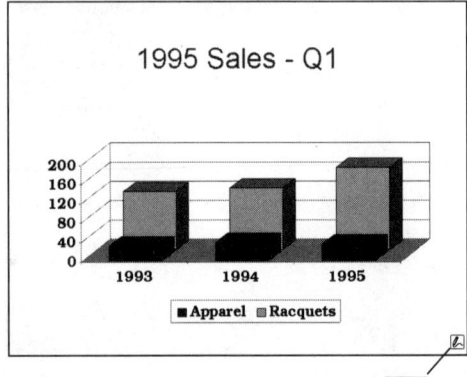

Figure 8. The Freehand Annotation icon

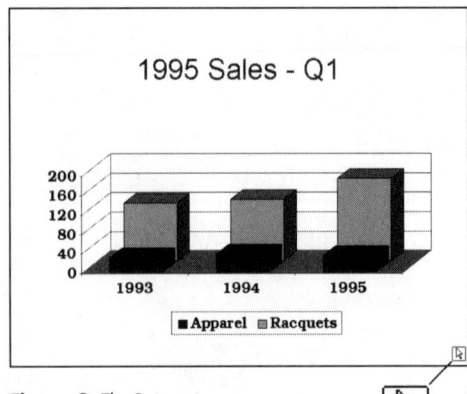

Figure 9. The Pointer icon

PRODUCING A SLIDE SHOW

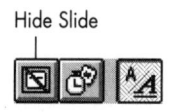

Figure 10. The Slide Sorter toolbar

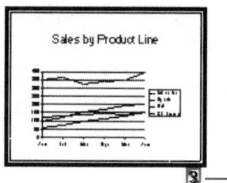

Figure 11. Slide 3 is hidden.

The slash across the slide number indicates the slide is hidden.

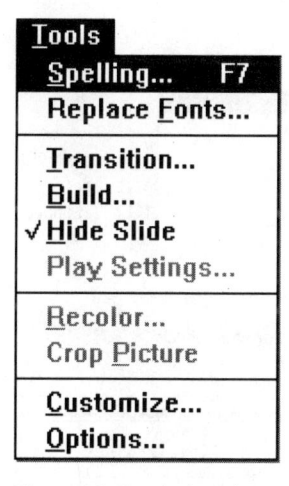

Figure 12. The check mark next to Hide Slide indicates the current slide is hidden.

Hiding a Slide

If you have a slide that you want to keep in your presentation but omit from a slide show, you can *hide* it. Hidden slides still appear in all views in your presentation, but they are skipped during a slide show.

1. In Slide Sorter view, click the slide you want to hide.

    or

    To select more than one slide, hold down Shift as you click each slide.

2. Click the Hide Slide button (Figure 10).

The slide number of a hidden slide has a slash through it (Figure 11).

■ Tips

✓ To redisplay a hidden slide, select the slide, and click the Hide Slide button again.

✓ You can hide slides in any view using the Tools/Hide Slide command. However, Outline and Slide view don't have an immediate way to tell that a slide is hidden. A check mark next to Hide Slide in the Tools menu (Figure 12) indicates the current slide is hidden.

177

CHAPTER 14

Adding a Transition Effect to a Slide

Transition effects control how slides are drawn on the screen during a slide show. Choosing appropriate effects not only holds your audience's attention, but it also adds a professional touch.

1. Switch to Slide Sorter view (Figure 13).
2. Click the slide for which you want to add a transition effect (Figure 14).

   or

   To add the same transition effect to multiple slides, hold down Shift as you click each slide.
3. In the Slide Sorter toolbar, click the Transition Effects field (Figure 14) to display the list of effects (Figure 15).
4. Click the desired transition effect.

Immediately after you choose an effect, the first selected slide is drawn with that effect, to give you an idea of what it looks like.

5. Repeat the above steps until all your slides have transition effects..
6. To see the effects during a slide show, press Ctrl+Home and then click the Slide Show button (Figure 13).

■ Tips

✓ To preview the effect chosen for a slide, click the transition icon beneath the slide in Slide Sorter view (Figure 16). When the slide is selected, the name of the effect appears in the Transition Effects field in the Slide Sorter toolbar.

✓ For consistency, don't use too many different transition effects in one show. Stick with a conservative transition effect for most slides, and, if you like, emphasize certain slides with special effects (such as a fade).

See the next page for another way to specify transition effects.

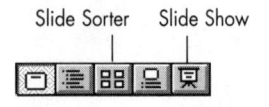

Figure 13. The view buttons

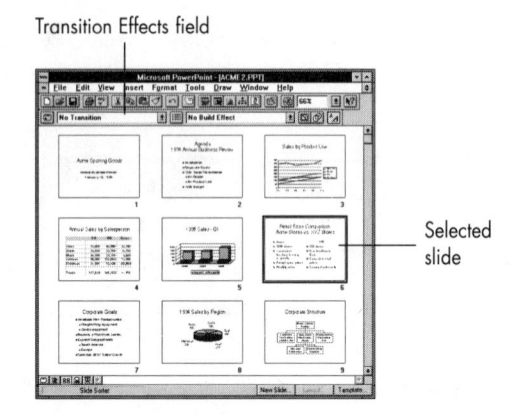

Figure 14. In Slide Sorter view, select the slide(s) and then choose a transition effect.

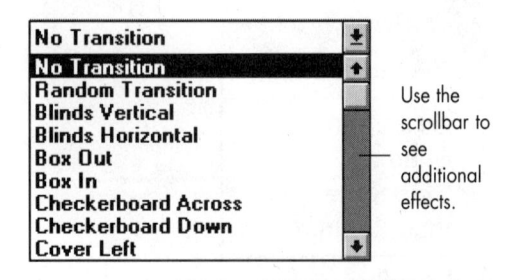

Figure 15. The list of transition effects

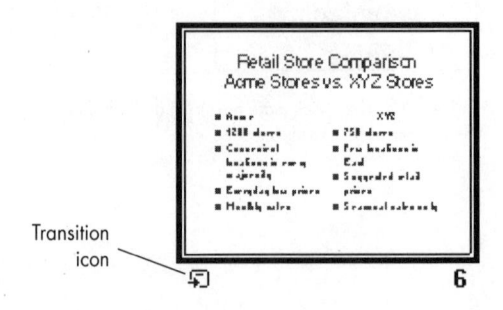

Figure 16. To preview the effect, click the transition icon.

Producing a Slide Show

178

PRODUCING A SLIDE SHOW

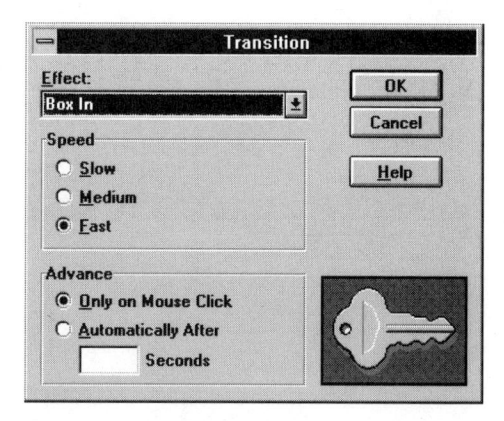

Figure 17. The Transition dialog box is another way to specify a transition effect.

Figure 18. The Slide Sorter toolbar

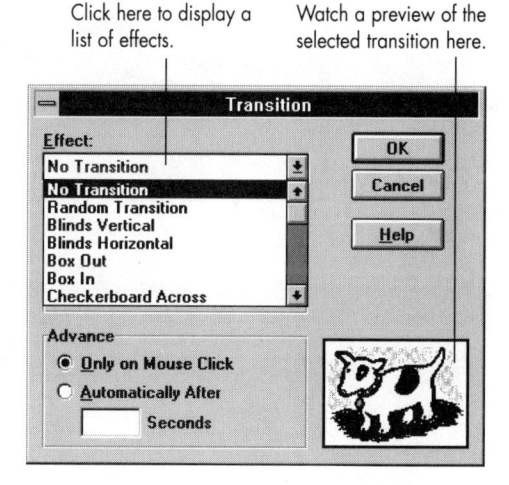

Figure 19. Choosing and previewing a transition

Figure 20. The view buttons

Adding a Transition Effect to a Slide (cont'd)

Another way to choose a transition effect is in the Transition dialog box (Figure 17). This way offers two advantages: You can do it from any view (not just Slide Sorter), and you can designate a speed at which the effect is drawn on the screen.

1. In any view, select the slides to which you want to add a transition effect.
2. Select Tools/Transition, or in Slide Sorter view, click the Transition button (Figure 18).
3. Click the Effect field to display a list of effects (Figure 19).
4. Click the desired transition effect. The preview box shows an example of how the effect looks.
5. You can click the preview box to see the effect again. If you don't like it, pick another one.
6. Choose a speed: Slow, Medium, or Fast.
7. Click OK.
8. Repeat the above steps until you have specified transition effects for all slides.
9. To see the effects during a slide show, press Ctrl+Home and then click the Slide Show button (Figure 20).

■ Tips

✓ To choose a single transition effect for the entire presentation, press Ctrl+A to select all slides. Then choose a transition.

✓ It's nice to be able to control the rate at which slides are drawn on the screen during a slide show because some effects draw more slowly than others. Furthermore, the speed of your computer influences the pace as well, so you may want to slow down or accelerate the transitions.

179

CHAPTER 14

Creating a Self-Running Slide Show

If you want to sit back and watch your slide show without having to click the mouse or press keys, you can tell PowerPoint to automatically advance each slide after a certain number of seconds. Self-running slide shows are useful during trade shows, for instance.

1. In Slide Sorter view, press Ctrl+A to select all slides.
2. Click the Transition button (Figure 21). The Transition dialog box appears (Figure 22).
3. In the Automatically After ___ Seconds field, enter the number of seconds you want the slide to remain on screen before the next is displayed.
4. Click OK. The time is indicated beneath each slide (Figure 23).
5. If you want a particular slide to remain on screen for a longer or shorter time, select it and then repeat steps 2 through 4.
6. Select View/Slide Show.
7. In the Slide Show dialog box (Figure 24), choose Use Slide Timings and click Show.

■ Tips

✓ Although you can enter only seconds in the Automatically After ___ Seconds field, you can enter a value greater than 60 seconds to indicate minutes.

✓ You can always advance a slide before the specified time has passed, by clicking the left mouse button, pressing the right arrow key, etc.

✓ To end a self-running slide show, press Esc.

✓ Choose the Manual Advance option in the Slide Show dialog box to return to the manual method of advancing slides.

Transition

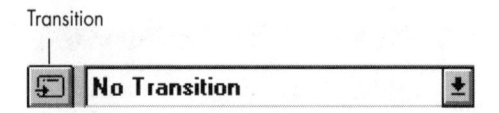

Figure 21. The Slide Sorter toolbar

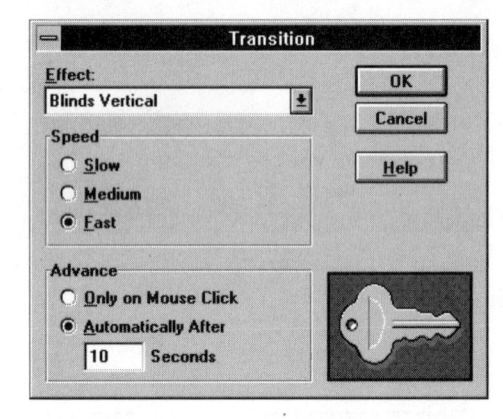

Figure 22. With these transition settings, slides will automatically advance every 10 seconds.

Slide time

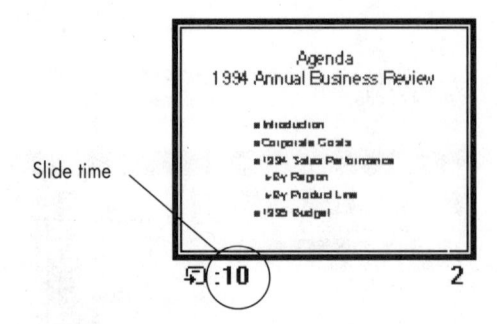

Figure 23. In Slide Sorter view, the slide time is displayed beneath each slide.

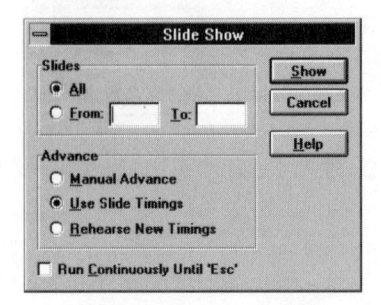

Figure 24. Starting a self-running slide show

Producing a Slide Show

PRODUCING A SLIDE SHOW

Rehearse Timings

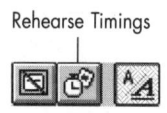

Figure 25. The last several buttons on the Slide Sorter toolbar

0:00:15

Figure 26. The counter that appears in the lower-left corner of the screen during a slide show rehearsal functions as a "stop watch."

Records slide timings and creates a self-running slide show

Microsoft PowerPoint

? The total time for the slide show was 8:27 minutes. Record new slide timings to see them in Slide Sorter view?

Yes   No

Figure 27. This dialog box lets you know the total time of your slide show rehearsal.

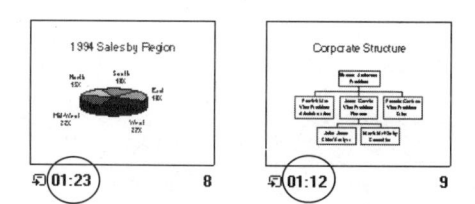

1994 Sales by Region   Corporate Structure

🔊 01:23   8   🔊 01:12   9

Figure 28. After the rehearsal, slide times are recorded beneath each slide in Slide Sorter view.

Rehearsing the Slide Show

To make sure your slide show is timed properly, you can have PowerPoint time your show as you rehearse your presentation.

1. In Slide Sorter view, click the Rehearse Timings button (Figure 25). The first slide in the show appears full screen, and a digital counter displays in the lower-left corner (Figure 26).
2. Either aloud or in your head, rehearse what you want to say when the slide is displayed.
3. When you are ready to advance to the next slide, click the left mouse button. The next slide appears and the counter resets to 0:00:00.
4. Repeat steps 2 and 3 for each slide.
5. When you are finished, PowerPoint displays the total time for the slide show (Figure 27) and asks if you want the slide times to be displayed in Slide Sorter view.
6. Select Yes to record the slide times or No if you don't want to record them. If you record the times, they display underneath each slide (Figure 28).

After recording the slide times, you have essentially created a self-running slide show. If you choose Use Slide Timings in the Slide Show dialog box when you run the show, each slide is automatically advanced after the indicated time has elapsed.

See Creating a Self-Running Slide Show on the previous page.

■ **Tip**

✓ On the average, two to three minutes per slide is a good pace and will keep the audience's attention. Slides that have more than three minutes worth of material can be broken up into several slides.

181

CHAPTER 14

Creating a Build for a Bullet Slide

During a slide show, a *build* reveals bullet items progressively in a Bulleted List slide. By using a build, you can display each successive bullet item when you are ready to discuss it. Optionally, you can dim previous items so the current item stands out. Figures 29 through 31 show a build in progress.

1. In Slide Sorter view, select the Bulleted List slide for which you want to create a build.
2. Click the Build button (Figure 32), or select Tools/Build.
3. In the Build dialog box (Figure 33), turn on the Build Body Text check box.
4. If you would like previous text to dim when new text appears, turn on the Dim Previous Points check box. Use the drop-down list to choose a color for dimmed text (Figure 34).
5. Click the arrow in the Effect field to display a list (Figure 35), and choose an effect for bullet items.
6. Click OK.
7. Click the Slide Show button (Figure 36). Only the slide title is displayed. To build successive bullet items, click the left mouse button.

■ Tips

✓ The best transitions for builds are Fly From Left, Fly From Right, Fly From Bottom, and Wipe Right.

✓ Another way to create or modify a build is with the Build Effects field (Figure 32). In this field, you can only choose an effect; you can't specify that you want to dim previous points.

✓ To remove a build from a Bulleted List slide, choose No Build Effect in the Build Effects field.

Agenda
1994 Annual Business Review

■ Introduction

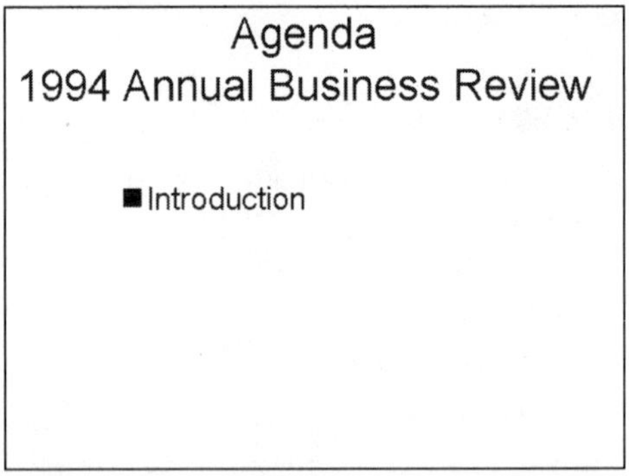

Figure 29. After the first mouse click, the first bullet item is displayed.

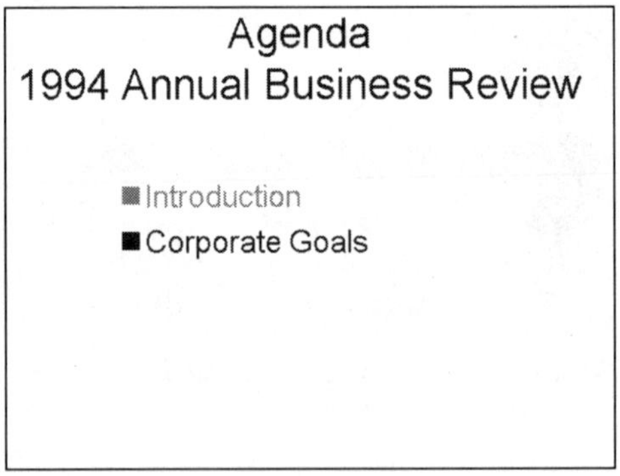

Agenda
1994 Annual Business Review

■ Introduction
■ Corporate Goals

Figure 30. After the next mouse click, the first item is dimmed and the next item is displayed.

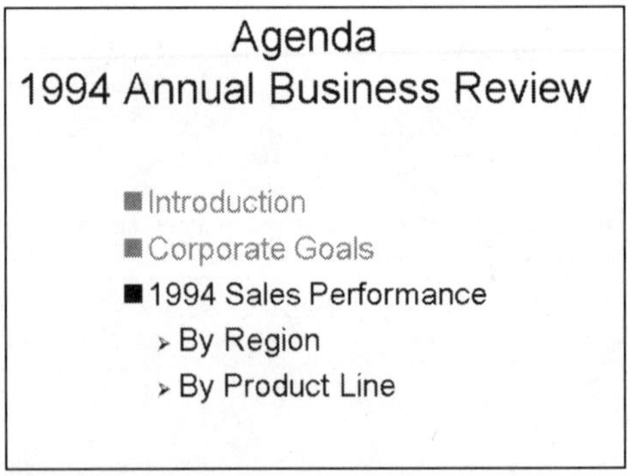

Agenda
1994 Annual Business Review

■ Introduction
■ Corporate Goals
■ 1994 Sales Performance
  ➢ By Region
  ➢ By Product Line

Figure 31. After the next mouse click, the previous two items are dimmed and the next set of bullets is displayed.

PRODUCING A SLIDE SHOW

Figure 32. The Slide Sorter toolbar

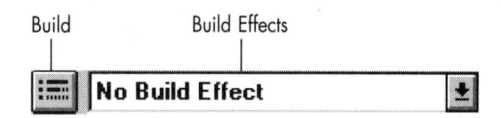

Creating a Build for a Bullet Slide (cont'd)

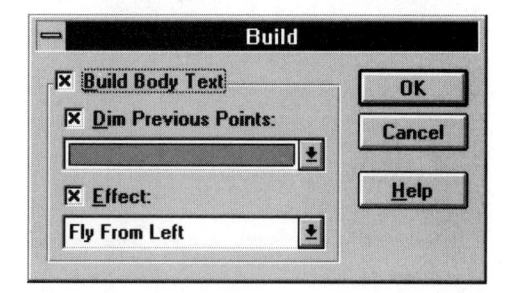

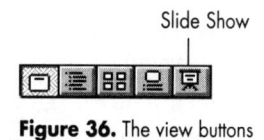

Figure 33. Creating a build

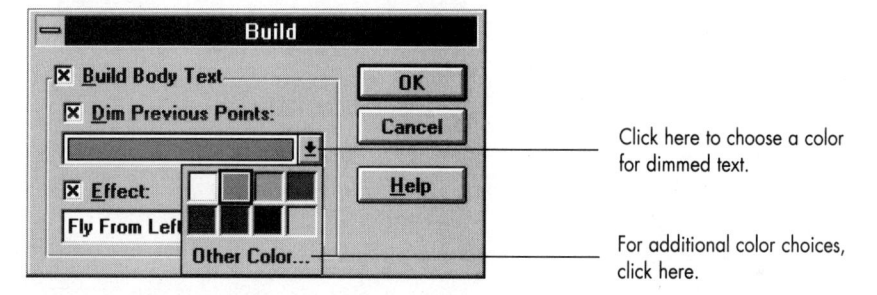

Figure 36. The view buttons

Figure 34. Choosing a color for dimmed text

Click here to choose a color for dimmed text.

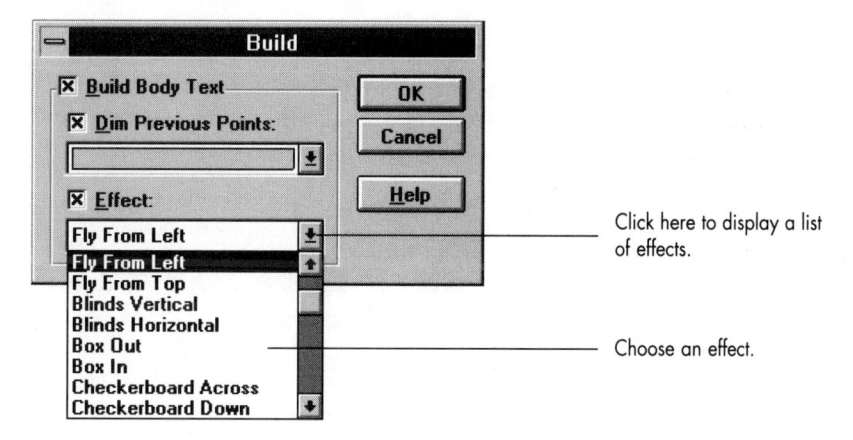

For additional color choices, click here.

Figure 35. Choosing an effect for the build

Click here to display a list of effects.

Choose an effect.

Producing a Slide Show

183

CHAPTER 14

Using the PowerPoint Viewer

The *PowerPoint Viewer* is a separate application (included with PowerPoint) whose sole purpose is to run slide shows. Viewer is a convenient way to give a presentation because you don't need to launch PowerPoint, open the presentation, and then begin the slide show. Instead, you launch Viewer and specify the presentation file; the slide show instantly begins.

1. In Program Manager, double-click the PowerPoint Viewer icon (Figure 37). You can find this icon in the Microsoft Office or PowerPoint program group.

2. In the PowerPoint Viewer dialog box (Figure 38), click a presentation name on the File Name list.

3. If you want the slide show to repeat itself after the last slide is displayed, turn on Run Continuously Until 'Esc'.

4. If your slide show was set up to automatically advance to the next slide and you want to use the preset times, turn on Use Automatic Timings.

5. Click Show. The Slide Show begins.

6. Press the left mouse button (or any of the other slide show navigation keys) to advance to the next slide.

■ Tips

✓ You can create an icon that, when double-clicked, launches Viewer and starts a slide show for a particular presentation. To create this icon in Program Manager, copy the PowerPoint Viewer icon by holding down Ctrl as you drag. Then select File/Properties and change the dialog box as indicated in Figure 39.

✓ To present a slide show on a computer that doesn't have PowerPoint, you can install just the Viewer. (It's self-contained on a single floppy disk.)

Figure 37. The PowerPoint Viewer icon

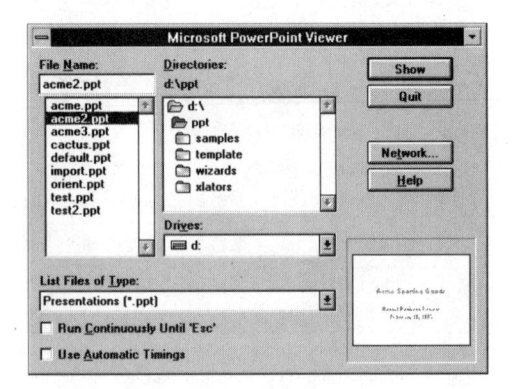

Figure 38. Choose a presentation file name in the Viewer dialog box.

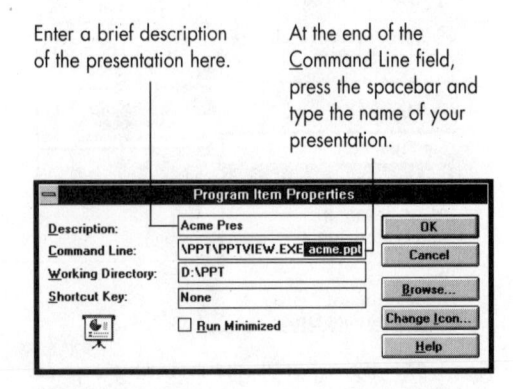

Enter a brief description of the presentation here.

At the end of the Command Line field, press the spacebar and type the name of your presentation.

Figure 39. Creating an icon to view a slide show

Producing a Slide Show

184

PRESENTATION OUTPUT 15

Figure 1. The types of output you can produce with PowerPoint

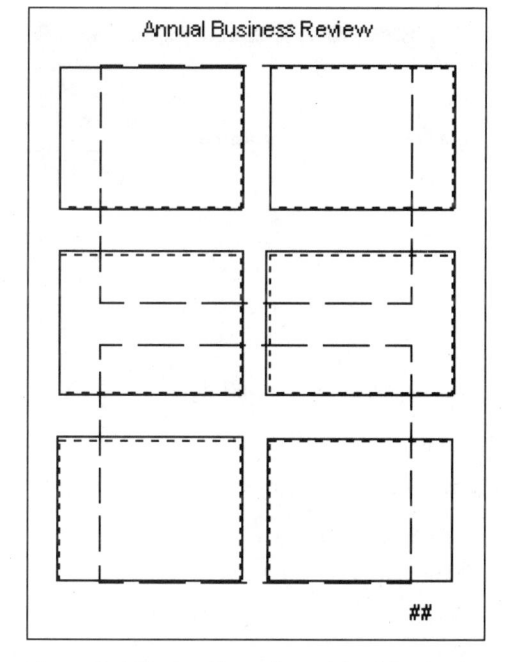

Figure 2. A Handout Master formatted with borders for six slides per page, with a title at the top and a page number at the bottom

Types of Output

You can output your presentation to the screen (in the form of a slide show), to a printer (on paper or on overhead transparencies), or to a file (to produce 35mm slides or high-resolution output).

In the Print dialog box (Figure 1), you indicate what you want to print: slides, handouts, speaker notes, or an outline of the presentation.

Handout are copies of your slides that the audience can use to follow along with your presentation. They can consist of either two, three, or six slides per page. Handouts are formatted on the *Handout Master* (Figure 2), where you can enter text or add background objects.

Each *notes page* contains a slide on top and notes at the bottom. Notes pages can be used to aid the speaker during a slide show, or to provide further information to the audience. You enter notes in Notes Pages view (Figure 3) and format the text on the *Notes Master*.

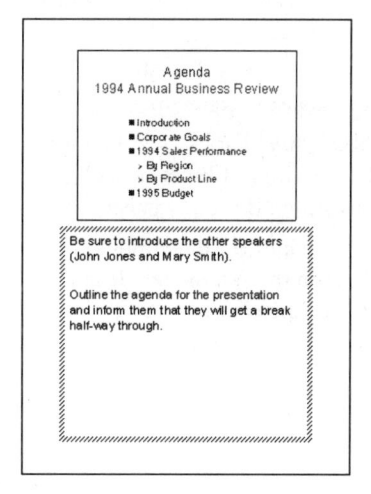

Figure 3. Notes Pages view

185

CHAPTER 15

Selecting a Printer

The Print dialog box (Figure 4) indicates the current printer. If you are connected to more than one printer and would like to specify a different one, follow these steps.

1. Select File/Print or press Ctrl+P.
2. Click the Printer button. The Print Setup dialog box appears (Figure 5).
3. In the Printers list, choose the printer you want to use.
4. Click OK to close the Print Setup dialog box. Your new choice appears at the top of the dialog box.
5. Finish filling in the Print dialog box and click OK to begin printing.

■ Tips

✓ By choosing Set as Default Printer in the Print Setup dialog box, the selected printer becomes the default for all Windows applications, not just PowerPoint.

✓ To set printer-specific options (such as paper size), click the Options button in the Print Setup dialog box.

Setting the Slide Size for Printing

Before printing, make sure that your slides are set to the desired size.

1. Select File/Slide Setup. The Slide Setup dialog box appears (Figure 6).
2. In the Slides Sized For list, select Letter Paper (8.5x11 in), A4 Paper (210x297 mm), or Custom (for other paper sizes).
3. If necessary, adjust the dimensions of the printed size in the Width and Height boxes. (The difference between the paper size and the slide dimensions is the margins.)
4. Click OK.

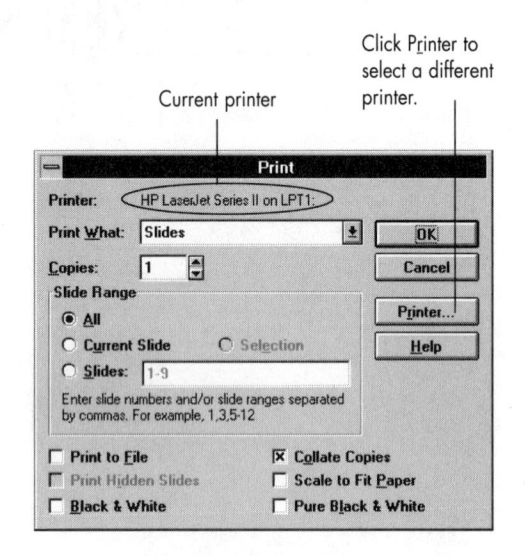

Figure 4. The current printer is listed at the top of the Print dialog box.

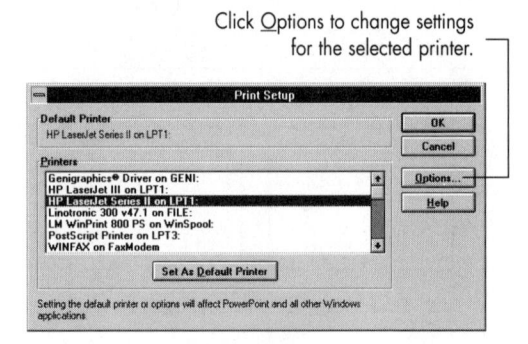

Figure 5. Selecting a different printer

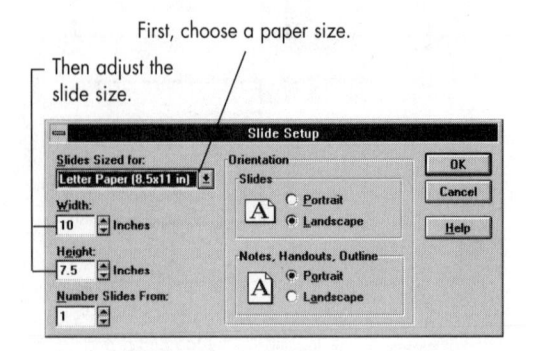

Figure 6. Setting the slide size

PRESENTATION OUTPUT

Be sure to select a slide range.

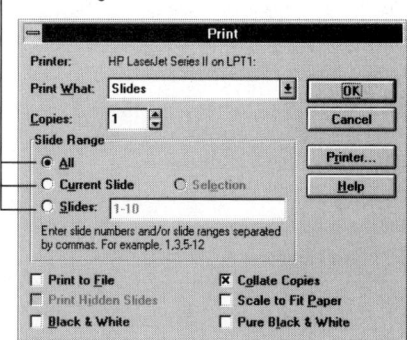

Figure 7. To display the Print dialog box, choose File/Print.

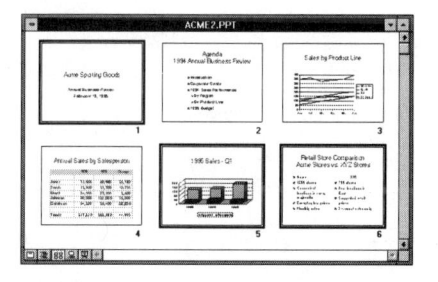

Figure 8. Slides 1, 5, and 6 are selected in Slide Sorter view.

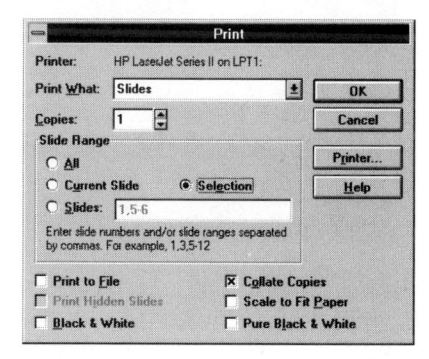

Figure 9. Choose Selection to print the slides you have selected in Slide Sorter view.

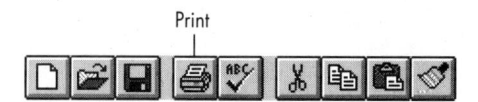

Figure 10. The Standard toolbar

Printing Slides

Probably the most common type of printing is full-page slides on paper or on overhead transparencies.

1. Select File/Print or press Ctrl+P to display the Print dialog box (Figure 7).

   To choose a different printer, see Selecting a Printer on the previous page.

2. In the Print What list box, choose Slides. If your presentation contains builds, choose either Slides (without Builds) or Slides (with Builds). To ignore builds during printing, choose Slides (without Builds).

3. Choose All for the Slide Range.

   or

   To print certain slides, choose Slides and then enter the range of slides you want to print. Use a dash to indicate a range of slides (as in 1-5), and a comma to indicate non-consecutive slides (as in 1-5, 7, 10).

4. Click OK.

■ Tips

✓ Another way to specify a range of slides is by first selecting them in Slide Sorter view (Figure 8). Then, in the Print dialog box, choose Selection as the Slide Range (Figure 9).

✓ The Print button (Figure 10) is another way to print. However, this button does not display the Print dialog box—it immediately prints the slide range last specified.

✓ When you print a color presentation on a black-and-white printer, PowerPoint converts the colors to shades of gray. If you want the fill colors to convert to white, and the line and text colors to convert to black, choose Pure Black & White in the Print dialog box.

CHAPTER 15

Printing the Outline

You can print your presentation's outline as it appears in Outline view. For instance, if only the slide titles are displayed in Outline view, only the slide titles are printed (Figure 11). Or, if the outline is completely expanded, all the slide titles and bullet items are printed (Figure 12). In addition, if formatting is hidden, the text and bullets are not formatted (Figure 13).

To get the results you want, go into Outline view and set your options—before printing your outline.

1. Switch to Outline view (Figure 14).
2. Make any of the following changes:
   - To display only the slide titles, click the Show Titles button (Figure 15). *See Displaying Slide Titles Only on page 157.*
   - To display the entire outline, click the Show All button (Figure 15).
   - To hide or display formatting, click the Show Formatting button (Figure 15). *See Hiding Text Formatting on page 156.*
3. Select File/Print or press Ctrl+P to display the Print dialog box (Figure 16).

   To choose a different printer, see Selecting a Printer on page 186.

4. In the Print What list box, choose Outline View.
5. Click OK to begin printing.

■ **Tip**

✓ Don't use the Print button on the Standard toolbar, as this doesn't give you a chance to specify you want to print Outline view.

```
1  Acme Sporting Goods
2  Agenda
     1994 Annual Business Review
3  Sales by Product Line
4  Annual Sales by Salesperson
5  1995 Sales - Q1
6  Retail Store Comparison
     Acme Stores vs. XYZ Stores
7  Corporate Goals
8  1994 Sales by Region
9  Corporate Structure
```

Figure 11. A printed outline of slide titles only

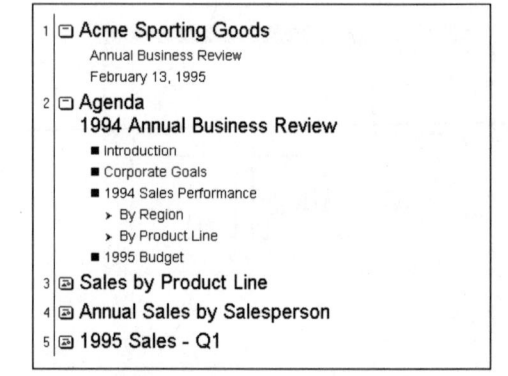

```
1  Acme Sporting Goods
     Annual Business Review
     February 13, 1995
2  Agenda
     1994 Annual Business Review
     ■ Introduction
     ■ Corporate Goals
     ■ 1994 Sales Performance
       ▸ By Region
       ▸ By Product Line
     ■ 1995 Budget
3  Sales by Product Line
4  Annual Sales by Salesperson
5  1995 Sales - Q1
```

Figure 12. A printed outline of slide titles and bullet items

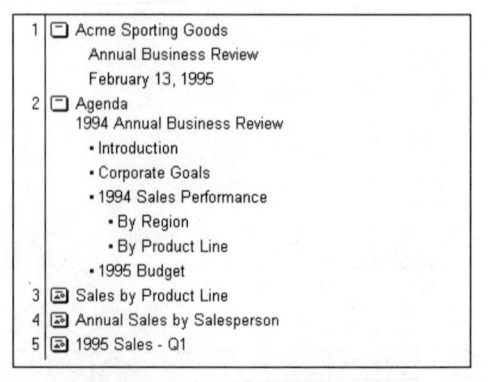

```
1  Acme Sporting Goods
     Annual Business Review
     February 13, 1995
2  Agenda
     1994 Annual Business Review
     • Introduction
     • Corporate Goals
     • 1994 Sales Performance
       • By Region
       • By Product Line
     • 1995 Budget
3  Sales by Product Line
4  Annual Sales by Salesperson
5  1995 Sales - Q1
```

Figure 13. A printed outline with unformatted text

PRESENTATION OUTPUT

Printing the Outline (cont'd)

Outline View

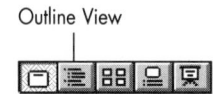

Figure 14. The view buttons

- Show Titles
- Show All
- Show Formatting

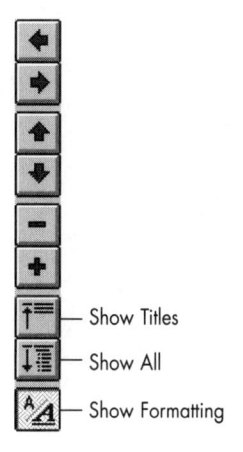

Figure 15. Outlining toolbar

Click here to display a list.

Choose Outline View.

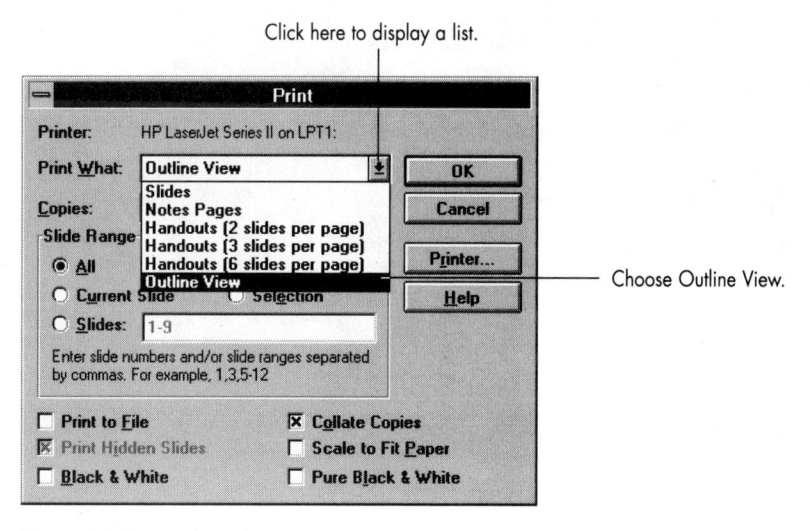

Figure 16. Printing the outline

189

CHAPTER 15

Adding Notes

To help remind you of what to say when you present each slide during a slide show, you can refer to *notes pages*. Each page of notes consists of a half-page slide along with the remarks you want to make when presenting that slide.

You enter your remarks in Notes Pages view (Figure 17).

1. Click the Notes Pages View button.
2. Press Ctrl+Home to display the notes page for Slide 1.
3. Click the text placeholder, and type your remarks.
4. To enter remarks for the next slide, click the Next Slide button.
5. Repeat steps 3 and 4 for each slide.

■ Tips

✓ To enlarge your text on the screen so that you can read it easily, choose a higher zoom percentage in the Zoom Control field.

✓ The default font size for note text is 12 points. You may want to choose a bigger size for easier reading in a dimly lit room during your slide show.

✓ You can also use notes pages as handouts for your audience, giving them pertinent information, with perhaps extra room to write their own notes.

See Editing the Notes Master and Printing Notes Pages on the following pages.

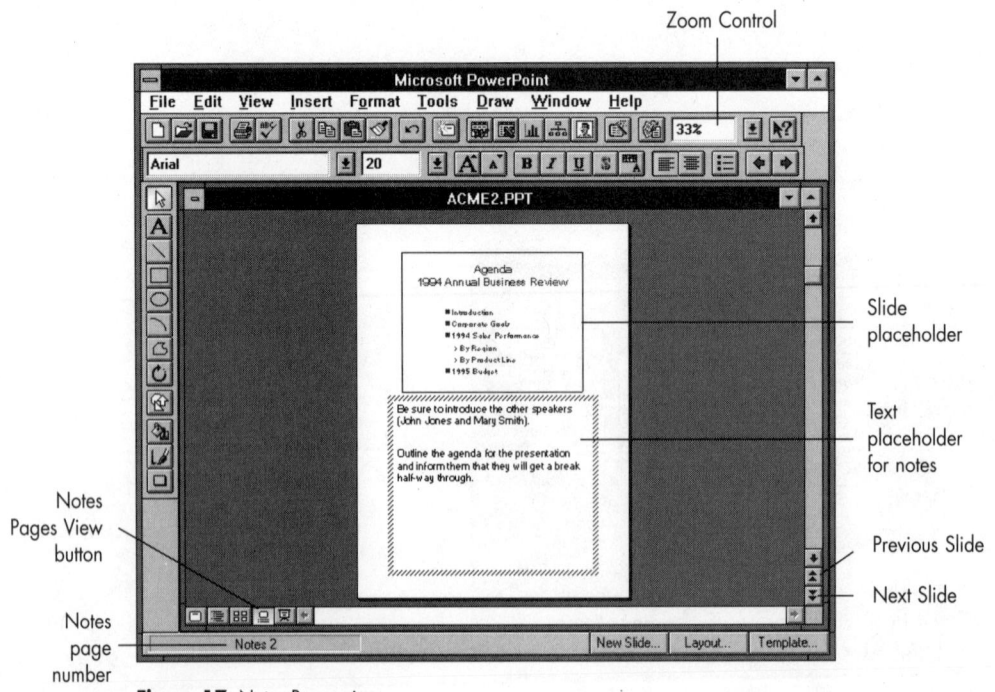

Figure 17. Notes Pages view

PRESENTATION OUTPUT

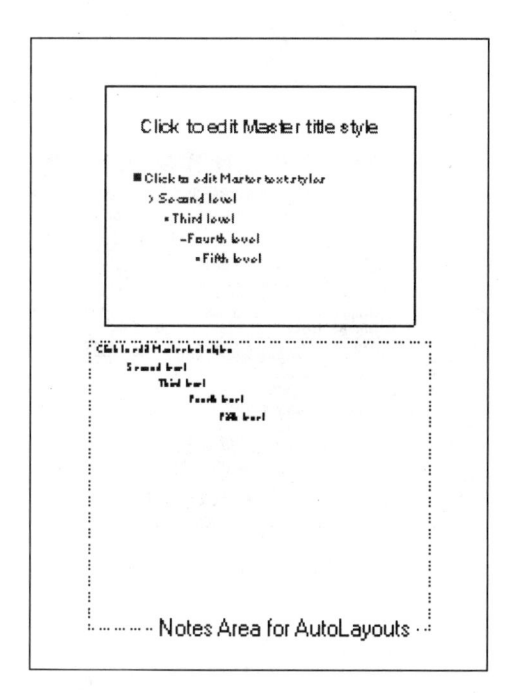

Figure 18. The Notes Master

Figure 19. Zooming in on the notes area

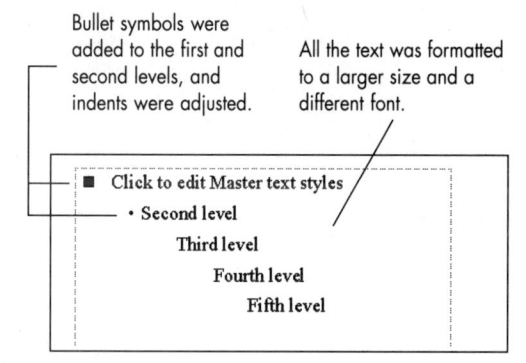

Bullet symbols were added to the first and second levels, and indents were adjusted.

All the text was formatted to a larger size and a different font.

Figure 20. A formatted notes area

Editing the Notes Master

You can perform global formatting of your notes pages on the Notes Master. (It's similar to the Slide Master discussed in Chapter 11.) For instance, by editing the Notes Master, you can have bullet symbols automatically appear when you enter your notes on all notes pages. You might also want to add a page number, format the text in a different font, or resize the slide and text placeholders.

1. Select View/Master/Notes Master or hold down Shift as you click the Notes Pages View button. The Notes Master appears (Figure 18).

2. You may want to zoom in so that you can clearly see the notes area (Figure 19).

3. Make any of the following changes:

   - Adjust the size and position of the slide and text placeholders.
     See Manipulating Text Placeholders on page 33.

   - Format the text as desired—add bullet symbols, adjust indents, change the font, and so forth. Figure 20 shows the text placeholder after formatting.
     See pages 39-43 for more information on formatting text.

   - To add text that you want to appear on each page (such as the presentation title), insert text placeholders and type the text.
     See Creating a Text Placeholder on page 32.

     To add a page number text placeholder, see Inserting Page Numbers on page 151.

   - Add any background graphics.
     See Chapter 9, starting on page 115, for information on adding graphic objects.

4. When finished, click the Notes Pages View button. All notes pages are now formatted identically.

Presentation Output

191

CHAPTER 15

Printing Notes Pages

Once you have typed your notes and formatted the Notes Master, you are ready to print the notes pages.

1. Select File/Print or press Ctrl+P to display the Print dialog box (Figure 21).

   To choose a different printer, see Selecting a Printer on page 186.

2. In the Print What list box, choose Notes Pages.

3. Choose All for the Slide Range.

   or

   To print certain notes pages, choose Slides and then enter the range of pages you want to print. Use a dash to indicate a range of slides (as in 1-5), and a comma to indicate non-consecutive slides (as in 1-5, 7, 10).

4. Click OK.

■ Tip

✓ Don't use the Print button on the Standard toolbar, as this doesn't give you a chance to specify you want to print notes pages.

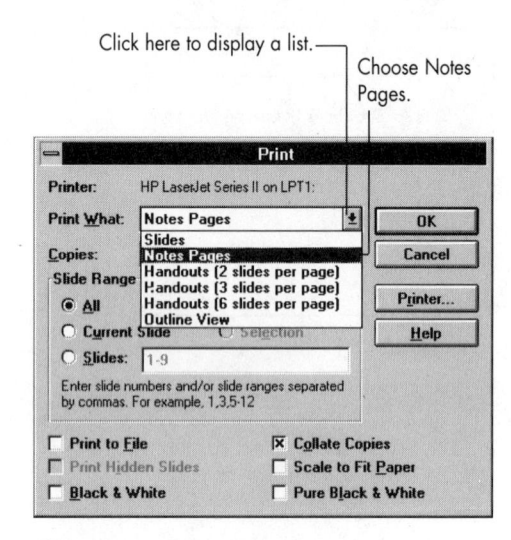

Figure 21. Printing notes pages

PRESENTATION OUTPUT

Placeholders for handouts with 3 slides per page (the three on the left)

The six small boxes are placeholders for handouts with 6 slides per page.

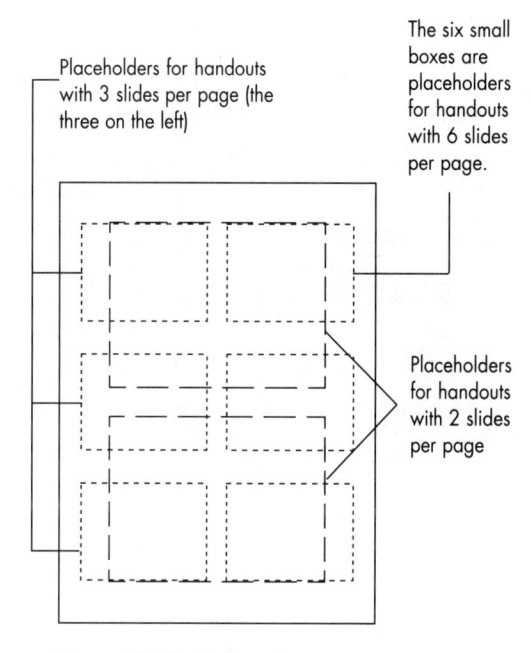

Placeholders for handouts with 2 slides per page

Figure 22. The Handout Master

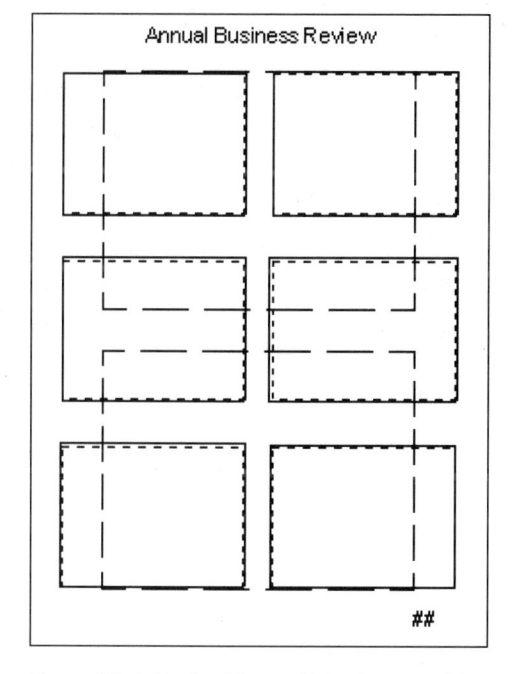

Figure 23. A Handout Master with borders around the six small placeholders

Formatting Handout Pages

Handouts help the audience follow along in your presentation. They can consist of 2, 3, or 6 slides per page. Before printing them, you may want to add a title to each page, number the pages, or create borders around each slide. You can perform all these tasks on the Handout Master.

1. Select View/Master/Handout Master or hold down Shift as you click the Slide Sorter View button. The Handout Master appears (Figure 22).
2. Make any of the following changes:
   - To add text that you want to appear on each page (such as the presentation title), insert text placeholders and type the text.
     See Creating a Text Placeholder on page 32.

     To add a page number text placeholder, see *Inserting Page Numbers on page 151.*
   - Draw borders around the slide placeholders using the Rectangle tool. (The placeholders you format depend upon the layout you plan to choose when printing. See Printing Handouts on the next page.) For instance, if you want six slides per page, draw rectangles around the six small placeholders (Figure 23).
     See Drawing Rectangles on page 118.
   - Add any other background graphics. *See Chapter 9, starting on page 115, for information on adding graphic objects.*
3. When finished, go to a view of your choosing.

■ Tip

✓ When drawing rectangles around the slide placeholders, draw the box slightly larger than the placeholder. If the box is smaller than the placeholder, the slide will overprint the box.

Presentation Output

193

CHAPTER 15

Printing Handouts

After formatting the Handout Master (described on the previous page), you are ready to print your handouts.

1. Select File/Print or press Ctrl+P. Figure 24 shows the Print dialog box.

   To choose a different printer, see Selecting a Printer on page 186.

2. In the Print What list box, choose one of the Handouts options.

3. Choose All for the Slide Range.

   or

   To print certain slides, choose Slides and then enter the range of slides you want to print. Use a dash to indicate a range of slides (as in 1-5), and a comma to indicate non-consecutive slides (as in 1-5, 7, 10).

4. Click OK.

■ **Tip**

✓ Don't use the Print button on the Standard toolbar, as this doesn't give you a chance to specify you want to print handouts.

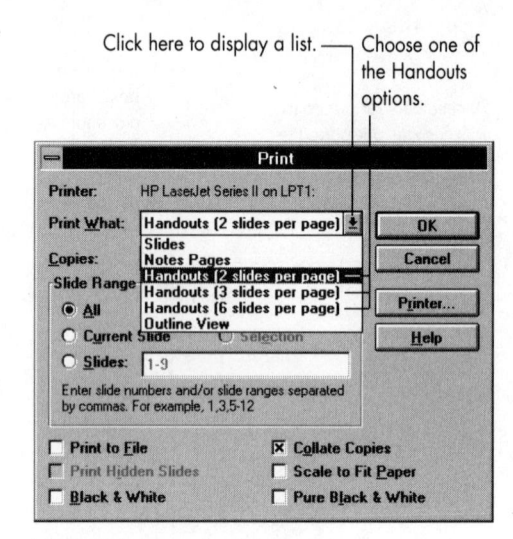

Figure 24. Printing handouts

194

PRESENTATION OUTPUT

When you choose 35mm Slides for the size...

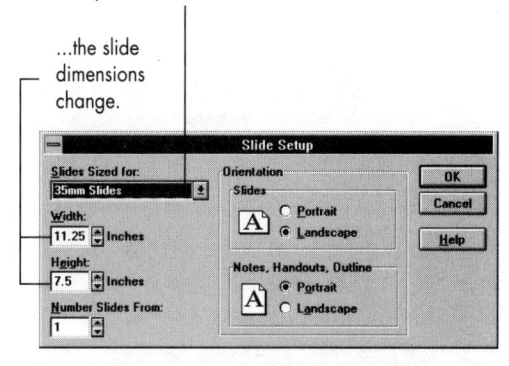

...the slide dimensions change.

Figure 25. Changing the slide setup for 35mm slides

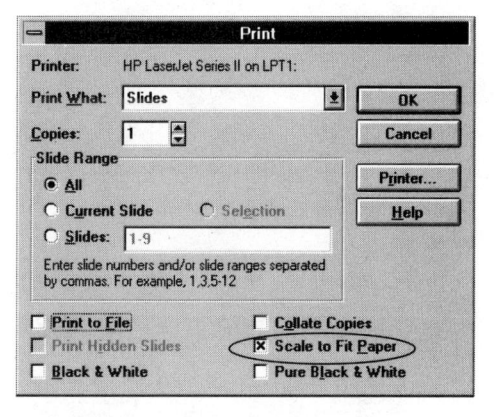

Figure 26. The Scale to Fit Paper option is automatically enabled for you.

Producing 35mm Slides

To produce 35mm slides of your presentation, you need to specify the proper slide dimension, and then create an output file that can be used by a service bureau.

Since 35mm slides have a slightly different dimension than printed slides, you will need to change the slide size.

1. Select File/Slide Setup. The Slide Setup dialog box appears (Figure 25).
2. In the Slides Sized For list, select 35mm Slides.
3. Click OK.

PowerPoint automatically scales your slides to fit the new format.

■ Tips

✓ For highest legibility on 35mm slides, choose a dark background with a contrasting color for text.

See Changing Default Colors in a Presentation on page 145.

✓ If you want to print the slides on paper, you don't need to change the setup again. PowerPoint will automatically enable the Scale to Fit Paper option in the Print dialog box (Figure 26).

Once your slides are ready for production, refer to the next page to learn how to prepare them for a service bureau.

CHAPTER 15

Producing 35mm Slides (cont'd)

The second step to producing 35mm slides is creating a PostScript file for a *service bureau* (a business that specializes in high-resolution production work).

You don't need a PostScript printer to create a PostScript file—you just need a PostScript driver. Your service bureau may give you a driver you can use, or you can use one of the ones included with Windows (such as a Linotronic driver). Once you have installed a driver, follow the steps below to create a PostScript file of the slides in your presentation.

1. Select File/Print or press Ctrl+P.
2. Click the Printer button to display the list of installed printers on your system (Figure 27).
3. Click your PostScript driver, and click OK.
4. In the Print dialog box, enable the Print to File check box (Figure 28).
5. Click OK. You are then prompted for a file name (Figure 29).
6. Type the complete file name, including the path and file extension (for example, C:\PPT\ACME.PS).
7. Click OK.

You can then copy this file to a floppy disk and take it to your local service bureau.

■ Tips

✓ To install a printer driver, open the Windows Control Panel and double-click the Printers icon.

✓ Included with PowerPoint is a driver for a service bureau called *Genigraphics*. This driver not only creates a PostScript file, but it also displays order forms for your print job and generates an electronic report to accompany your presentation.

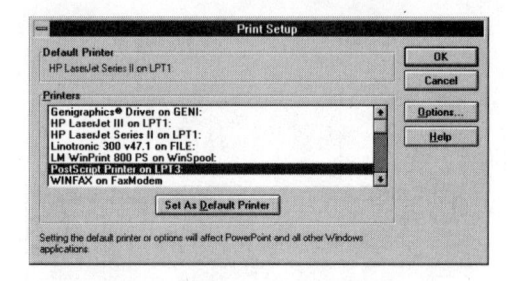

Figure 27. Select your PostScript driver.

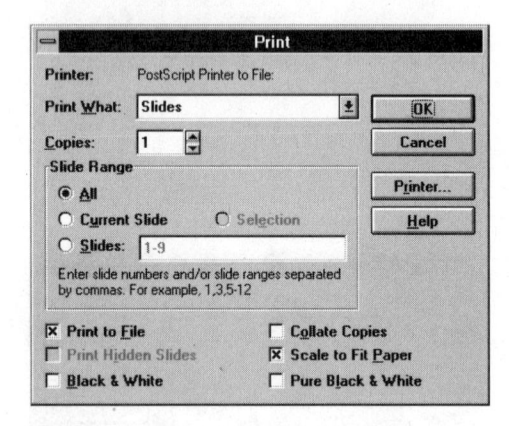

Figure 28. Enable the Print to File check box.

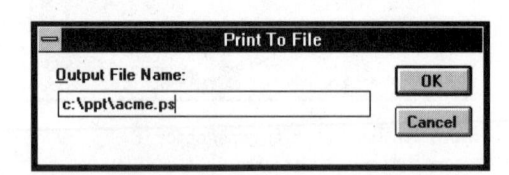

Figure 29. Enter a name for the PostScript file.

Index

Symbols

2-D charts 22, 51
3-D charts 22, 51
   formatting 68, 81
35mm slides 195, 196

A

adding slides
   graphs 47
   organization charts 86
   pie charts 74
   tables 100
aligning
   objects 133
   text 41, 93
      in a table 112
anchor points 42
annotating a slide 176
Apply Object Style command 44
Arc tool 122
arcs
   drawing 122
   filling 120
   reshaping 122
   resizing 122
arrows 117
audience handouts. *See* handouts
AutoContent Wizard 154
AutoFit
   column widths in a table 104
AutoFormats
   applying built-in 22, 70
   applying custom 72
   for graphs 70
   for tables 113
AutoLayouts. *See also* layout
   choosing 19
   text 30
autoshapes
   creating 124
   filling 120
   replacing 124
   typing text inside 124
AutoShapes button 124
AutoShapes toolbar 115, 124
axis. *See also* category axis; value axis
   adding tick marks 64
   scaling 65

B

backgrounds
   adding background items 150
   choosing a color 145, 147
   creating a shade 146
bold 39, 67, 77, 93, 109
borders
   on a table 110, 113
   on organization chart boxes 94
branches. *See* organization charts: branches
Bring Forward command 139
Bring to Front command 139
Build Effects field 182
builds 182, 183
bullet items
   moving 34, 158
   selecting 34
   typing 20
Bulleted List slides
   creating in Outline view 158
   creating in Slide view 20
bullets
   changing shapes 37
      for all slides 37, 149
   placement 38
   removing 37
By Column button 75
By Row button 75

C

canceling slide shows 28, 175
case
   changing 36
   sentence case 36
   title case 36
   toggle case 36
category axis
   defined 46
   scaling 65

197

INDEX

cells
   defined 48, 101
   editing 54
   selecting 103
centering
   objects 133
   text 41
Change Case command 36
chart
   depth 68
   dimension 51, 74, 83
chart type
   button 51
   choosing 22, 51, 83
   pie charts 74
Chart Type command 22, 51
ChartWizard 50
circles. *See* ellipses
clip art
   inserting 125
   moving 125
   placeholder 125
   resizing 125
   searching 126
ClipArt Gallery
   launching 125
closing presentations 24
co-managers. *See* organization charts: co-managers
co-workers. *See* organization charts: co-workers
Collapse Selection button 157
collapsing an outline 157
color
   changing the defaults 145
   data series 60
   fills 145
   lines 117, 145, 147
   objects 120
   organization chart boxes 94, 95
   palette 40, 60, 79, 120, 145
   pie slices 79
   replacing 136
   scheme 145, 147, 152
   shadow 145
   slide background 145, 147
   text 40, 145, 147
   titles 145
Colors and Lines dialog box 117, 120

columns
   adjusting widths in a table 104
   deleting in a table 108
   inserting in a table 107
   specifying in a table 100
Copy button 168
copy-and-paste technique 168
copying
   formatting attributes 44, 135
   graph placeholders 55
   slides 168
   slides between presentations 170, 171
   text placeholders 33
creating new presentations
      18, 152, 154, 161, 169
cropping 138
Current Slide indicator 4, 5, 23
cursor movement 31
custom AutoFormats
   applying 72
   creating 71
Cut button 160, 167
cut-and-paste technique 34, 160, 167

D

data labels
   inserting 53
      on pie charts 76
   moving 53
data markers
   formatting 61
data points
   changing the symbols 61
   defined 46
data series
   changing the color 60, 79
   changing the pattern 60, 79
   defined 46
   in columns versus rows 75
datasheet
   closing 21, 48
   displaying 21, 48, 75
   editing cells 54
   entering data 21, 48
   entering pie data 75
   erasing sample data 21, 48, 75

INDEX

deleting
   boxes in organization charts 88
   rows and columns in a table 108
   slides 172
   text 31
   text placeholders 33
delimiters
   defined 49
Demote button 158
dialog boxes
   explained 14
dimension. *See* chart: dimension
doughnut charts
   creating 83
   sizing the hole 83
drag-and-drop technique 34, 159, 167, 168
Draw menu 12
Draw/Align command 133
Draw/Group command 134
Draw/Scale command 137
Draw/Snap to Grid command 131
drawing
   arcs 122
   ellipses 119
   freehand 123
   lines 116
   polygons 123
   rectangles 118
Drawing toolbar 4, 5, 15, 115, 116, 118, 119, 121, 122, 123, 124
Drawing+ toolbar 117, 121, 134, 139, 140, 141
drop shadows. *See* shadow
duplicating slides 168

E

Edit menu 9
Edit/Duplicate command 168
editing
   graphs 54, 55
   organization charts 97
   tables 102
editing cells
   in a datasheet 54
   in a table 101
editing text 31
elevation of 3-D charts 68, 81
Ellipse tool 119

ellipses
   changing the size 118
   drawing 119
   filling 120
   moving 118
   typing text inside 119
embedded objects 128
emboss 40
ending slide shows 28, 175
Enlarge tool. *See* organization charts: zooming in and out
Exclude Row/Col command 48
Expand Selection button 157
expanding an outline 157
exploding pie slices 78

F

File menu 9
File/Slide Setup command 186, 195
files
   closing 24
   creating 169
   opening 24
   printing 25
   saving 24
Fill On/Off button 120
filling an object 120
   changing the default color 145
   removing a fill 120
first slide
   going to 23
Flip Horizontal button 141
Flip Vertical button 141
flipping objects 141
font
   changing 39
      in a graph 67, 77
      in a table 109
      in an org chart 93
   changing the default 149
   replacing 144
   size 39, 67, 77, 93, 109
   style 39, 67, 77, 93, 109
Format menu 11
Format Painter 44, 135
Format Painter button 44, 135
Format/Colors and Lines command 150
Format/Presentation Template command 152

199

INDEX

Format/Shadow command 120
Format/Slide Background command 146
Format/Slide Color Scheme command 145, 147
formatting
    axis numbers 66
    copying 44
    data markers 61
    data series 60
    graph text 67
    graphs 57–72
    gridlines 63
    legends 58
    plot area 69
    tick marks 64
Formatting toolbar 4, 5, 15, 39, 41
formulas in a table 114
Free Rotate tool 140
freeform objects
    filling 120
Freeform tool 123
Freehand Annotation icon 176
freehand drawing 123

G

gap depth 68
gap width 68
Genigraphics 196
gradient. *See* shaded background
Graph. *See* Microsoft Graph
Graph toolbar 45, 48, 49, 51, 54, 62, 75
graphic images
    inserting 127
    moving 127
    pasting 128
    resizing 127
graphs 45–72
    autoformatting 22
    creating two on a slide 55, 84
    entering data 21, 48
    formatting 22, 57–72
    formatting automatically 70
    inserting 21, 45, 47
    inserting titles 52
    placeholders 21, 47, 74
    revising 54, 55
grid snap 131

gridlines
    defined 46
    formatting 63
    inserting 62
    removing 62
    table 101
Group button 134
grouping objects 134
    deactivating a group 134
    ungrouping 134
groups. *See* organization charts: groups
guides
    displaying 130
    moving 130

H

Handout Master
    defined 185
    editing 193
handouts
    defined 185
    formatting 193
    printing 194
Help menu 13
hiding
    formatting in an outline 156
    formatting in Slide Sorter view 165
    slides 177
    text in an outline 157
Horizontal Gridlines button 62

I

Import Data command 49
importing
    graph data 49
    outlines 162
increments on an axis scale 65
indent markers
    adjusting 38
    in a table 112
indenting
    bullet items 20
    text in a table 112
Insert Clip Art button 125
Insert/Page Number command 151
Insert/Picture command 127
Insert/Slides from File command 171

INDEX

Insert/Slides from Outline command 162
inserting
    boxes in organization charts 88
    clip art 125
    data labels on a graph 53
    graph titles 52
    graphic files 127
    gridlines 62
    page numbers 151, 191, 193
    rows and columns in a table 107
    slides for graphs 47
    slides for organization charts 86
    slides for pie charts 74
    slides for tables 100
    slides from an outline 162
    slides from another file 171
italic 39, 67, 77, 93, 109

J

justified text. *See* aligning: text

L

labels. *See* data labels
last slide
    going to 23
layering objects 139
layout. *See also* AutoLayout
    Bulleted List 20
    button 4, 5
    choosing a different 19, 30, 161
    Clip Art & Text 125
    Graph 21, 47, 74
    Graph & Text 47, 55
    Org Chart 86
    Table 100
    Text & Clip Art 125
    Text & Graph 47, 55
legends
    defined 46
    enlarging 58
    entering legend labels 48
    formatting 58
    placement 59
    removing 76
line graphs
    formatting data markers 61
Line On/Off button 120

line spacing 43
Line tool 116
lines
    adding arrowheads 117
    adjusting the angle 116
    adjusting the length 116
    changing the default color 145
    connected segments 123
    drawing 116
    formatting 117
    moving 116
    removing 120
linking data 50
logo
    adding to every slide 150

M

major unit on an axis 65
managers. *See* organization charts: managers
maximum axis value 65
menus
    pulling down 7
    shortcut 7
    understanding 8
Microsoft ClipArt Gallery. *See* ClipArt Gallery
Microsoft Graph 21, 45
    exiting 21, 45
    formatting in 57–72
    loading 21, 22, 45
    revising a graph 54
Microsoft Organization Chart. *See also* organization charts
    exiting 85
    loading 85, 86
Microsoft Word 6
    creating tables 99–114
    editing outlines 163
    exiting 99
minimum axis value 65
misspellings. *See* spelling checker
mouse
    clicking 6
    clicking and dragging 6
    double-clicking 6
Move Down button 158, 159, 160
Move Up button 158, 159, 160

INDEX

moving
    boxes in organization charts 89
    bullet items 34, 158
    data labels on a graph 53
    legends 59
    lines 116
    objects 118
    pie charts 82
    slides between presentations 169
    slides in Outline view 26, 159, 160
    slides in Slide Sorter view 27, 167
    text 34
    text placeholders 33

N

new presentations 18, 152, 154, 161, 169
New Slide
    button 4, 5, 47, 55, 86, 158
    dialog box 19, 20, 21, 30, 47, 86
Next Slide button 4, 5, 23
Notes Master
    defined 185
    editing 191
notes pages
    defined 185
    formatting 191
    printing 192
    typing notes 190
Notes Pages view 185, 190
    button 4, 5
numbers
    formatting 66, 77

O

opening
    outlines 162
    presentations 24
Organization Chart toolbar 85, 88, 96
organization charts 85
    assistants 85
    Box tools 88
    branches 90
    co-managers 90
    co-workers 85
    colors 94, 95
    creating 86
    deleting boxes 88

    entering text 87
    formatting box text 93
    formatting boxes 94
    formatting lines 95
    groups 90
    inserting boxes 88
    managers 85
    moving boxes 89
    revising 97
    selecting boxes 90
    styles 91, 92
    subordinates 85
    zooming in and out 96
Outline view 26, 155–163
    bulleted lists 158
    button 4, 5
    collapsing 157
    expanding 157
    hiding formatting 26, 156, 188
    importing an outline 162
    inserting slides 158
    moving a slide 26, 159, 160
    showing all text 26, 157, 188
    showing formatting 26
    showing only titles 26, 157, 188
    switching to 155
    toolbar 155
    typing an outline 161
Outlining toolbar 26, 156, 157, 158, 159, 189
output 185–195
overhead transparencies 185, 187

P

page numbers 151, 191, 193
palette
    color 40, 60, 120, 145
    pattern 60
paragraphs
    aligning 41
    spacing 43
        in a table 112
Paste button 160, 167, 168
Paste Link command 50
pasting graphic images 128
patterns
    data series 60, 79
    object fills 120
percents on pie charts 76

INDEX

periods
  adding 36
  removing 36
perspective of a 3-D chart 68
Pick a Look Wizard 154
Pick Up Object Style command 44
pictures. *See* clip art; graphic images
pie charts 73–84
  3-D effects 81
  adding data labels 76
  coloring the slices 79
  creating 74
  entering data 75
  exploding a slice 78
  formatting slice labels 77
  moving 82
  resizing 82
  rotating 80
placeholders
  clip art 125
  graph 47, 74
  org chart 86
  table 100
  text 30
plot area
  formatting 69
  resizing 59, 82
  selecting 69, 82
polygons
  drawing 123
PostScript 196
PowerPoint Viewer 184
PowerPoint window
  explained 4
presentation graphics
  defined 2
presentations
  closing 24
  creating 18, 152, 154, 161, 169
  displaying side-by-side 169, 170
  opening 24
  printing 25
  saving 24
Previous Slide button 4, 5, 23
Print button 187
printers
  selecting 186
printing
  handouts 194

notes pages 192
outlines 188
slides 25, 187
Promote button 158

R

radar graphs
  formatting data markers 61
rearranging slides. *See* moving: slides
recoloring pictures 136
Rectangle tool 118
rectangles
  adjusting the size 118
  drawing 118
  filling 120
  moving 118
  typing text inside 118
Reduce tool. *See* organization charts: zooming in and out
rehearsing slide shows 181
removing gridlines 62
replacing fonts 144
Report It button 163
resizing
  objects 137
  pie charts 82
  text placeholders 33
revising
  graphs 54, 55
  organization charts 97
  tables 102
Rotate Left button 140
Rotate Right button 140
Rotate/Flip command 140, 141
rotating
  axis titles 52
  objects 140
  pie charts 80, 81
rows
  adjusting heights 106
  deleting in a table 108
  inserting in a table 107
  specifying in a table 100
rulers
  adjusting column widths in a table 104
  adjusting row heights in a table 106
  displaying 38, 130
  displaying in a table 102

INDEX

indent markers 38
indenting text in a table 112
running Slide Shows
  in PowerPoint 175
  in Viewer 184

S

Save As command 24
saving presentation files 24
scaling
  objects 137
  slides 195
scroll bar 5
  moving to other slides 23
Select All button 21, 48
selecting
  all text in a placeholder 43
  boxes in orgranization charts 90
  bullet items 34
  multiple objects 133, 134
  multiple slides 169, 170, 178
  text 31
selection box 33
Send Backward command 139
Send to Back command 139
Series in Columns command 48
service bureau 196
shaded background 146
shading cells in a table 110, 113
shadow
  color 145
  object 120
  organization chart boxes 94
  text 40
Shadow Color button 120
Shadow On/Off button 120
shapes
  drawing. *See* drawing
  filling 120
  flipping 141
  resizing 118
  rotating 140
  typing text inside 118, 119, 124
shortcut menus 7
  for formatting graphs 57
Show Formatting button 156, 165
Show Titles button 188

slice labels
  adding 76
  formatting 77
slices
  coloring 79
  exploding 78
slide icon 155, 159, 160
Slide Layout command 19
Slide Master
  defined 143
  editing 148, 149, 150, 151
slide placeholders 193
slide shows 173–184
  annotating a slide 176
  builds for bulleted lists 182, 183
  button 4, 5, 175
  canceling 28, 175
  navigating 175
  rehearsing 181
  self-running 180, 181
  slide order 174
  timing 181
  transition effects 173, 178, 179, 182
    speed 179
  viewing 28, 175, 184
Slide Sorter view 27, 165–172
  button 4, 5
  copying slides 168
  copying slides between presentations 170, 171
  deleting slides 172
  hiding formatting 165
  moving slides 27, 167
  moving slides between presentations 169
  switching to 165
  toolbar
    165, 173, 177, 178, 179, 180, 181, 183
slide timings 180, 181
Slide view
  button 4, 5
slides
  moving to 23
  setting the size 186, 195
Snap to Grid command 131
spacing
  line 43
  paragraph 43, 112
speaker notes. *See* notes pages
spelling checker 35
squares. *See* rectangles

stacking objects 139
Standard toolbar
    4, 5, 15, 24, 25, 125, 154, 160, 163, 166, 167, 168, 172, 187, 188, 192, 194
styles. *See* organization charts: styles
subordinates. *See* organization charts: subordinates
subscript 40
subtypes. *See also* chart type
    choosing 51
Summary Info dialog box
    filling in 24
    turning off 24
superscript 40
symbols
    at data points 61
    bullet 37

T

tables 99–114
    adjusting the size 100
    aligning text 112
    autoformatting 113
    borders 110
    cells 101
    column widths 104
        adjusting automatically 104
    creating 99, 100
    default size 100
    deleting rows and columns 108
    editing cells 101
    entering text into 101
    erasing cells 108
    formatting text 109
    formulas 114
    gridlines 101
    indents 112
    inserting rows and columns 107
    modifying 99
    moving the cursor 101
    paragraph spacing 112
    revising 102
    row heights 106
    rulers 102, 104
    selecting cells 103
    shading 110
    summing columns 114
templates
    applying 18, 152, 153, 154

button 4, 5, 152
    choosing a subdirectory 18
    defined 143
text
    anchoring 42
    changing the default color 145
    changing the default format 149
    changing the font 39
    formatting in a graph 67
    moving 34
Text Import Wizard 49
text placeholders
    copying 33
    creating 32
    deleting 33
    entering text into 20, 31, 47
    moving 33
    moving the cursor within 31
    positioning of text inside 42
    resizing 33
text slides
    creating 29
Text tool 32
tick marks
    defined 46
    formatting 64
timing slide shows 181
title placeholders 20, 21, 47
titles
    changing the default color 145
    inserting 52
    rotating 52
toolbar
    Drawing 116
toolbars 15
    Drawing
        4, 5, 15, 115, 118, 119, 121, 122, 123, 124
    Drawing+ 117, 121, 134, 139, 140, 141
    Formatting 4, 5, 15, 39, 41
    Graph 45, 48, 49, 51, 54, 62, 75
    Organization Chart 85, 88, 96
    Outlining 155, 156, 157, 158, 159, 189
    Slide Sorter
        173, 177, 178, 179, 180, 181, 183
    Standard
        4, 5, 15, 24, 25, 125, 154, 160, 163, 66, 167, 168, 172, 187, 188, 192, 194
    using 15
Tools menu 12

INDEX

Tools/Crop Picture command 138
Tools/Hide Slide command 177
Tools/Recolor command 136
Tools/Replace Fonts command 144
Tools/Transition command 179
transition
   button 179, 180
   icon 178
transition effects 173, 178, 179, 182
   speed 179
Transition Effects field 178
typeface. *See* font
typing text
   bullet items 20
   in a datasheet 21, 48, 75
   in a table 101
   in an outline 158, 161
   in organization chart boxes 87
   inside a rectangle 118
   inside an autoshape 124
   inside an ellipse 119
   inside text placeholders 20, 31
   on notes pages 190

U

underline 40
ungrouping objects 134
unindenting bullet items 20
user-defined AutoFormats 71

V

value axis
   defined 46
   formatting the numbers 66
   scaling 65
Vertical Gridlines button 62
View Datasheet button 21, 48, 54, 75
View/Slide Show command 175, 180
View/Zoom command 132, 166
Viewer. *See* PowerPoint Viewer
views
   Outline 2, 5, 26, 155–163
   Slide 5
   Slide Sorter 2, 5, 27, 165–172

W

Window menu 13
Window/Arrange All command 169, 170
Wizards
   AutoContent 154
   ChartWizard 50
   Pick a Look 154
   Text Import 49
Word 6. *See* Microsoft Word 6

X

x-axis. *See also* category axis
   defined 46
   labels 48
XY graphs
   formatting data markers 61

Y

y-axis. *See also* value axis
   defined 46

Z

z-axis. *See also* value axis
   defined 46
Zoom Control field 27
zooming in and out
   Microsoft Organization Chart 96
   Slide Sorter view 27, 166
   Slide view 132